# Exercises in Group Work

**Kurt L. Kraus**

*Shippensburg University of Pennsylvania*

Merrill
Prentice Hall

Upper Saddle River, New Jersey
Columbus, Ohio

**Vice President and Publisher:** Jeffery W. Johnston
**Executive Editor:** Kevin M. Davis
**Associate Editor:** Christina Kalisch Tawney
**Editorial Assistant:** Autumn Crisp
**Production Editor:** Mary Harlan
**Design Coordinator:** Diane C. Lorenzo
**Cover Design:** Ali Mohrman
**Cover Image:** Index Stock
**Production Manager:** Laura Messerly
**Director of Marketing:** Ann Castel Davis
**Marketing Manager:** Amy June
**Marketing Coordinator:** Tyra Poole

This book was printed and bound by Banta Book Group. The cover was printed by Phoenix Color Corp.

Pearson Education Ltd.
Pearson Education Australia Pty. Limited
Pearson Education Singapore Pte. Ltd.
Pearson Education North Asia Ltd.
Pearson Education Canada, Ltd.
Pearson Educación de Mexico, S.A. de C.V.
Pearson Education—Japan
Pearson Education Malaysia Pte. Ltd.
Pearson Education, *Upper Saddle River, New Jersey*

10  9 8 7 6 5 4 3 2 1

Merrill
Prentice Hall

ISBN: 0-13-098188-5

# INTRODUCTION

Welcome to *Exercises in Group Work*. This workbook is a study guide designed to accompany Gladding's *Group Work: A Counseling Specialty* (4th ed.). It also is designed to extend your learning through knowledge checks (mini quizzes), application and reflection (scenarios and vignettes to consider and respond to), individual and small group activities (reflecting on your classroom experiences, community opportunities, and others), a space to formalize reflections on any out-of-class group participation, and a variety of other opportunities to better develop your understanding of the complexities of group work.

This workbook offers students examples, vignettes, and scenarios pertaining to the diverse sphere of settings where groups happen, from classrooms with young children, adolescents, and adults to an assortment of meetings, to counseling and psychotherapy groups in school counseling offices, outpatient mental health centers, and hospital settings. The format mirrors Gladding's text *Group Work: A Counseling Specialty* (4th Ed.) and hopefully will parallel the life experiences of many students who are utilizing this workbook as a way to learn about groups. I ask students to consider examples from culturally diverse populations throughout. I encourage you not to see the world as an extension of yourselves, rather see where you are unique among so many others. So numerous are the variations of human experience it is likely some will be disappointed by my neglecting to mention one or many important differences; I promise such omissions are not intentional.

You will notice that ample writing space (lined sections and blank spaces) is provided where you are encouraged to keep notes, enter reflections, journal, and otherwise strengthen your personal growth and learning as you focus on the world of group work. I believe that this reflecting process will aid immeasurably in your continued group membership and eventual practice as a group leader, and as you continue your academic journey.

Answers to multiple choice and true and false questions are provided at the end of this book; however, much of what is asked of you throughout this workbook has many possible answers. Hence, I encourage working with partners, in small groups, and with your instructors in determining good, better, and best answers. Your course instructor will direct how she or he feels the use of this workbook will benefit you most. If you are completing this workbook as a self-directed learning experience, I trust you will chart an interesting course. Note that the pages of this workbook are perforated, thus allowing you to share your responses to some prompts and questions with other students, while keeping your more personal reflections private. The process of learning about group work can be divided into several, rather overlapping segments: text *knowledge*, where you learn of history and trends, pioneers, concepts, theories, methods, and research; *application*, where you practice putting text knowledge into guided practice; and *experiential*, where students transition into actual demonstration and participation by being an observer, member, coleader, leader, and perhaps supervisor and teacher. This workbook is designed to guide learning opportunities in each of these three areas.

## ORGANIZATION

This workbook design parallels *Group Work: A Counseling Specialty* (4th Ed.) by Samuel T. Gladding, chapter by chapter. However, students or their course instructors may wish to select in what order this material is covered, the time spent in each of the 3 parts of the text, and what learning strategies will be utilized and when. Students may find that the sequence of some writing activities or the need to clarify text content is best accomplished by flipping back and forth, skipping sections altogether, or returning to material a second time. Chapters in this Workbook have several common elements, which I outline below.

## Chapter Highlights, Key Terms, and Important People

Each chapter begins with highlighted excerpts extracted from Gladding's *Group Work: A Counseling Specialty* (4th Ed.) text. The purpose of this section is to help students fully understand the text material. Excerpts are presented here to assist your study and recall of key information; the same is true for important vocabulary and people. All vocabulary terms are included and defined in the glossary at the end of this workbook as well as in the Gladding text.

## Group Experience – Parallels and Reflections, Group Prompts

Many graduate-level group courses, as an adjunct to course content learned through experiential and didactic classroom instruction, require students to be members in one or more, often time-limited, personal growth groups. Such groups are typically counseling groups but can occasionally take the form of a psychoeducational group. For often-complex reasons including your course instructor taking on a dual role of group counselor and other ethical quandaries, these student groups are often led by group work specialists outside the counselor education faculty. Following the *written exercises* section in many chapters several prompts ask you to connect the chapter topic with your actual small group experiences. These prompts reflect the text content, and you are encouraged to write responses for your personal growth and development. No space for these assignments is provided in the workbook itself. You are asked to keep your responses separate and private to ensure privacy. Should you choose to share any or all of these exercises with your instructor or other group members, be sure to maintain everyone's confidentiality.

In Chapters 2 through 8 students study types of groups and their defining features, group dynamics, group leadership, the development and stages of groups, working with diverse membership, and ethical and legal issues in group work. For each of these 8 chapters, students will find prompts for reflection and space for personal commentary. Students are encouraged to write about their experiences with their external group membership. Caution, of course, will be needed to not write about confidential information shared within the group. The assumption is made that these workbook chapters will likely parallel your actual group experiences (although sequence and significance may differ, of course); the prompts and the spaces to record your thoughts and feelings are designed to assist students in making meaningful connections between the course content and your small group experiences.

Pages of this workbook are perforated so that students may easily remove certain pages for various reasons (e.g., to hand in particular pages to the professor/instructor or to store separately).

## Written Exercises

Students may respond to an array of questions, prompts, and queries based on vignettes, character sketches, scenarios, and stories, depending on the chapter. Students are encouraged to write their responses; however, the responses can lead to interesting discussions with others, self-reflections, and content check-ups. Although it is challenging to capture the dynamics and nuances present in any interpersonal interaction, these sections allow students to "try on" different skills in the safety of your workbook. I encourage students to flex your imagination; make the group members in these sections come to life.

## Self Assessment

In this section you can quiz yourself on the progress you are making comprehending the text content. True or false and multiple choice formats are utilized. As you work your way through this workbook you will be able to return to your responses, and rethink them where necessary, in order to best prepare for course examinations or perhaps for certification and licensure exams.

## Journal and Reflection

As mentioned earlier, there is ample space for journaling. This space is provided for students' use (e.g., notes and reflections) and to respond to instructor's prompts and assignments. Possibilities include reflections on course presentations, thoughts about class activities, the group dynamics of class, and general opportunities to comment thoughtfully. Recording your thoughts and feelings will provide a written history, a personal narrative, of this current phase of your group work education and development.

## Glossary and Answers Section

The glossary from *Group Work: A Counseling Specialty* (4th ed.) is reproduced in this section. The glossary is a rich resource that you will likely refer to repeatedly. In the answers section you will find the answers for selected of items in the self-assessment section of each chapter.

## REQUEST FOR FEEDBACK

Learning about group work is a lifelong enterprise indeed, considering that the field itself is continuously developing, the desire some may have to become specialists in group work cannot possibly end at the completion of this workbook. So that I may be responsive to your thoughts, suggestions, and creative ideas, please write to me (in care of the publisher) or e-mail me at klkrau@ship.edu with your feedback about how you have used this workbook. I would greatly enjoy simply hearing from you about your journey thus far into the world of group work.

Kurt L. Kraus

# ACKNOWLEDGEMENTS

I wish to thank:

- my incredible counselor education mentors and role-models Diana Hulse-Killacky, Marguerite (Peg) Carroll, Jerry Donigian and so many others, with whom I have been blessed to learn and love group work;
- my wonderful, skilled, and caring colleagues at Shippensburg University of Pennsylvania; and,
- my wife and partner on life's journey, Sally, and our children who are forever the greatest joy in my life.

A note of heartfelt appreciation to Sam Gladding—an extraordinary individual, and to my editor, Christina Kalisch Tawney, and editorial assistant, Autumn Crisp, at Merrill/Prentice Hall, thank you.

# ABOUT THE AUTHOR

Kurt L. Kraus is an Assistant Professor of Counseling in the Department of Counseling at Shippensburg University of Pennsylvania. Kurt received his doctorate from the University of Maine. He has held professional positions as a counselor in schools for grades k-12; and in community-based, hospital, and private practice. Prior to beginning his counseling and counselor educator career in 1987, Kurt taught English. He also taught adolescents with special needs in both public schools and in residential treatment. Dr. Kraus is an active member of the Association for Specialists in Group Work (ASGW), the Association for Counselor Education and Supervision (ACES) and the American Counseling Association (ACA). He is a Licensed Professional Counselor in Pennsylvania, a Nationally Certified Counselor and an Approved Clinical Supervisor. Kurt has professional interests in the areas of group work, counseling adolescents, clinical supervision, and ethics. He is the current chairperson of the school counseling program at Shippensburg and chair of the University's Institutional Review Board for Human Subject Research.

# CONTENTS

# HISTORY AND TRENDS OF GROUP WORK

**Outcome Objectives**
1. I am knowledgeable about the history of and trends in group work.
2. I am able to chronicle highlights and describe uses of groups throughout the past century.
3. I comprehend current trends in group work.
4. I am able to describe and discuss:
    a. Current training & education in group work
    b. Impact of technology on group work
    c. Studies on group effectiveness
    d. Brief group work
5. I am able to speculate on future directions for group work.

## Chapter Overview

     *History and Trends of Group Work* focuses on the emergence and development of group work across many contexts and in the counseling professions. Along with the history of groups in general, key individuals responsible for the growth of group work are discussed. Different types of groups are defined, and the reader is introduced to the wide scope of group work.

## Chapter Highlights

Groups are defined in many ways.

A **group** is a collection of two or more individuals, who meet in face-to-face interaction, interdependently, with the awareness that each belongs to the group and for the purpose of achieving mutually agreed-on goals. (adapted from Johnson and Johnson, 2000)

The concept *group work* encompasses all types of activities performed by organized groups — for example, task/work, psychoeducation, psychotherapy, and counseling.

The Association for Specialists in Group Work (ASGW, 2000) defines **group work** as "a broad professional practice involving the application of knowledge and skill in group facilitation to assist an inter-dependent collection of people to reach their mutual goals, which may be intrapersonal, interpersonal, or work related." (p. 330).

### GROWTH OF GROUP WORK

#### 1900 to 1909
Joseph Hersey Pratt started a psychotherapy group for tuberculosis outpatients in 1905 at the Massachusetts General Hospital in Boston.

In 1907, Jesse B. Davis, principal of Grand Rapids High School in Michigan, directed that one English class per week be devoted to "Vocational and Moral Guidance" (Glanz & Hayes, 1967).

Davis stressed the functionality of a group as an environment in which to learn life skills and values.

## 1910 to 1919

At select American schools and organizations there was growth on group psychoeducational approaches to learning.

In Europe, J. L. Moreno published a paper on group methods, written under the name of J. M. Levy, that stressed the psychoanalytic and social psychological perspectives of individuals working together.

## 1920 to 1929

In 1922 Alfred Adler initiated a new and systematic form of group guidance and counseling that became known as collective counseling.

In his creation of psychodrama, Jacob L. Moreno challenged old methods of working with individuals.

During the 1920s formal research investigations of small groups began.

## 1930 to 1939

Group guidance and psychoeducation in schools centered on vocational and personal themes.

Jacob Moreno introduced the terms *group therapy* and *group psychotherapy* into the vocabulary of helping professionals in 1931 and 1932.

Studies of groups in natural settings used various investigative methods to gather data.

Alcoholics Anonymous (AA), a support group, was established to help alcoholics gain and maintain control of their lives by remaining sober.

Psychoanalytic group analysis emerged in the 1930s (Gazda, 1968).

## 1940 to 1949

The 1940s are often seen as the beginning of modern group work.

Kurt Lewin is generally recognized as the most influential founder and promoter of group dynamics during this era. His approach, field theory, emphasizes the interaction between individuals and their environments.

Lewin is responsible for the formation of the **National Training Laboratories (NTL)** and the growth of the **basic skills training (BST) group**, which eventually evolved into the **training group (T-group)** movement.

Lewin is credited for emphasis on a here-and-now orientation to the environment, and it was he who first applied the concept of *feedback* to group work.

Wilfred Bion (1948), a member of the **Tavistock Institute of Human Relations** in Great Britain, like Lewin, stressed the importance of group dynamics. His focus was on group cohesiveness and forces that foster the progression or regression of the group.

Two major group organizations and publications were founded: the **American Society of Group Psychotherapy and Psychodrama (ASGPP),** and the **American Group Psychotherapy Association (AGPA).**

### 1950 to 1959

The 1950s were characterized by a greater refinement in group work and more emphasis on research.

Rudolph Dreikurs employed Adler's theory and ideas in setting up primarily psychoeducational groups working with parent groups.

### 1960 to 1969

Group work, especially group counseling and psychotherapy, was immensely popular in the 1960s, though at times controversial.

Many forms of group work were initiated or refined during the 1960s, including encounter groups, sensory awareness groups, growth groups, marathons, and minithons.

Carl Rogers coined the term "basic encounter group." Encounter groups are often known as *personal growth groups* because the emphasis in these groups is on personal development.

Among the most popular theorists-practitioners of this decade were those who took a humanistic-existential orientation.

### 1970 to 1979

Group work continued to grow, but not without controversy. Irving Janis (1971) created the term **groupthink** to emphasize the detrimental power that groups may exert over their members to conform.

The controversy surrounding groups in the 1970s was due to their rapid, almost uncontrolled growth in the late 1960s and to the fact that guidelines for leading and conducting group experiences themselves were not well defined.

The Association for Specialists in Group Work (ASGW) was formed in 1973 as a divisional affiliate within the American Personnel and Guidance Association (now the American Counseling Association).

Group research also came into prominence during the 1970s with the important work of Irvin Yalom and George Gazda.

### 1980 to 1989

The popularity of group work for the masses increased, as did the continued professionalism of the group movement itself.

Self-help groups and psychoeducational groups also received increased attention during this decade.

### 1990 to 1999

The Group Psychology and Group Psychotherapy division of the American Psychological Association was established.

Group work became increasingly utilized in school settings. Group work also focused on groups for special populations, such as those in the midst of divorce, adult offenders, people from different cultures, and people with disabilities.

The ASGW published professional standards for the training of group workers in task/work groups, psychoeducational groups, counseling groups, and psychotherapy groups.

## CURRENT TRENDS IN GROUP WORK

Counselors, coaches, teachers, politicians, and corporate researchers have made group work more a part of their personal and professional lives than ever before.

Specialty group practice and research into specialty areas flourish.

### Training/Education in Group Work
The training and educating of group leaders has become more sophisticated as the dynamics within groups have become better understood.

### Technology and Group Work
Increasing interest in computer technology has taken numerous forms including the use of chat rooms, computer conferencing, listservs, and news groups (Bowman & Bowman, 1998; Hsiung, 2000).

Computer support for something a group does is referred to as *groupware*.

Computers promote psychoeducational and task/work group development, at least in regard to the exchange of information.

Web sites on the Internet have emerged for group associations that are national and international in scope, such as the International Association of Group Psychotherapy (IAGP).

Computers in groups hold promise for the future, especially as ways of helping group members stay in contact with one another and exchange information.

Software programs, such as *The Palace*, can simulate visual, auditory and spatial cues, and the group virtual room and experience can become more personal.

### Research on Group Effectiveness
Research shows that group work is an effective method of providing services to others (Kivlighan, Coleman, & Anderson, 2000).

Group research is in its infancy compared with research in many other social sciences (Christensen & Kline, 2000; Stockton & Morran, 1982).

Meta-analyses of different group formats have been published. Meta-analyses make it possible to more clearly compare group outcomes with each other and group work with individual treatment.

Increased concern and attention is being devoted to group research.

Professional group associations are giving awards and grants for group research.

Greater emphasis is being placed on investigating the effectiveness of important concepts crucial to group work, such as feedback through the development of measurements.

Resources for identifying both methods and measures of evaluating group outcome and process are being published.

Qualitative methods of conducting research on groups hold promise for exploring dynamics within groups.

### Brief Group Work: Solution-Focused Counseling Groups

Brief group work began as a response to managed care and other health management programs that limited the number of sessions that were reimbursed for group treatment (Cornish & Benton, 2001).

Solution-focus theory and therapy was one of the first forms of brief group work practiced.

### THE FUTURE OF GROUP WORK

Group work has come a long way in its brief formal history, and undoubtedly it will be robust and permeate almost all segments of society on a global level in the future.

A greater variety of groups are being created, including approaches that are more educational and growth inducing rather than ameliorative or adjustment focused.

Groups that are able to harness the resources within themselves are more constructive and effective in promoting change and fostering support.

### Key Terms and Concepts

*Can you define and describe each of the following terms? Be able to offer a brief example or relevant context for these concepts.*

> Alcoholics Anonymous (AA)
> American Group Psychotherapy Association (AGPA)
> American Society of Group Psychotherapy and Psychodrama (ASGPP)
> Association for Specialists in Group Work
> asynchronous online groups
> "BA" (Basic Assumption) activity
> basic encounter group
> Basic Skills Training (BST)
> collective counseling
> cooperative learning groups
> curative (therapeutic) factors within groups
> developmental group counseling
> family councils
> field theory
> focus groups
> general systems theory
> group
> group work
> groupthink
> groupware
> 'guidance hour'
> marathon groups

National Training Laboratories (NLT)
phyloanalysis
process-play
psychodrama
sensitivity groups
simulated group counseling model
social group work
synchronous online groups
Tavistock Institute of Human Relations
Training group (T-group)
Transactional analysis (TA)
Theatre of Spontaneity (*Stegreiftheatre*)
total quality groups
"W" group (work group)


## Key Personalities

*Can you identify and discuss the contributions of the following experts?*

Ackerman, Nathan
Addams, Jane
Adler, Alfred
Allen, R. D.
Bach, George
Bateson, Gregory
Bell, John
Berne, Eric
Bion, Wilfred
Burrow, Trigant
Davis, Jesse B.
Dreikurs, Rudolph
Gazda, George
Gibb, Jack
Horney, Karen
Lewin, Kurt
Moreno, J. L. (aka J. M. Levy)
Perls, Fritz
Pratt, Joseph Hersey
Rogers, Carl
Satir, Virginia
Schilder, Paul
Schutz, William
Slavson, Samuel R.
Solotaroff, Paul
Stoller, Fred
Sullivan, Harry Stack
Wender, Louis
Yalom, Irvin

## Self Assessment Questions

**True or False Statements**

The following statements check your comprehension of terms and identification of individuals (knowledge and comprehension level); your ability to apply that knowledge to solve more challenging questions (application level), and your ability to evaluate given information (analysis and evaluation level).

Indicate whether each statement is true or false. If you believe a statement is false, identify the error in the space provided. When necessary, refer to your text, Gladding's *Group Work: A Counseling Specialty* (4th ed.). An answer key appears at the end of this book.

1. Johnson and Johnson's (2000) definition of "group" includes two or more individuals, mutually agreed upon goals, and face-to-face meeting.

   _____
   _____
   _____

2. Jesse B. Davis began his group work in part for "humane and economic reasons."

   _____
   _____
   _____

3. "Phyloanalysis" is best defined as an interest in social forces and political priniciples in groups.

   _____
   _____
   _____

4. "Field theory" emphasizes the interaction between individuals and their environment, according to Lewin.

   _____
   _____
   _____

5. Jane Addams is credited with having conducted early formal group experiences with the poor and immigrants.

   _____
   _____
   _____

6. The group style that was designed by Fritz Perls was known as the "encounter group."

   _____
   _____
   _____

7. Behaviorism was the group counseling orientation most popular in the 1960s.

   _____
   _____
   _____

8. Alcoholics Anonymous is a type of self-help group.

_____

_____

_____

9. "Groupthink" describes the detrimental power that groups may exert on their members to conform.

_____

_____

_____

10. The Association of Group Psychotherapy was formed in 1973 as a division within the American Personnel and Guidance Association (now the American Counseling Association).

_____

_____

_____


## Multiple Choice Questions

1. The early growth of group work as a specialization beginning in the late 1800s is best explained by which of the following statements? The group work movement developed because of the _____.
   a. need for social reform and education
   b. burgeoning of professional psychology
   c. demand for competent vocational guidance
   d. beginning of the social work profession

2. The notion that group work could have a detrimental personal and social effect was coined by Irving Janus in the early 1970s as _____.
   a. groupspeak          c. socialism
   b. groupthink          d. anti-intellectualism

3. The purpose of unique group work training opportunities (such as simulated group counseling model, process-play) is to allow students to learn and to practice group work skills in

_____.
   a. a professional and ethical manner
   b. ways that protect trainees from self-disclosure
   c. ways without relying on traditional roleplays
   d. (all of the above)

**Written Exercises**
Respond in writing to several of the following questions, prompts, and inquiries, designed to deepen your comprehension of the text. Student responses can lead to self-reflection and interesting discussions with others. You are encouraged to flex your imagination and make your understanding of group work as presented in these chapters come to life.

## Questions & Prompts for Written Reflection and Discussion

## Chapter 1

1. Select one decade from the last century with a rich group work history. Use a variety of references to place group work development in a broader social context. Attempt to capture the significance of that decade's historical events on the United States and globally. Speculate as to how these events might have shaped our group work history. Attempt to include issues of social development (e.g., the economy, health care, political events, world events, civil rights, issues unique to underrepresented groups). Share your findings with class members. Imbed the decade you have researched with the findings of others in your class. Does the continuity of group work development seem smooth, erratic, logical, et cetera? What decade of group work development do you find to be the most extraordinary? Discuss.

_____
_____
_____
_____
_____
_____
_____
_____
_____
_____
_____
_____
_____

2. Review several selections from the professional literature in the allied mental health fields pertaining to group work. What stands out for you? What do you find that has truly changed in the years since the article was published? What, on the other hand, seems relatively stable over this period of time?

_____
_____
_____
_____
_____
_____
_____
_____
_____
_____
_____
_____

3. Given the current sociopolitical picture of today, what next steps seem logical in the progression of group work development? What do you envision as trends, new horizons, pitfalls for the near future in group work? Support your hypotheses with current relevant evidence. Discuss your thoughts with others in the class; what similarities emerge? Differences?

_____
_____
_____
_____
_____
_____
_____
_____
_____
_____
_____
_____
_____
_____
_____

## Prompts for Group Members

1. Consider the question: What is group work anyway? What are your preconceptions about joining a "group"? What do you hope will emerge from your experience?

2. Given the history of group development, current trends, and speculation on the future of group work, how does the group you are joining seem to fit in this ever-developing world of group work?

## Journal and Reflection

Space for journaling about your group work experiences is provided below. Use this space to reflect on your reading about group work, your classroom presentations and activities, the group dynamics of your classes themselves, and any simulations or actual group participation opportunities you may have. Comment here thoughtfully. Be sure to carefully honor your ethical commitment to uphold the confidentiality of others in your group. Reflections are yours and are not to reveal anyone else's information. Recording your thoughts and feelings will provide a written history of this phase of your group work education. (Reproduce and/or attach additional sheets of paper if desired.)

_Entry date_ _____

# TYPES OF GROUP WORK

**Outcome Objectives**
    1. I understand and can describe types of group work
    2. I am able to define and give examples for each of the following models of specialty groups:
        (a) psychoeducational groups
            an example of psychoeducational group work:
                life-skills development group
        (b) counseling groups
            an example of a counseling group:
                a counseling group for counselors
        (c) psychotherapy groups
            an example of group psychotherapy:
                group work with abusers and the abused
        (d) task/work groups
            an example of task/work groups:
                teams
        (e) mixed groups and a proposed regrouping of categories
            an example of a mixed group:
                a consumer-oriented group
    3. I am able to compare and contrast models of specialty groups.

## Chapter Overview

In this chapter you are introduced to *core group skills* and the *four major types of groups*. Also included are the hybrid groups that do not fall neatly into one specific category, and you will read a proposed reorganization of group types. Mastering these basic group skills is essential for a group leader to be effective in leading all varieties of groups.

## Chapter Highlights

In 1991 the Association for Specialists in Group Work (ASGW) developed standards and competencies for the preparation of group workers in four distinct group work specializations: psychotherapy, counseling, psychoeducation, and task/work.

By explicitly defining what group workers need to do in specific group settings, the standards identify, define, and establish skills that need to be acquired and developed.

Training models have been set up in educational institutions. Specialists from a variety of disciplines can now point to examples of what should be done in the preparation of group leaders (Conyne, Wilson, & Ward, 1997).

Awareness of different types of groups and their purpose and function allows one to conduct and participate in a variety of groups effectively and ethically.

## MODELS OF SPECIALTY GROUPS

**Contact-focused group theory** was an early forerunner to the specialty group model. Three primary contact groups described in this theory were group guidance, group counseling, and group psychotherapy.

Saltmarsh, Jenkins, and Fisher (1986) pioneered the TRAC model of group work: tasking, relating, acquiring, and contacting.

ASGW's *Professional Standards for the Training of Group Workers* focuses on psychoeducational, counseling, therapy, and task/work groups.

## PSYCHOEDUCATIONAL GROUPS

**Psychoeducational groups** were originally developed for use in educational settings, specifically public schools.

Sometimes these types of groups are simply referred to as **"educational groups"** or **"guidance" groups**.

"Psychoeducation group work emphasizes using education methods to acquire information and develop related meaning and skills" (Brown, 1997, p. 1).

Psychoeducation groups can be preventive, growth oriented, or remedial in their purpose and focus. They are increasingly being used in various settings outside of schools, including hospitals, mental health agencies, social service agencies, and universities (Jones & Robinson, 2000).

"The overarching goal in psychoeducational group work is to prevent future development of debilitating dysfunctions while strengthening coping skills and self-esteem" (Conyne, 1996, p. 157).

Because of their flexibility and efficiency, psychoeducational groups may even be preferred in counseling and psychotherapy environments "when managed care policies demand brief and less expensive treatment" (Brown, 1997, p. 1).

The size of psychoeducational groups will vary across settings, but a range from 20 to 40 individuals is not unusual. In such large groups, discussion and skill practice can take place in subgroups.

The leader of psychoeducational groups is in charge of managing the group as a whole, disseminating information, and breaking groups into subgroups when necessary.

Timing is crucial and the group leader must be cognizant of group members' readiness to approach certain activities (Jones & Robinson, 2000).

Psychoeducational group leaders should take steps before the group's first session, including planning for session length, session frequency, number of sessions, and what will occur within sessions (i.e., the curriculum). Follow-up planning for subsequent sessions is crucial.

Psychoeducational groups stress growth through knowledge (ASGW, 1991, 2000).

## COUNSELING GROUPS

**Counseling groups** are preventative, growth oriented, and remedial.

The focus of group counseling and interpersonal problem solving is on each person's behavior and development or change within the group. Although goals are personal, the group as a whole may also share them.

These groups emphasize group dynamics and interpersonal relationships.

Counseling groups are ideal for individuals experiencing "usual, but often difficult, problems of living" (ASGW, 1991, p. 14) that information available in psychoeducational groups alone will not solve.

The size of these counseling groups varies with the ages of the individuals involved, ranging from 3 or 4 in a children's group to 8 to 12 in an adult group.

The number of group meetings also fluctuates but will generally be anywhere from 6 to 16 sessions.

The leader is in charge of facilitating the group interaction but becomes less directly involved as the group develops.

The leader is often theory-driven in leading the group.

A major advantage of counseling groups is the interpersonal interaction, feedback, and contributions group members experience from each other over a period of time.

## PSYCHOTHERAPY GROUPS

A psychotherapy group is sometimes simply called **group psychotherapy**.

"Psychotherapy groups address personal and interpersonal problems of living . . . among people who may be experiencing severe and/or chronic maladjustment" (ASGW, 2000, p. 331).

Psychotherapy groups may be either **open ended** (admitting new members at any time) or **closed ended** (not admitting new members after the first session).

One of the primary aims of the group psychotherapy process is to reconstruct, sometimes through depth analysis, or rectify through various treatment modalities the personalities or intrapersonal functioning of those involved in the group (Brammer, Abrego, & Shostrom, 1993; Gazda, 1989).

The size of the group varies from 2 or 3 to 12 members and the duration of the group is measured in months, or even years.

The leader of the psychotherapy group is always an expert in one of the mental health disciplines (psychiatry, psychology, counseling, social work, or psychiatric nursing), who has training and expertise in dealing with people who have major emotional problems.

It is not wise or effective to just include individuals with personality disorders or diagnosable mental disorders (Yalom, 1995). Instead, a variety of individuals, a heterogeneous group, works best.

Group leaders must prescreen carefully and are wise to use prescreening instruments.

Most often leaders of psychotherapy groups operate from a theoretical position (e.g., psychoanalysis, gestalt, existential).

## TASK/WORK GROUPS

**Task/work groups** "promote efficient and effective accomplishment of group tasks among people who are gathered to accomplish group task goals" (ASGW, 2000, p. 330) including: "task forces, committees, planning groups, community organizations, discussion groups, and learning groups" (ASGW, 1991, p. 14).

Task/work groups emphasize accomplishment and efficiency in successfully completing identified work goals (a performance or a finished product) through collaboration.

Task/work groups do not focus on changing individuals.

Successful task/work groups depend on group dynamics — the interactions fostered through the relationships of members and leaders in connection with the complexity of the task involved.

The number of members within a task/work group may be large, but this type of group usually works best with fewer than 12 people because unintended subgrouping does not occur.

Task/work groups may disband abruptly after accomplishing their goal.

Task/work group members and leaders may have considerable contact with others in an organization in which the group is housed.

## MIXED GROUPS AND A PROPOSED REGROUPING OF CATEGORIES

Some groups don't fit any of the four major categories of groups.

Groups that defy classification are sometimes described as **mixed groups** because they encompass multiple ways of working with their members and may change their emphasis at different times in the development of the group.

Waldo and Bauman (1998) have proposed the use of at least five dimensions that could be used in describing groups – goals, process, members, setting, and leader.

A mixed group might begin with multiple purposes, i.e., psychoeducational, psychotherapeutic, and task oriented. The prototype for such an actual group can be found among a number of self-help groups.

<u>**Key Terms**</u>

*Can you define and describe each of the following terms? Be able to offer a brief example or relevant context for these concepts.*

> airtime
> closed-ended
> contact-focused group theory
> counseling groups
> counseling/interpersonal problem-solving groups
> "educational groups"
> GAP matrix for groups
> group psychotherapy
> "guidance groups"
> psychoeducational groups
> life-skill group
> life-skills training
> mixed groups
> open-ended
> self-help groups
> specialty/standards model
> support groups
> task/work groups
> team
> TRAC model of groups
> yearbook feedback

## Group Experience – Parallels and Reflections

1.  Describe the "out of class" group experience that you have begun. What "type" of group is it? What are some of your early before-the-group-begins feelings?

2.  Based on your understanding of the specialty models described in this chapter, what evidence have you seen so far that the group you have joined will in fact match the definitions of group type?

3.  What has your group facilitator, or the literature that you have read regarding the group, told you about the purpose of the group; the role of the leader or facilitator, the duration of the group, and your role as member?

<u>**Self Assessment Questions**</u>

**True or False Statements**

The following statements check your comprehension of terms and identification of individuals (knowledge and comprehension level); your ability to apply that knowledge to solve more challenging questions (application level), and your ability to evaluate given information (analysis and evaluation level).

Indicate whether each statement is true or false. If you believe a statement is false, identify the error in the space provided. When necessary, refer to your text, *Group Work: A Counseling Specialty* (4th ed.). An answer key appears at the end of this book.

1. Gazda distinguished among the 'three group types' by leader responsibility.

_____
_____
_____

2. "Work groups" are often categorized as personal growth groups.

_____
_____
_____

3. Counseling group leaders recommend that the number of children in children's counseling groups be greater than the number of members in adult counseling groups.

_____
_____
_____

4. Relationship enhancement in psychotherapy groups means to improve personalities or intrapersonal functioning.

_____
_____
_____

5. Task/work groups differ from the other three types of groups most dramatically in that they do not focus on changing individuals.

_____
_____
_____

6. Teams are a specific subtype of task/work groups.

_____
_____
_____

7. The acronym "GAP" in the GAP Matrix (Waldo & Bauman, 1998), stands for "goals and process."

_____
_____
_____

8. Leadership and membership are key distinctions between "self-help groups" and "support groups."

_____
_____
_____

9.  Group psychotherapy leaders are thought to facilitate members' growth in small groups.

_____
_____
_____

10.  Brief therapy with abusive individuals in groups is proving to be quite effective.

_____
_____
_____

11.  Saying "nice" but insignificant things about a person in a group is called "microcounseling."

_____
_____
_____

12.  Guidance/psychoeducational groups have expanded from educational settings to many others, including mental health treatment.

_____
_____
_____

13. Life-skills groups are an example of psychoeducational groups.

_____
_____
_____

**Multiple Choice Questions**

1. The ends of the *nature of group process* axis on the TRAC map of group processes and management are _____ and _____.
   a.  task achievement/process enhancement
   b.  facilitation/leadership
   c.  preventative and remedial
   d.  (none of the above)

2. Psychoeducational groups are one of the earliest types of group work to evolve. A premise upon which psychoeducational groups is based is _____.
   a.  that a group format is convenient
   b.  membership in a group is natural
   c.  education is treatment
   d.  all people need guidance

3. In the revised goals and process (GAP) matrix, "Goal" is best illustrated by which of the following?
   a.  Evoking emotional response
   b.  Applying principles of group dynamics
   c.  Purpose that guides direction of group
   d.  Use of interactive feedback and support

**Written Exercises**
Respond in writing to several of the following questions, prompts, and inquiries, designed to deepen your comprehension of the text. Student responses can lead to self-reflection and interesting discussions with others. You are encouraged to flex your imagination and make your understanding of group work as presented in these chapters come to life.

## Questions & Prompts for Written Reflection and Discussion

### Chapter 2

1. Consider the current literature on models of specialty groups. Select several articles from the professional literature that specifically address one or more of the four Association for Specialists in Group Work types of groups (i.e., psychoeducational, counseling, psychotherapy, and task/work groups). Compare and contrast these models. What stands out for you as the delimiters for each group type? Do you think that the four models adequately classify these group types based on the evidence that you have before you in these articles? If you see limitations to this existing model, speculate on solutions.

_____
_____
_____
_____
_____
_____
_____
_____
_____
_____
_____
_____
_____
_____

2. Access the full text of one or more of the journal articles that underpin the *specialty group model* cited in the reference section in Chapter 2. Thoroughly read the article and write up a brief critique of this original work. What do you view as this article's greatest strengths? Weaknesses? How does this article support your current understanding of specialty group models?

_____
_____
_____
_____
_____
_____
_____
_____
_____
_____
_____
_____

**Prompts for Group Members**

1. What "type" of group have you joined? In what ways do the defining features of the four types of group work covered in the text help you to define what is to happen during this experience? Are there any discrepancies between the text and your actual experience? Explain.

2. Take a look at the goals and process (GAP) model in your text. What have you experienced so far in your group that this model illustrates particularly well?

## Journal and Reflection

Space for journaling about your group work experiences is provided below. Use this space to reflect on your reading about group work, your classroom presentations and activities, the group dynamics of your classes themselves, and any simulations or actual group participation opportunities you may have. Comment here thoughtfully. Be sure to carefully honor your ethical commitment to uphold the confidentiality of others in your group. Reflections are yours and are not to reveal anyone else's information. Recording your thoughts and feelings will provide a written history of this phase of your group work education. (Attach additional sheets of paper if desired.)

_Entry date_ _____

# GROUP DYNAMICS

## Outcome Objectives

1. I can demonstrate my understanding of group dynamics.
2. I am able to define and give examples of:
   a. Group content
   b. Group process
3. I am able to describe and illustrate the balance between content and process
4. I can describe the "group as a system" as one way of explaining group dynamics.
5. I can describe and give examples of factors that influence group dynamics including:
   a. Preplanning
   b. Group structure
   c. Group exercises
   d. Group interaction
   e. Members' roles
   f. Types of roles
   g. Problems in carrying out roles
6. I can identify and describe possible effects of positive and negative variables on group dynamics.
7. I am able to describe the use of the following activities for learning the dynamics of a group:
   a. Videotaping
   b. Journaling
   c. Outdoor experiences
   d. Simulation games for team building
   e. Sociometrics and learning integration
8. I can identify, compare, and contrast group, individual, and family dynamics in relationship to these factors:
   a. Person
   b. Processing
   c. Consequences

## Chapter Overview

Both members and leaders should be aware of group dynamics as they can have either a positive or negative impact on the development of the group. Group structure, the purpose of the group, and members' roles are important areas to be considered under the broad umbrella of group dynamics.

## Chapter Highlights

Groups are dynamic entities that have a direct and indirect impact on their members (Bion, 1959; Yalom, 1995).

People act differently in groups than they do by themselves. As a general rule, **primary affiliation groups** exert greater pressure on individuals than do **secondary affiliation groups**.

The influence of groups on members, and what has grown to be known as **group dynamics,** was first studied as a phenomenon in work environments.

Changes in behavior as a result of observation and manipulation of conditions in an environment became known as the **Hawthorne effect**.

Many factors contribute to the overall concept of group dynamics, including the group's purpose, communication patterns, power/control issues, and member roles. Lewin (1948), believed group dynamics includes everything that goes on in a small group.

## GROUP CONTENT AND GROUP PROCESS

These are two powerful elements in a group's development and productivity. The amount and mixture of group content and group process are what ultimately determine the dynamics within a group.

Group content involves the actual words, ideas, and information exchanged within a group, as well as the purpose of the group.

Group process is the interaction of group members with each other.

As groups develop, less time generally is spent on content material and more is focused on process functions.

Donigian and Malnati (1997) outlined seven types of frequent group processes: contagion, conflict, anxiety, consensual validation, universality, family reenactment, and installation of hope.

Groups that work well are those in which group members and leaders are aware of the need to have content and process balanced.

## THE GROUP AS A SYSTEM: A WAY OF EXPLAINING GROUP DYNAMICS

A **system** is a set of elements standing in interaction with one another (Agazarian, 1997). Each element in the system is affected by whatever happens to any other element.

A system is only as strong as its weakest part; likewise, the system is greater than the sum of its parts (Gladding, 2002).

A group can be conceptualized as a system that is made up of three crucial parts: the group leader, the group members, and the group as a whole (Donigian & Malnati, 1997).

In a systems context, group members are always deciding between their needs for *differentiating themselves* (i.e., taking care of their needs to do things by themselves) and *integrating with others* (i.e., doing things with others) (Matthews, 1992).

From a systems perspective, group leaders must orchestrate their efforts in helping members and the group as a whole achieve a balance of individual and collective needs as the group develops.

From a systems perspective, even small or seemingly insignificant events make a difference in the group.

## INFLUENCING GROUP DYNAMICS

Group workers are wise to spend time and energy attending to the preplanning part of a group, the group structure, group exercises, group interaction, and members' roles.

### Preplanning
The dynamics of a group begin before the group ever convenes.

In the pregroup stage, the leader(s) plan for what type of group to conduct, in what setting it should be held, how long it will last, who should be included, and how it will be evaluated.

Three factors that must be considered in preplanning are clarity of purpose, a group's setting, and time.

Size makes a difference in the dynamics of the group.

Membership affects dynamics with regard to both the mixture and number of people in it.

**Heterogeneous groups** (those composed of persons with dissimilar backgrounds) can broaden members' horizons and enliven interpersonal interactions. Such groups may be helpful in problem solving, such as in psychotherapy and counseling groups.

**Homogeneous groups** (those centered around a presenting problem or similarity in gender, ethnicity, sexual orientation, or sociocultural background) are extremely beneficial in working through specific issues.

It is the nature and purpose of the group that usually determines what its member composition will be.

### Group Structure
**Group structure** refers to the physical setup of the group and the interaction of each group member in relation to the group as a whole. Structure will vary according to the type of group.

The **physical structure** (i.e., the arrangement of group members) has a strong influence on how a group operates.

Many groups, regardless of purpose, use a **circle** format. In this configuration, all members have direct access to each other (Yalom, 1995) as well as implied equality in status and power.

Leavitt (1951) devised three communication networks (i.e., structure) in addition to the circle: the "chain," the "Y," and the "wheel."

In a psychoeducational group, members may be seated in lines and rows in **theater style**.

### Group Exercises
There are certain advantages and disadvantages to employing exercises in a group setting (Carroll et al., 1997; Jacobs, 1992).

Leaders may wish to use exercises as catalysts, especially early in the group's life, to bring people together. In this capacity, games and exercises can play a vital part in promoting group dynamics.

**Group exercises** can be used anytime and can be beneficial through promoting a positive atmosphere in a group.

There are also some ethically questionable games and exercises that promote anxiety and do harm; Gazda (1989) advises that group leaders who use them do so cautiously.

## Group Interaction

**Group interaction,** which can be described as the way members relate to each other, consists of nonverbal and verbal behaviors and the attitudes that go with them.

Group interaction exists on a continuum, from extremely nondirective to highly directive.

**Nonverbal behaviors** make up "more than 50 percent of the messages communicated in social relationships" and are usually perceived as more honest and less subject to manipulation than verbal behaviors (Vander Kolk, 1985, p. 171).

The four main categories of nonverbal behavior, according to Vander Kolk, are *body behaviors, interaction with the environment, speech,* and *physical appearance.*

**Verbal behavior** is also crucial in group dynamics. One of the most important variables to track is who speaks to whom and how often each member speaks.

In task, psychoeducational, counseling, and psychotherapy groups, discussion allows members to process information relevant to making decisions (Forsyth, 1999).

## Members' Roles

A **role** is "a dynamic structure within an individual (based on needs, cognitions, and values), which usually comes to life under the influence of social stimuli or defined positions" (Munich & Astrachan, 1983, p. 20).

The manifestation of a role is based on the individual's expectation of self and others and the interaction one has in particular groups and situations.

When groups change or when people change groups, roles are frequently altered.

### *Types of Roles*

One way to conceptualize most roles in groups is to view them as primarily functioning in one of three ways: facilitative/building, maintenance, or blocking (Capuzzi & Gross, 1992).

Four major forms of role difficulties are role collision, role incompatibility, role confusion, and role transition.

## THE EFFECT OF POSITIVE AND NEGATIVE VARIABLES ON GROUP DYNAMICS

Many group specialists (e.g., Corey, 2000; Jacobs et al., 2002) have listed a number of **positive group variables** within groups essential to group life and functioning. These variables include member commitment; readiness of members for the group experience; the attractiveness of the group for its members; a feeling of belonging, acceptance, and security; and clear communication.

Yalom (1995) was among the first to delineate positive primary group variables; he called these positive forces **curative (therapeutic) factors within groups**.

The following therapeutic factors (Yalom, 1995) constitute both the "actual mechanisms of change" and "conditions for change" (p. 4): installation of hope, universality, imparting of information, altruism, corrective recapitulation of the primary family group, development of socialization techniques, imitative behavior, interpersonal learning, group cohesiveness, catharsis, and existential factors.

Bemak and Epp (1996) have added to Yalom's list what they consider to be a 12th therapeutic factor—love.

Negative group variables operate as well. These variables include, but are not limited to, avoiding conflict, abdicating group responsibilities, anesthetizing to contradictions within the group, and the group becoming narcissistic.

## LEARNING GROUP DYNAMICS

Knowledge of group dynamics that is both experiential and cognitive can help a group worker either lead or be in a group.

One model involves the following five activities that help participants gain greater insight into the ways their group is functioning: videotaping, journaling, outdoor experiences, simulation games for team building, and sociometrics and learning integration (Marotta, Peters, & Paliokas, 2000).

## GROUP, INDIVIDUAL, AND FAMILY DYNAMICS

Individual, group, and family approaches to helping have some parallels in history, theory, technique, and process, but because of the unique composition of each, the dynamics of these ways of working are distinct (Gladding, 2000).

A complexity of working with others is a process that involves knowing what to do, when to do it, and what the probable outcomes may be.

### Persons

In working with individuals, only one person is the focus of attention. Therefore, attention is almost always centered on intrapersonal issues.

With groups and families, the focus is on more than one person. It is often simultaneously intrapersonal and interpersonal.

Groups are distinct from families in that the members come together initially as strangers for a common purpose (Becvar, 1982; Hines, 1988). They have no experience of working together. Families, on the other hand, have members with a shared history of interactions.

In groups, intrapersonal change may be just as important as interpersonal change, whereas in families the focus is usually on changing the family system.

## Processing

"**Processing** refers to helping group members identify and examine what happened in the group and their individual experiences of the event, as well as how the event occurred and how different members responded to it (Glass & Benshoff, 1999, p. 16).

## Consequences

A major difference in working with individuals, groups, and families is what happens once helping ends.

Individual, group, and family approaches overlap and yet are distinct from each other. Persons involved, how they are involved, and how they relate to the professional clinician and the others outside of treatment sessions must be taken into consideration in any comparison.

## Key Concepts

*Can you define and describe each of the following terms? Be able to offer a brief example or relevant context for these concepts.*

> altruism
> anxiety
> avoiding conflict
> blocking role
> catharsis
> chain
> circle
> clarity of purpose
> conflict
> consensual validation
> contagion
> corrective recapitulation of the primary family group
> curative (therapeutic) factors within the group
> development of socializing techniques
> existential factors
> facilitative/building role
> family reenactment
> group cohesiveness
> group content
> group dynamics
> group exercises
> group interaction
> group process
> group setting
> group structure
> Hawthorne effect
> heterogeneous groups
> homogeneous groups
> imitative behavior
> imparting of information
> instillation of hope
> interpersonal learning
> Law of Triviality

linear
maintenance role
narcissistic groups
negative group variables
nonverbal behaviors
PARS Model
physical structure
positive group variables
primary affiliation groups
processing
psychic numbing
role
role collision
role confusion
role incompatibility
role transition
secondary affiliation groups
social influence
sociogram
sociometry
subgrouping
system
systemically
systems theory
theater style
universality
verbal behavior
wheel
"Y"

## Key Personalities

*Can you identify and discuss the contributions of the following experts?*

Lewin, Kurt
Mayo, Elton
Yalom, Irvin

### Group Experience –Parallels and Reflections

1. In your "out of class" group, what dynamics have you become aware of? Describe these dynamics and speculate on how and why they have emerged.

2. What influences on the dynamics can you identify? Mention observations about group content and process. Can you find examples of a balance between the two?

3. Consider the structure, the leader/facilitator's use of exercises, and the group interaction. What influence do these appear to have on your group?

4. From your text's definition and descriptions of *positive* and *negative group variables*, what variables are you witnessing in the small group?

## Self Assessment Questions

### True or False Statements

The following statements check your comprehension of terms and identification of individuals (knowledge and comprehension level); your ability to apply that knowledge to solve more challenging questions (application level), and your ability to evaluate given information (analysis and evaluation level).

Indicate whether each statement is true or false. If you believe a statement is false, identify the error in the space provided. When necessary, refer to your text, *Group Work: A Counseling Specialty* (4th ed.). An answer key appears at the end of this book.

1. Research on "group dynamics" began in laboratory settings.

_____
_____
_____

2. "Process" is the interaction of group members with one another.

_____
_____
_____

3. Universality is a therapeutic factor that allows members to recognize that others may have similar life experiences.

_____
_____
_____

4. Balance between content and process is an ideal, according to Hulse-Killackcy, Schumacher, and Kraus (1999).

_____
_____
_____

5. Sitting in a circle, as the physical structure for a group, promotes a nonhierarchical, equal access structure.

6. Yalom's curative factor where members accept responsibility for their own lives is labeled altruism.

_____
_____
_____

7. Family members exert greater pressure on individuals than do "primary affiliation" groups.

_____

_____

_____

8. The actual words, ideas, and information exchanged within a group is referred to as content.

_____

_____

_____

9. Nonverbal behaviors make up more than 70% of interaction and are perceived as more honest and less subject to manipulation.

_____

_____

_____

10. "Blocking" is NOT a type of leader role in a group setting.

_____

_____

_____

11. Systems theory is a way of looking at a group as an organism and acknowledging the group as greater than the sum of its parts.

_____

_____

_____

## Multiple Choice Questions

1. As a result of Mayo's workplace research in the mid-1940s, changes in behavior as a result of observation and manipulation of conditions in an environment is known as the _____.

    a. Hawthorne effect        c. Law of Triviality
    b. primary affiliation groups    d. secondary affiliation groups

2. The complexity of group dynamics are reflected in our attempt to classify the ways factors influence others directly (i.e., cause-and-effect) or indirectly (i.e., circularly). One theoretical explanation that attempts to account for such complexities is _____ theory.
    a. sociogram         c. specialty/standards
    b. systems           d. critical incident

3. You are invited to participate in a "planning group" for a community service organization that you belong to, and when you arrive the chairs in your meeting room are arranged in a "chain" configuration. You might speculate that the planning group will be characterized by _____.

    a.   an implied equality in status and power
    b.   people being seated in some hierarchical order
    c.   the leader being the "conduit" of all information
    d.   an emphasis on obtaining cognitive information

**Written Exercises**

Respond in writing to several of the following questions, prompts, and inquiries, designed to deepen your comprehension of the text. Student responses can lead to self-reflection and interesting discussions with others. You are encouraged to flex your imagination and make your understanding of group work as presented in these chapters come to life.

## Questions & Prompts for Written Reflection and Discussion

### Chapter 3

1. Create your own brief scenario that describes some imbalance between process and content in group work. Using the basic graphic design to visually conceptualize the balance of process and content (see pages 49-50) in groups, illustrate your imbalance. Share your graphic design with others but withhold your verbal scenario. Ask them to create a narrative to accompany your illustration. How close is it to yours? Discuss the similarities.

_____
_____
_____
_____
_____
_____
_____
_____
_____
_____
_____
_____
_____
_____

2. Observe several group structures in your environment. What physical structures do you observe (pp. 53-55)? How well does the physical structure match your impressions of both the leader and member roles?

_____
_____
_____
_____
_____
_____
_____
_____
_____
_____
_____
_____
_____
_____

3. Watch carefully the interpersonal dynamics of a group in which you are a member (e.g., classroom, club, community organization). What member roles (pp. 60-63) can you detect? Do you observe any excellent models for the facilitative/building role, the maintenance role, or members who are blockers? Describe the effect of each role on the group. Report what you have observed (ensuring anonymity where appropriate).

_____
_____
_____
_____
_____
_____
_____
_____
_____
_____
_____
_____
_____
_____
_____
_____

## Prompts for Group Members

1. What dynamics are you particularly aware of in your out-of-class group experience? Write about your personal reaction to these dynamics. Are you able to determine how or where these dynamics occur?

2. What member roles are emerging in group? Are you able to see yourself taking on any particular role at this point? If the roles you are observing are not facilitative of a positive group experience, what do you see your group leader "doing," if anything?

3. Of the curative (therapeutic) factors with groups, as discussed in your text, are any becoming observable at this stage of your group? If the group you are participating in is not counseling or psychotherapeutic, how is your psychoeducation or task/work group dealing with conflict?

**Journal and Reflection**

Space for journaling about your group work experiences is provided below. Use this space to reflect on your reading about group work, your classroom presentations and activities, the group dynamics of your classes themselves, and any simulations or actual group participation opportunities you may have. Comment here thoughtfully. Be sure to carefully honor your ethical commitment to uphold the confidentiality of others in your group. Reflections are yours and are not to reveal anyone else's information. Recording your thoughts and feelings will provide a written history of this phase of your group work education. (Attach additional sheets of paper if desired.)

_Entry date_ _____

## CHAPTER 4

# EFFECTIVE GROUP LEADERSHIP

## Outcome Objectives

1. I comprehend and can describe effective group leadership.
2. I can identify and describe group leadership styles.
3. I am able to differentiate between leadership styles for different groups.
4. I can describe personal qualities of effective group leaders including:
   a. The trait approach
   b. Personality and specific groups
5. I comprehend and can discuss the role of theory and effective group leaders.
6. I understand the following skills of effective group leaders:
   a. Core group skills
   b. Specific group skills
7. I understand and describe group leadership functions including:
   a. Main functions of group leaders
   b. Leaders and group conflict
8. I can explain the advantages and the limitations of the use of coleaders in groups.
9. I comprehend and can discuss group leadership training.
10. I can describe the processes and benefits of group supervision.

## Chapter Overview

A group leader must be flexible and have some personal qualities such as warmth and empathy in order to be effective. The role and function of group leaders varies, but group leaders must always be knowledgeable about group operations and skilled in helping individual members and the group as a whole.

## Chapter Highlights

Caring, openness, strength, awareness, warmth, flexibility, and sensitivity are characteristics group leaders often display.

Many issues surround group leaders and leadership. Some of them deal with substance, such as the mastery of skills, others with style and personality.

There are different types of leaders, just as there are distinct types of groups, and the appropriateness of an individual to a particular group depends on many complex and interrelated factors.

It is assumed that a leader is one who implements a number of facilitative qualities in a group, such as envisioning goals, motivating people, and achieving a workable unity, in an appropriate and timely way (Carroll, Bates, & Johnson, 1997; Gardner, 1990).

## GROUP LEADERSHIP STYLES

The style that a group leader displays has a direct effect on the behavior of group members and group dynamics (Sampson & Marthas, 1981).

Most effective group leaders show versatility (Kottler, 1994). They modify their leadership pattern to coincide with the purpose of the group and its membership.

Lewin (1944) identified three basic styles of group leadership: authoritarian, democratic, and laissez-faire.

Lieberman, Yalom, and Miles (1973) describe six basic styles: energizers, providers, social engineers, impersonals, laissez-faires, and managers.

**Authoritarian group leaders** envision themselves as experts and tend to be rigid and conventional in their beliefs (Cheng, Chae, & Gunn, 1998).

Authoritarian leaders often interpret, give advice, and generally direct the movement of the group much like parents control the actions of a child. They demand obedience and expect conformity from their followers.

Authoritarian leaders are often charismatic and manipulative (McClure, 1994).

Frequently, they structure their groups using the wheel model (explained in chapter 3), which results in an autocratic **leader-centered group**.

An authoritarian style of leadership is also sometimes referred to as *guru oriented* (Starak, 1988), and McGregor (1960) characterizes this type of leader as a so-called **Theory X leader**.

**Democratic group leaders** are more group centered and less directive.

Leaders operating from this perspective, such as Carl Rogers (1970), trust group participants to develop their own potential and that of other group members.

These leaders serve as facilitators of the group process and not as directors of it. They cooperate, collaborate, and share responsibilities with the group.

McGregor (1960) refers to leaders who are group centered as **Theory Y leaders**.

Leaders who are inwardly comfortable and trust group members to take care of themselves and others often use this approach.

**Laissez-faire leaders** are leaders in name only. They fail to provide any structure or direction for their groups, so members are left with the responsibility of leading.

Laissez-faire leaders "lead" groups from a **group-centered perspective**, focusing on members and interpersonal processes.

A disadvantage to this type of leadership is that the group as a whole may be slow to establish agendas and achieve goals.

At the extreme of a group-centered approach is what Ouchi (1981) describes as a **Theory Z leader**.

So-called **leaderless groups** rotate the leadership role among their members. In these groups, leaders emerge as the group develops.

In many forms of these groups, this style of peer leadership works well. Nonprofessional leaders in such cases develop as their group progresses.

Another type of leaderless group meets alternatively with and without a leader (Mullan & Rosenbaum, 1978; Wolf, 1963; Yalom, 1995). However, notable group specialists (Gazda, 1989; Yalom, 1995) warn about the potential dangers of these groups.

## LEADERSHIP STYLES FOR DIFFERENT GROUPS

Different types of groups demand specific styles of leadership (Association for Specialists in Group Work, 2000).

In psychoeducation and task/work groups, leaders do best when they are direct and keep the group focused on the topic or job at hand.

Psychotherapy and counseling groups require that leaders provide support, caring, and sometimes confrontation and structure.

The **interpersonal style of group leadership** focuses on transactions between individuals in the group, whereas the **intrapersonal style of group leadership** stresses the inward reactions of individual group members.

Ideally, counseling group leaders begin by concentrating on the group's interpersonal dimension. Later, when members are more comfortable with one another, the leaders integrate intrapersonal material into the group

Leadership may also focus on the accomplishment of tasks versus the development of personal relationships.

**Core mechanisms of group leadership** are emotional stimulation, caring, meaning attribution, and executive function. Lieberman et al. (1973) first described these universal central factors and distinguished them from a group leader's orientation (i.e., theoretical approach).

## PERSONAL QUALITIES OF EFFECTIVE GROUP LEADERS

Every group leader brings his or her personal qualities to a group, including preferred ways of perceiving the world and experiences in relating to oneself and others.

Personal qualities of effective leaders have traditionally been explained through examining their personality traits or learned skills.

### The Trait Approach

Some group work specialists have compiled long lists of ideal qualities they believe are essential to the personality of an effective group leader, a so-called **trait approach** to group leadership (Johnson & Johnson, 2000).

Slavson (1962) advocates that the personal qualities of group leaders include poise, judgment, empathy, ego strength, freedom from excessive anxiety, a desire to help people, tolerance of frustration, imagination, intuition, perceptiveness, and an ability to avoid self-preoccupation.

Corey and Corey (2002) include such qualities as courage, willingness to model, presence, goodwill and caring, belief in group process, openness, nondefensiveness in coping with attacks, personal power, stamina, willingness to seek new experiences, self-awareness, humor, and inventiveness.

The trait view of leadership, although popular and appealing, has little support in research. No single personality type is best suited to be a group leader.

## PERSONALITY AND SPECIFIC GROUPS

Studies point out that persons who are effective in some groups, such as those that are relationship oriented, may not be skilled in other groups, such as those that are task oriented (Forsyth, 1999).

Research indicates that ineffective group leaders are characterized as aggressive, authoritarian, pressure oriented, disrespectful of members, confrontational, egocentric, inappropriate self-disclosurers, and poorly timed interveners (Lieberman et al., 1973).

Experienced leaders act more like each other than inexperienced leaders do (Kottler, 1994).

Would-be group leaders need to explore through both experience and reflection whether they are suited by temperament and skills to operate as the leader of a group.

## THEORY AND EFFECTIVE GROUP LEADERS

The principles by which group leaders are guided are known as **theory**. The word *theory* receives mixed reactions in the field of group work because it is often misunderstood and overused.

Among the advantages of theories is that they are practical. A good theory helps a practitioner understand and find meaning in experiences by providing a conceptual framework.

A second advantage of theory is it serves as a guide to expected behavior.

A third advantage of a theory is its **heuristic** (i.e., research) dimension.

Group leaders without any theory behind their interventions will probably find that their groups never reach a productive stage.

A further argument for the employment of theory in groups is that it helps practitioners formulate their own personalized approach to the groups in which they work.

Group leaders may have difficulty choosing a theory because some theories tend to be "either too specific or too general to account for all the elements involved in the complexity of human behavior" (Ohlsen, Horne, & Lawe, 1988, pp. 48–49).

A second problem in selecting a theory is that theories may become political. Practitioners of specific approaches tend to reinforce each other and exclude others.

A third drawback of theories is that they have many overlapping dimensions. The meaning of many theoretical concepts can be quite different from their origins.

A further limitation of theories, and a potentially dangerous one, is that group leaders who use theory may notice only select aspects of their group members (Kottler, 1994).

## SKILLS OF EFFECTIVE GROUP LEADERS

Group leader skills are displayed in different ways and at various stages during the life of a group. Therefore, to make appropriate leadership decisions, group leaders must be well educated and know what skills are at the core of leading an effective group.

### Core Group Skills
Regardless of the type of group people are participating in, some critical core skills need to be exercised if the group is to be successful.

The ASGW's (1991) *Professional Standards for the Training of Group Workers* lists 16 core group skills. Some of the core group skills are solely the responsibility of the leader. Other core group skills depend more on the cooperative efforts of a group leader and members.

### Specific Group Skills
Group leaders should recognize that a number of group skills are the same as those displayed in working with individuals. Skills that differ significantly between group and individual work include facilitating, protecting, blocking, linking, diagnosing, reality testing, modification, delegating, and creativity.

By being familiar with skills and how they are employed, group leaders increase their range of alternative actions (Ivey & Ivey, 1999).

## GROUP LEADERSHIP FUNCTIONS

A group leader must be able to function in a variety of ways at different times. Experience, coupled with training, permits leaders to operate in such a manner.

### Main Functions of Group Leaders
Bates et al. (1982) characterize four main functions that group leaders need to display at various times: traffic director, modeler of appropriate behavior, interactional catalyst, and communication facilitator. Each of these roles takes specific skills.

### Leaders and Group Conflict
A primary function of group leaders is dealing constructively with conflict. The display of conflict is normal within a group and offers a potential opportunity for growth within the group if managed properly.

Five specific techniques for managing conflict in groups have been proposed by Simpson (1977) and elaborated by Kormanski (1982): withdrawal from the conflict, suppressing the conflict, integrating conflicting ideas to form new solutions, working out a compromise, and using power to resolve the conflict.

Overall, a prerequisite to becoming an effective leader is learning what strategies and roles to employ in conflict situations and when.

## COLEADERS IN GROUPS

A **coleader** is a professional or a professional-in-training who undertakes the responsibility of sharing the leadership of a group with another leader in a mutually determined manner.

The efficacy of using coleaders depends on many factors, including economic considerations, advantages to the group, and the compatibility of the leaders.

According to experts, strengths associated with coleading a group include: ease of handling the group in difficult situations, uses of modeling, feedback, shared specialized knowledge, and pragmatic considerations.

Among the potential liabilities of coleading are the lack of coordinated efforts, being too leader-focused, competition, and collusion.

Coleading requires that both leaders be competent to begin with and that they be able to express a wide range of facilitative skills (e.g., self-disclosure, timing) in an appropriate manner.

The three main models of co-led groups are those in which the lead is (a) **alternated** (b) **shared** or (c) **apprenticed** (a more experienced leader takes charge of the group to show a novice how to work with groups).

## GROUP LEADERSHIP TRAINING

In the early days of group work (the 1950s and 1960s) before training standards were established, almost anyone could claim to be a group leader and consequently start a group. Such an approach is no longer recognized or considered ethical by major group associations.

It takes time and training to perfect group leadership skills.

Yalom (1995) strongly advocates that potential group psychotherapy leaders participate in groups as a part of their training.

Jacobs et al. (2002) point out the importance of being in groups to fine-tune skills; people must first experience the power of the group as followers before they can become group leaders.

Group leaders must have specialized knowledge in the theories, dynamics, interpersonal, ethical, research, and stage components of group work (Association for Specialists in Group Work, 2000).

Among the methods that have been established to train group leaders are (a) group-based training, (b) the group generalist model, (c) the educational and developmental procedure, (d) systematic group leadership training, (e) the critical-incident model and intervention cube, and (f) skills-based training models.

Yalom (1995) concurs with a holistic, research-based, balanced, and multidimensional emphasis in training.

"Supervised experiential training is a key component of group leader instruction" (Stockton & Toth, 1996, p. 280).

Supervision for group workers is essential after formal training. Without ongoing supervision and evaluation, original errors made by a group leader may be reinforced by simple repetition (Yalom, 1995).

One way to minimize problems and processes in group supervision is to make it developmental and comprehensive.

The American Group Psychotherapy Association recommends a minimum of 180 hours of supervision for group leaders in training.

Trotzer (1999) states that one good way of being supervised is to have two potential group leaders colead a group under the supervision of a more experienced leader.

"Support for **peer group supervision** is based on the belief that it offers opportunities for vicarious learning in a supportive group environment" (Christensen & Kline, 2001, pp. 81-82). This type of supervision also may reduce hierarchy and dependency needs found within individual supervision.

A less effective way of supervising is through listening to an audiotape of a group.

The least effective way of conducting group supervision is through having a supervisee report either orally or in writing what occurred in the group.

If supervision is successful, group leader trainees will grow in four areas (Bernard, 1979; Freeman & McHenry, 1996; Lanning, 1986): process skills, conceptual skills, personalization skills, and professional skills.

## Key Concepts

*Can you define and describe each of the following terms? Be able to offer a brief example or relevant context for these concepts.*

> alternated (coleadership)
> apprenticed (coleadership)
> authoritarian group leaders
> blocking
> burnout
> caring
> coleader
> communication facilitator
> conceptual skills
> core mechanisms of group leadership
> creativity
> critical-incident model
> cutting off
> delegating

democratic group leaders
diagnosing
drawing out
educational and developmental procedure
emotional stimulation
executive function
facilitating
group-based training
group-centered perspective
group generalist model
Group Leader Self-Efficacy Instrument (GLSI)
heuristic
holding the focus
integrating conflicting ideas to form new solutions
interactional catalyst
interpersonal style of group leadership
intervention cube concept
intrapersonal style of group leadership
laissez-faire leaders
leader-centered group
leaderless groups
linking
meaning attribution
mediation
modeler of appropriate behavior
modification
peer group supervision
personalization skills
personal power
position power
process skills
professional skills
protecting
reality testing
self-efficacy
settling-down period
shared (coleadership)
shifting the focus
Skilled Group Counseling Model
Skilled Group Counseling Scale
suppressing conflict
systematic group leadership training
theory
theory X leader
theory Y leaders
theory Z leaders
traditional leader
traffic director
trait approach
transformational leader
tying things together

using eyes
using power to resolve the conflict
we/they mentality
withdrawal from the conflict
working out a compromise

## Group Experience –Parallels and Reflections

1. At this stage of your small group experience, characterize your group leader's style. What evidence do you have that supports your belief? How does her or his leadership style feel for you as a member?

2. Consider the *core mechanisms of group leadership* (e.g., caring, executive function). What mechanisms have begun to emerge in your small group? Can you pinpoint any leader behaviors that contribute to these core mechanisms?

3. Referring to the list of *core group skills* (p. 86), contrast what you notice about your group leader's skills. Find examples (anonymous) from group sessions that illustrate these skill areas.

4. If your small group is co-facilitated/coled what advantages are you able to identify at this stage of group development? Are there any limitations that you notice at this point? Assess the communication between your two leaders. How well do you think or feel they work together?

## Self Assessment Questions

### True or False Statements

The following statements check your comprehension of terms and identification of individuals (knowledge and comprehension level); your ability to apply that knowledge to solve more challenging questions (application level), and your ability to evaluate given information (analysis and evaluation level).

Indicate whether each statement is true or false. If you believe a statement is false, identify the error in the space provided. When necessary, refer to your text, *Group Work: A Counseling Specialty* (4th ed.). An answer key appears at the end of this book.

1. Leaders who attempt to empower members of a subcommittee to make critical decisions are practicing traditional leadership.

_____
_____
_____

2. A "Theory X leader" leads in an authoritarian style.

_____
_____
_____

3. One of the *core mechanisms of group leadership* is "executive function," which provides cognitive explanations for what is occurring in the group.

_____
_____
_____

4. The trait approach takes into consideration a group leader's *personal qualities*, those characteristics of personality that influence the group.

_____
_____
_____

5. *Heuristic* dimensions are research dimensions of a group leadership theory.

_____
_____
_____

6. Clarifying accomplishes the goal of "honest self-investigation; to promote full use of potentials; to bring about awareness of self-contradictions" (Corey, 2000).

_____
_____
_____

7. Position power conflict is often seen between mature individuals.

_____
_____
_____

8. Collusion and competition between co-leaders are two limitations in group work.

_____
_____
_____

9. The "critical-incident model" for training group leaders has the trainee studying group dynamics, observing the instructor leading, and then coleading under supervision.

_____
_____
_____

10. With successful supervision, group leader trainees will improve their conceptual, process, and professional skills.

_____
_____
_____

11. Democratic group leaders envision themselves as experts.

_____
_____
_____

12. Laissez-faire group leaders do not provide structure for their groups and are actually leaders in name only.

_____

_____

_____

13. Meaning attribution is a core mechanism of group leadership.

_____

_____

_____

14. Group leaders help to open up communication between group members by facilitation.

_____

_____

_____

15. Acting as an interactional catalyst requires the group leader to promote interaction between group members while not drawing attention to him/herself.

_____

_____

_____

16. A mediator is a professional or a professional-in-training who undertakes the responsibility of a group with another leader in a mutually determined manner.

_____

_____

_____

17. Interpersonal leadership focuses on transactions between individuals in the group as opposed to the inward reactions of individual members.

_____

_____

_____

18. Group leaders are guided by principles.

_____

_____

_____

**Multiple Choice Questions**

1. The *trait approach* of group leadership is supported by long lists of personality qualities that advocates believe are essential for success as a group leader. Which of the following pairs is NOT a *personality characteristic* with its corresponding *type of relationship*.
    a. adaptability/positive      c. extroversion/unclear
    b. dominance/negative      d. (none of the above)

2. Which of the following best exemplifies the *executive function* in group leadership?
    a. clarifying      c. setting rules
    b. encouragement      d. offering support

3. Group conflict places some measure of stress on the leaders. Conflict can be viewed positively as _____.
  a.  an opportunity for growth within the group
  b.  a microcosm of effective problems-solving
  c.  unique moments that test a leader's skills
  d.  (none of the above)

4. Which of the following is NOT an apparent advantage to coleadership in group work?
  a. feedback                          c. collusion
  b. use of modeling                   d. shared specialized knowledge

5. Stockton and Toth (1996) summarized four components necessary for successful group leadership training. They include grounding in theory and each of the following EXCEPT _____.
  a.  opportunities to observe group leaders in action
  b.  participation in a personal growth group experience
  c.  practice in leading or coleading a group under supervision
  d.  a minimum of 600 hours of supervised group leadership

**Written Exercises**
Respond in writing to several of the following questions, prompts, and inquiries, designed to deepen your comprehension of the text. Student responses can lead to self-reflection and interesting discussions with others. You are encouraged to flex your imagination and make your understanding of group work as presented in these chapters come to life.

**Questions & Prompts for Written Reflection and Discussion**

**Chapter 4**

1. Reflect back on your personal experiences in different types of groups (e.g., task/work groups, psychoeducation groups) and the group leaders who led them. What do you remember about their leadership styles? Are there any outstanding examples of *transformative leadership*? How about *traditional leadership*? How did each group leader enhance your experience as a member? Do you recall any leader behaviors that were detrimental to your participation or your potential for success in those groups?

_____
_____
_____
_____
_____
_____
_____
_____
_____
_____
_____
_____

2. Describe a current group membership experience to others in your class (be aware of and honor any confidentiality obligations, of course). Envision that group under the leadership of a variety of leader styles. What do you foresee would be the result of each leadership style? Speculate on the current leader's self-perception of his or her leadership style. If appropriate, ask the group leader to describe "how" she or he leads. Share your findings with others in class.

_____
_____
_____
_____
_____
_____
_____
_____
_____
_____
_____
_____
_____
_____
_____

3. Consider some of your personality traits or attributes. Given what you think is true about them at this point in your development, what do you see as particular strengths and potential limitations for yourself as a group leader? Record some of your thoughts on paper. Share your hypotheses in a small group. What are others' reactions to your perceptions? Are your team members in agreement or do they perceive you differently than you see yourself? What about your perceptions of them?

_____
_____
_____
_____
_____
_____
_____
_____
_____
_____
_____
_____
_____

**Prompts for Group Members**

1. Write about your group leader's leadership style. What do you notice about his or her way of leading? Are you aware of anything that you struggle with in this regard?

2. What *specific group skills* have you noticed? What reactions have you had as you recognize the leader's skills actually being applied in real group work?

**Journal and Reflection**

Space for journaling about your group work experiences is provided below. Use this space to reflect on your reading about group work, your classroom presentations and activities, the group dynamics of your classes themselves, and any simulations or actual group participation opportunities you may have. Comment here thoughtfully. Be sure to carefully honor your ethical commitment to uphold the confidentiality of others in your group. Reflections are yours and are not to reveal anyone else's information. Recording your thoughts and feelings will provide a written history of this phase of your group work education. (Attach additional sheets of paper if desired.)

_Entry date_ _____

## CHAPTER 5

# BEGINNING A GROUP

## Outcome Objectives

1. I can describe and I am able to discuss the following 5 steps in the forming stage of groups.
   a. Step 1: Developing a rationale for the group
   b. Step 2: Deciding on a theoretical format
   c. Step 3: Weighing practical considerations
   d. Step 4: Publicizing the group
   e. Step 5: Pretraining and selecting members and a leader
2. I comprehend the tasks involved in beginning a group including:
   a. Dealing with apprehension
   b. Reviewing goals and contracts
   c. Specifying group rules
   d. Setting limits
   e. Promoting a positive interchange among members
3. I am able to identify and resolve potential group problems during the forming stage of group including:
   a. People problems
   b. Group procedural problems
4. I can identify and am able to demonstrate useful procedures for the beginning stage of a group including:
   a. Joining
   b. Linking
   c. Cutting off
   d. Drawing out
   e. Clarifying the purpose

## Chapter Overview

The beginning stage of a group involves many complex steps that can become overwhelming for the group leader if he or she is not sufficiently prepared. Two important factors that a group leader must deal with are the roles that group members take on and the structure of the group itself. This stage of group development is emphasized because groups that begin well tend to do well in all the other stages.

## Chapter Highlights

By understanding how to begin and nurture a group, chances significantly improve that the goals of the group and its members will be achieved and chaos will be avoided (Zimpfer, 1986).

Almost all healthy groups go through developmental stages.

Tuckman and Jensen (1977) identify the stages as *forming, storming, norming, performing,* and *adjourning,*

Ward (1982) characterizes developmental stages as *power, cohesiveness, working,* and *termination.*

**49**

Kormanski and Mozenter (1987) state that groups develop out of *awareness* and then move on to *conflict, cooperation, productivity,* and finally *separation.*

Trotzer (1999) conceptualizes groups as moving through the stages of *security, acceptance, responsibility, work,* and *closing.*

Prior to the initial group meeting many processes have already been completed — for example, formulating the idea for the group, screening members, and selecting preliminary individual and group goals.

## STEPS IN THE FORMING STAGE

Forming is a process that involves several steps. Although some of these steps may be completed concurrently, none may be skipped if the group is going to form properly and prosper.

### Step 1: Developing a Rationale for the Group
Behind every successful group is a *rationale* for its existence; a clear rationale and focus are of uppermost importance in planning.

### Step 2: Deciding on a Theoretical Format
Group workers must consider the theoretical format from which they will work.

In choosing a theoretical format, the limitations and strengths of such an approach must be considered.

A theoretical format should function on intrapersonal, interpersonal, and extrapersonal matters, but in varying degrees. The theoretical base of the group should match the needs of participants and the group as a whole.

Despite the approach chosen, the planning for a group must consider that groups contain many variables, among them people, processes, and products.

### Step 3: Weighing Practical Considerations
Group proposals should stress specific, concrete, and practical objectives and procedures.

Considerations such as meeting time, place, and frequency cannot be overlooked if the group is to be successful (Jacobs, Masson, & Harvill, 2002).

Group leaders must be sensitive to political and practical realities as well.

### Step 4: Publicizing the Group
Corey and Corey (2002) note that how a group is announced influences both the ways it will be received by potential members and the kind of people who will join.

*Best Practice Guidelines* (Association for Specialists in Group Work, 1998) provide guidance on the proper conduct expected of those who lead groups, including preparation procedures

### Step 5: Pretraining and Selecting Members and a Leader
#### *Pretraining*
The maturity, readiness, and composition of members play a major role in determining the success of a group (Riva, Lippert, & Tackett, 2000).

**50**

Potential group members should be **screened** (interviewed either individually or in a group prior to the group's first meeting in regard to their suitability for the group) and carefully chosen whenever possible.

In the pregroup screening process, the leader must address potential group members' readiness to be in a group and their goals (MacNair-Semands, 1998) as well as myths and misconceptions they may have about groups (Childers & Couch, 1989).

One way to ensure that members are ready for the group besides screening is through **pretraining** (i.e., orienting them on what to expect of the group before it ever meets).

Group pretraining is not required, but the more thoroughly prepared potential members and the group leader are, the more likely the dropout rate will be low, the communication clearer, and the cohesion of the group as a whole greater (Yalom, 1995).

Facts concerning the formation and procedure of a group are preferably put in writing.

### *Selecting Group Members*
Group member selection is usually a two-way process. (Exceptions are found in some psychoeducational groups and in some task/work groups.)

When potential group members and the leader are mutually involved in the selection process, both have input into deciding who will be included or excluded.

Most experts in the group field endorse either an **individually conducted pregroup screening procedure** or a **group conducted pregroup screening process** (Couch, 1995; Riva, Lippert, & Tackett, 2000). Both formats are essentially intake interviews -- ways of determining who will join a particular group and who should not.

In pregroup screening sessions, the goal is to determine whether a particular group is right for a particular person at a specific time.

Through screening members, premature termination is avoided, goals and processes involved with the group are clarified, and members are empowered to take an active part in the group.

Individuals who do not appear likely to contribute to the growth of the group or who lack personal maturity are prime candidates for exclusion from it.

### *Selecting a Group Leader*
Selection of a leader by a potential group member hinges partly on professional qualities and partly on personal qualities.

If the potential group member does not think that the group leader is one with whom he or she can comfortably work, it is best to find another group to join.

### TASKS OF THE BEGINNING GROUP

Group leaders and members have varied tasks to accomplish during the first sessions of a group, including: (a) dealing with apprehension, (b) reviewing members' goals and contracts, (c) specifying more clearly or reiterating group rules, (d) setting limits, and (e) promoting a positive interchange among members so they will want to continue (Weiner, 1984).

### RESOLVING POTENTIAL GROUP PROBLEMS IN FORMING

One of the best ways of handling potential group problems is to prevent them.

When prevention is not possible, the leader and group members can work together to bring about resolution.

### People Problems

Despite careful screening, some group members display difficult behaviors early on in the group process. In counseling groups, those who cause the most concern are individuals who monopolize, withdraw, intimidate, verbally ventilate, focus on others, seduce, or show intolerance (Edelwich & Brodsky, 1992).

Six common membership roles often displayed during the first session include: manipulators, resisters, monopolizers, silent members, users of sarcasm, and those who focus on others.

**Subgroups** are cliques of members who band together. They may be troublesome.

Group leaders may help prevent subgroup formation by focusing on the uniqueness of each individual and his or her connectedness with the group as a whole.

Leaders may also discourage the formation of subgroups by making their expectations known in regard to such groups in the screening interview, pregroup training, and the initial group session.

### Group Procedural Problems

Beginning the first group session is often a difficult experience, especially for the novice leader. How it is handled can make a major difference in what happens later in the group.

Overall, no one single type of introduction will work consistently for every group and every group leader. The style of introduction is largely determined by the interpersonal skill of the leader and the nature of the group.

#### *Structure*

Group leaders in the initial stage of a group must make decisions on **structuring the group** (i.e., running the group according to a prescribed plan or agenda).

The advantages of structuring a group are that it promotes group cooperation, lessens anxiety, highlights individual performance, and facilitates the inclusion of everyone in the group (Bach, 1954).

The disadvantages of structuring are that it may discourage personal responsibility and restrict freedom of expression. Unstructured groups, though promoting more initial anxiety and discontent, also ultimately create high group cohesiveness and morale (Trotzer, 1999).

#### *Involvement*

**Involvement** of group members, in which they actively participate with each other and invest themselves in the group, is necessary for first sessions to work best.

During the first sessions, group leaders need to facilitate member interaction. The use of structured activities is one way to accomplish this goal.

### *Group Cohesion*

"The effective development of any group requires that members share an image of the group" (Hansen et al., 1980, p. 492).

One way to build **group cohesion** — that is, a sense of "we-ness" — is to allow individuals to voice their concerns freely and fully.

Group cohesiveness may be aided through the use of the arts (e.g., drawing, photography, and literature) in helping group members express their feelings and thoughts more clearly (Shechtman & Perl-Dekel, 2000).

Although group cohesion usually does not manifest itself fully until the norming (or identity) stage of the group, the seeds for its development are planted early in the group.

### *Hope and Risk Taking*

**Promoting hope** is one of the basic "therapeutic" factors described by Yalom (1995).

Leaders can instill hope during the initial sessions of the group by conveying information, validating commonalties, accentuating the positive (Couch & Childers, 1987), and using humor (Gladding, 1994).

If members are able to experience a sense of **universality** (i.e., commonness with others) within the group, they will feel more cohesive (MacKenzie & Livesley, 1983).

Leaders who can facilitate the appropriate disclosure by members of limited and nonthreatening information in the early stages of the group are on their way to conducting a successful group.

### *Termination of the Session*

It is just as important to end a group session appropriately as it is to begin it correctly.

To avoid group member frustrations and failure to gain insight into themselves and others, Corey and Corey (2002) recommend that at least 10 minutes be set aside at the end of a group for reflection and summarization.

### USEFUL PROCEDURES FOR THE BEGINNING STAGE OF A GROUP

Some universal group procedures seem to work well for beginning most groups; they include: joining, linking, cutting off, drawing out, and clarifying the purpose.

## Key Concepts

*Can you define and describe each of the following terms? Be able to offer a brief example or relevant context for these concepts.*

apprehension
clarifying the purpose
confidentiality
contract
critical incident in the life of a group
cutting off
cyclotherapy process
drawing out
eclectic
focusers on others
forming, or orientation, stage of the group
goals
group cohesion
group-conducted pregroup screening process
icebreaker
individually conducted pregroup screening procedure
interactive journal writing
involvement
I/We/It
joining
limits
linking
manipulators
monopolizers
pretraining
promoting hope
promoting a positive interchange
publicizing a group
reframing
resisters
rules
screened
silent members
structuring the group
subgroups
universality
users of sarcasm

## Group Experience –Parallels and Reflections (Beginning a Group)

1.  Consider issues of selecting group members and pretraining members. What screening process did you undergo? Did you have an individual pregroup experience or a small pregroup screening process? Or did you have neither?

2. Did you have questions for the pre-group screener? If you asked, how did you feel about the reply? And what of the pre-group screener's questions for you? How did the selection process strengthen (or weaken) the early formation of the group itself? Can you speculate as to what the group leader(s) were looking for through this pre-group session?

3. Recollect one or two limit-setting statements that were made by your group leader(s) early on during the group formation stage. What about *rules*?

4. Do you note any *people problems* (pp. 120-123) emerging? If so, do the problem behaviors seem to fit into any of the broad categories listed in your text? Are you aware of any leader interventions that appear to be contributing to or discouraging any problem behaviors?

5. Of the five *useful procedures for the beginning stage of a group* (p. 127), did you notice your group leader utilizing any or all of them? How did one or more of the procedures seem to work?

6. How are you feeling as a member about the beginning of your group?

## Self Assessment Questions

### True or False Statements

The following statements check your comprehension of terms and identification of individuals (knowledge and comprehension level); your ability to apply that knowledge to solve more challenging questions (application level), and your ability to evaluate given information (analysis and evaluation level).

Indicate whether each statement is true or false. If you believe a statement is false, identify the error in the space provided. When necessary, refer to your text, *Group Work: A Counseling Specialty* (4th ed.). An answer key appears at the end of this book.

1. Yalom's (1995) "cyclotherapy process" is best described as leaders anticipating a certain amount of storming.

_____
_____
_____

2. An "eclectic" theoretical approach is "atheoretical."

_____
_____
_____

3. In Waldo's (1985) "I/We/It" conceptualization of group functioning, "I" is intrapersonal, "We" is interpersonal, and "It" is extrapersonal.

_____
_____
_____

4. Pre-screening is a process whereby potential group members are met with either individually or in a group to assess their suitability for membership in the group before the group's first session.

_____

_____

_____

5. Implicit limits are conveyed through nonverbal reinforcement by the leader and group members.

_____

_____

_____

6. Members' personal responsibility may be discouraged if the group leader exerts too much structure.

_____

_____

_____

7. Group cohesion occurs as members' different images as to what the group will be like become shared.

_____

_____

_____

8. The forming/orientation stage of the group is usually characterized by excitement.

_____

_____

_____

9. Linking is a way for leaders to connect members with one another by helping them know what they share in common.

_____

_____

_____

10. Goals are specific objectives that individuals or the group wish to accomplish.

_____

_____

_____

11. Borders are the outer boundaries of a group in regard to behaviors that will be accepted within the group.

_____

_____

_____

12. A critical incident in the life of a group has the power to shape or influence the group positively or negatively.

_____

_____

_____

13. Joining is the process by which group members connect both physically and psychologically with one another.

_____

_____

_____

14. In pretraining, members are oriented to what to expect of the group before it ever meets.

_____

_____

_____

15. A person who is often angry and/or frustrated and who brings these feelings into the group might be known as a manipulator.

_____

_____

_____

16. The sense of "we-ness" in group work is called group cohesion.

_____

_____

_____

**Multiple Choice Questions**

1. The forming, or orientation, stage of a group is often a time when new members attempt to

_____.

    a. stay at arm's-length
    b. be accepted and safe
    c. assert their individualism and autonomy
    d. ensure others see them as competent and able

2. Prior to the beginning of group, leaders should interview potential members with the goal of assessing each individual's readiness and appropriateness for membership. This process is called

_____.

    a. publicizing          c. pretraining
    b. screening           d. referral

3. Three of the four *types of groups* frequently share rather universal goals across the membership, but _____ groups often do not. Goals for this type of group may vary widely.

    a. psychoeducation     c. psychotherapy
    b. counseling          d. task/work

4. Shaheen has joined a career-transition counseling group, following the closing of the computer programming company where he had worked for 11 years. During the first session he seems unable to talk at all about the impact of his loss. He makes remarks about the futility of "crying" about what's done. "What is done is done, all I need is another job." This potential challenging behavior labels him and his behavior as _____.

    a. manipulator            c. monopolizer

    b. resister               d. focusers on others

### Written Exercises

Respond in writing to several of the following questions, prompts, and inquiries, designed to deepen your comprehension of the text. Student responses can lead to self-reflection and interesting discussions with others. You are encouraged to flex your imagination and make your understanding of group work as presented in these chapters come to life.

### Questions & Prompts for Written Reflection and Discussion

### Chapter 5

1. Investigate some group membership opportunities in your environment. Where do you find groups being publicized? What groups (e.g., type, purpose) are available? What selection processes are evident, if any? If appropriate, contact one or more of these opportunities and see if someone there is willing to talk about some of the more challenging points.

_____
_____
_____
_____
_____
_____
_____
_____
_____
_____
_____

2. Consider the list of potential *people problems* (pp. 120-122). What "problems" from this list would be particularly challenging for you to work with if you were leading the group? What if a member in your group demonstrated one or more of these behaviors; what would your internal reaction(s) be? What would your reaction look like to the group leader or to others in the group?

_____
_____
_____
_____
_____
_____
_____
_____
_____
_____
_____

3. Have you observed any of the procedures for the beginning stage of group being utilized by your class instructor? What about in other courses? What are these procedures and how have they seemed to work?

_____
_____
_____
_____
_____
_____
_____
_____
_____
_____
_____

**Prompt for Group Members**

What is most memorable about the beginning (forming) of your out-of-class group? Is there anything about the screening, selection, or pretraining that stands out? If you did not have one or more of these forming activities, do you have any ideas why? Do you think there will be a "cost" associated with their omission?

**Journal and Reflection**

Space for journaling about your group work experiences is provided below. Use this space to reflect on your reading about group work, your classroom presentations and activities, the group dynamics of your classes themselves, and any simulations or actual group participation opportunities you may have. Comment here thoughtfully. Be sure to carefully honor your ethical commitment to uphold the confidentiality of others in your group. Reflections are yours and are not to reveal anyone else's information. Recording your thoughts and feelings will provide a written history of this phase of your group work education. (Attach additional sheets of paper if desired.)

_Entry date_ _____

# THE TRANSITION PERIOD IN A GROUP: NORMING AND STORMING

## Outcome Objectives

1. I can describe and am able to discuss the stages encountered during the transition period in groups.
2. I am able to identify what happens during the storming stage, including:
   a. Peer relationships in storming
   b. Resistance during storming
   c. Task processing in storming
   d. Working through storming
   e. Results of working through storming
3. I am able to describe norms and norming, including:
   a. Peer relations during norming
   b. Task processing during norming
   c. Examining aspects of norming
   d. Promoting norming
   e. Results of norming

## Chapter Overview

The transitional stage of a group is sometimes difficult in that it has many parts. The two major elements of the transitional stage are storming and norming. When storming and norming occur successfully, the group generally becomes cohesive and begins to move onto the process of working.

## Chapter Highlights

The **transition period** in the group is the time after the forming process and before the working stage. In groups that last 12 to 15 sessions, this period begins in the second or third group session and usually extends for one to three meetings.

Transition begins with a **storming** stage in which members start to compete with others to find their place in the group.

Storming involves struggles over power and control anxiety; resistance, defensiveness, conflict, confrontation, and transference are frequent feelings that surface at this time (Corey & Corey, 2002; Gladding, 1994a).

Once the group successfully weathers storming, it moves on to a **norming** stage in which there are resolutions, the building of cohesiveness, and the opportunity to move forward in growth (Ward, 1982).

The purpose of the group and the skill of its leader influence the general ebb and flow of these processes, but the personalities and needs of members and their levels of trust, interest, and commitment also play a major part (Gordon & Liberman, 1971; Jacobs, Masson, & Harvill, 2002; Zimpfer, 1986).

## STORMING

Storming is a time of conflict and anxiety when the group moves from **primary tension** (i.e., awkwardness about being in a strange situation) to **secondary tension** (i.e., intragroup conflict) (Bormann, 1975).

During storming, group members and leaders struggle with issues related to structure, direction, control, catharsis, and interpersonal relationships (Hershenson & Power, 1987; Maples, 1988).

Members need to work through past nonproductive ways of relating, create new repertoires, and establish their place in the group.

Some groups may encounter all the problems associated with this period, whereas others may have few difficulties.

**Conflict resolution** "is based on the underlying notion that conflict is essentially negative and destructive" (Rybak & Brown, 1997, p. 31). Therefore, the primary focus is on ending a specific conflict.

**Conflict management** is premised on the "basis that conflict can be positive" (Rybak & Brown, 1997, p. 31); thus, the focus is on directing conflict toward a constructive dialogue (McRoy & Brown, 1996).

When group leaders employ either a conflict resolution or a conflict management approach during the storming stage, the potential benefits of conflict in a group are numerous.

### Peer Relationships in Storming
During the storming stage, group members are initially more anxious in their interactions with each other because they are afraid of losing control, being misunderstood, looking foolish, or being rejected (Corey & Corey, 2002).

Some members avoid taking a risk by remaining silent at this time; others who want to establish their place in the group deal with their anxiety by being more open and assertive (Bach, 1954; Yalom, 1995).

The concern for power is also prevalent during storming. **Power** is "the capacity to bring about certain intended consequences in the behavior of others" (Gardner, 1990, p. 55).

Power within a group can take many forms: informational power, influential power, and authoritative power.

Members' attitudes about trusting the group and its leader are also an issue during storming.

Negative comments, judgments, and criticisms are frequent during storming as members deal with issues of control, conflict, and dominance in the establishment of a hierarchy (Maples, 1988; Schutz, 1971; Yalom, 1995).

### Resistance During Storming
**Resistance** is best defined as any behavior that moves the group away from areas of discomfort, conflict, or potential growth.

Group leaders who are unprepared for such resistance may be put on the defensive when this kind of behavior happens.

The most prevalent forms of resistance are subtle *indirect resistances,* which include intellectualization, questioning, advice giving, band-aiding, dependency, monopolizing, and attack on the group leader.

## Task Processing in Storming
During storming there is a great deal of member attention on personal matters, such as group safety, leader competence, trust, and ways of interacting.

**Task processing** (i.e., ways of accomplishing specific goals) appears to regress during storming. No longer do members or leaders concentrate as directly on objectives as they did at the beginning of the group.

A potential problem in this suspension of effort to accomplish a task is that someone in the group may be blamed, or scapegoated, for the group's lack of achievement (Rugel, 1991).

## Working Through Storming
One way to help group members work through their feelings in storming is to use a **process observer** (i.e., a neutral third-party professional who observes the group and gives it feedback on its interpersonal and interactive processes).

A second way to work through the storming stage is to use the process of **leveling**, in which members are encouraged to interact freely and evenly (Kline, 1990; Kottler, 1994); the leader draws out group members who are underparticipating, and those who are excessively active are helped to understand the impact of their actions through group feedback.

A global way of dealing with the storming part of transition is to get **feedback** from members on how they are doing and what they think needs to be done (Ponzo, 1991).

The process of feedback can take place in a formal or informal way. Using **informal feedback**, the leader may ask members to give their reactions to a group session in an unstructured way at any time they wish. **Formal feedback** is structured. It may be set up, for example, through the use of what is known as **rounds** (i.e., having each person in the group make a comment).

## Results of Working Through Storming
When the group works through storming, especially in regard to resistance, the group will take on a new dimension characterized by members making emotional space for each other and being accommodating to one another.

Members may also decide to revise their goals or alter their style of interpersonal relationships as a result of working through storming.

Different types of groups will vary in the length and depth of their experience in storming and the amount of conflict they may have (Jacobs et al., 1994).

For most groups, the interdependency among group members and the stability of the group as a whole cannot deepen until intragroup hostility has surfaced, been acknowledged, and dealt with (Bennis & Shepard, 1956).

## NORMS AND NORMING

**Norms** are expectations about group members' behaviors that should or should not take place (Forsyth, 1999).

"Group norms function to regulate the performance of a group as an organized unit, keeping it on the course of its objectives" (Napier & Gershenfeld, 1989, pp. 117–118).

In most groups, norms are clear and are constructed both from expectations of the members for their group and from the explicit and implicit directions of the leader and more influential members (Yalom, 1995).

As the group develops, group members and leaders become more aware of the verbal and nonverbal rules they wish to follow to achieve their goals (Vander Kolk, 1985).

Norming is a crucial part of the group process because it sets the pattern for the next stage: performing (i.e., working). In the norming stage, often enthusiasm and cooperation are expressed (Hershenson & Power, 1987).

### Peer Relations During Norming

Group members usually have a positive attitude toward others in the group and the experience itself during norming.

This positive mind-set is likely to result in learning, insight, and feelings of support and acceptance.

Peer interactions are manifested through identification, here-and-now experiences, hope, cooperation, collaboration, and cohesion.

### Task Processing During Norming

One main task objective in the norming stage is for members to reach an agreement on the establishment of *norms,* or rules and standards from which to operate the group.

Groups typically accept both *prescriptive norms,* which describe the kinds of behaviors that should be performed, and *proscriptive norms,* which describe the kinds of behaviors that are to be avoided (Forsyth, 1999).

Norms are value laden and give a degree of predictability to the group that would not be there otherwise (Luft, 1984). Often, they evolve so gradually that they are never questioned until violated.

### Examining Aspects of Norming

Norming is generally characterized in terms of behaviors and feelings expressed by group members toward each other. Although it is difficult to measure the impact of emotion on the group, there are ways of examining behaviors during this stage that are both concrete and scientific.

The SYMLOG model yields a field diagram that pictures how members of a group are rated on three dimensions: dominance versus submissiveness, friendliness versus unfriendliness, and instrumentally versus emotionally expressive.

## Promoting Norming

Norming can be promoted through actions by either the group leader or group members.

Several human relations and specific group skills can be used in this process, including supporting, empathizing, facilitating, and self-disclosure.

## Results of Norming

If the process of norming goes well, members will feel connected with the group and will be able to concentrate on being productive rather than protecting themselves.

When members feel secure and linked with others, they are free to begin cooperating and coordinating their efforts in achieving specific goals.

Norming allows members to clear their minds, reassess their goals from a realistic perspective, feel good about themselves and the group's progress, and make new plans for the working stage of the group.

## Key Concepts

*Can you define and describe each of the following terms? Be able to offer a brief example or relevant context for these concepts.*

accommodating
advice giving
attack on the group leader
authoritative power
avoiding
band-aiding
cohesion
collaborating
collaboration
commitment
competing
compromising
conflict management
conflict-management orientations
conflict resolution
cooperation
dependency
empathizing
existential variables
facilitating
feedback
formal feedback
group norming
hope
identification
influential power
informal feedback
informational power
intellectualization

leveling
logs/journals
monopoloizing
norming
norms
power
primary tension
process observer
pseudo-acceptance
questioning
resistance
rounds
scapegoat
secondary tension
self-disclosure
storming
supporting
SYMLOG
task processing
transition period

## Group Experience –Parallels and Reflections

1. Are you able to find evidence of the *storming stage* of your small group experience? What did you notice? How might you define the storming in terms of *power*?

2. Recall some examples of *resistance* that were observed during a recent session. Can you label any of these examples? Consider the list: intellectualization, questioning, advice giving, band-aiding, dependency, monopolizing, or attacking the group leader. What effect did such resistance seem to have on the transition of the group?

3. Using the SYMLOG model, attempt to identify the three dimensions (pp. 148-149) by rating your tendency to engage in any of the 26 possible roles. Observe your behaviors within the group, especially during this transition period. Comment on the roles you identified as most like you and the actual roles you appear to be taking on in the group.

4. Pay attention to members' self-disclosures. Do you see a relationship between trust and self-disclosure? Can you identify aspects of member behavior and group leadership that contribute to this relationship? (Be sure not to inadvertently breach member confidences as you write about self-disclosure.)


## Self Assessment Questions

## True or False Statements

The following statements check your comprehension of terms and identification of individuals (knowledge and comprehension level); your ability to apply that knowledge to solve more challenging questions (application level), and your ability to evaluate given information (analysis and evaluation level).

Indicate whether each statement is true or false. If you believe a statement is false, identify the error in the space provided. When necessary, refer to your text, *Group Work: A Counseling Specialty* (4th ed.). An answer key appears at the end of this book.

1. During the "storming" phase of group development, group members move from primary tension to secondary tension. Secondary tension in the storming phase of a group is best defined as developmental conflict.

_____

_____

_____

2. The aim of conflict resolution is based on the underlying notion that conflict is welcomed.

_____

_____

_____

3. Moving forward into norming signals successful navigation through the storming phase.

_____

_____

_____

4. Goal setting is one of the group members' most prevalent concerns during the storming phase.

_____

_____

_____

5. A "process observer" gives feedback on interpersonal processes to aid in resolving storming challenges.

_____

_____

_____

6. Empathizing means putting oneself in another's place in regard to subjective perception and objective emotion (Brammer & MacDonald, 2000).

_____

_____

_____

7. Structure is the capacity to bring about certain intended consequences in the behavior of others.

_____

_____

_____

8. Resistance moves the group away from areas of discomfort, conflict, or potential growth.

_____

_____

_____

9. A scapegoat is someone who might enter a group in order to help the group through their feelings during the storming process.

_____

_____

_____

10. Competing, accommodating, and sharing are three of the five dominant conflict-management orientations.

_____

_____

_____

11. Norms are expectations about group members' behaviors that should or should not take place.

_____

_____

_____

12. Facilitating refers to putting oneself in another's place in regard to subjective perception and emotion while maintaining objectivity.

_____

_____

_____

13. Informational power is based on the idea that those who know more are able to exert control over all situations, even those that include people.

_____

_____

_____

14. To project the group's problems onto a single individual instead of the group taking responsibility is to level.

_____

_____

_____

## Multiple Choice Questions

1. The transition period in the group is the time after the forming stage and before the working stage. In a group that lasts 18 sessions, one can predict that transition will last between _____.

      a. one and two sessions        c. three and four sessions
      b. one and four sessions       d. three and nine sessions

2. Conflict can be viewed in two ways. One, that conflict is essentially negative and destructive, and second, that conflict can be positive. If conflict management is employed during the *storming* phase in group work, the leader likely views conflict as _____.

      a. negative            c. (both a & b)
      b. positive            d. (there is no way of knowing)

3. During the storming phase, Paul attempts to build a coalition of power in the group by agreeing to basically everything that other men in the group say; however, he rejects and argues forcefully with practically everything that the women in the group offer. This is an example of
_____.

    a. informational power        c. authoritative power
    b. antagonistic power        d. influential power

4. Peer relations during the norming phase evolve with a newfound sense of belongingness. Which of the following is NOT reflective of the interaction among peers at this phase?
    a. identification        c. here-and-now experience
    b. anxiety        d. cohesion

### Written Exercises
Respond in writing to several of the following questions, prompts, and inquiries, designed to deepen your comprehension of the text. Student responses can lead to self-reflection and interesting discussions with others. You are encouraged to flex your imagination and make your understanding of group work as presented in these chapters come to life.

## Questions & Prompts for Written Reflection and Discussion

### Chapter 6

1. Do you tend to be someone who works toward "conflict resolution" or are you more of a "conflict manager"? Locate one or more members of your class who share your inclination. Discuss these self-perceptions. What influences do you believe this attribute might exert on members during the transition period in your group or perhaps in a group that you might eventually lead?

_____
_____
_____
_____
_____
_____
_____
_____
_____
_____
_____
_____
_____

2. Think of some real-life examples of people you have encountered who have demonstrated various types of *power* in peer relationships (groups). How did these individuals use their power? What was your reaction to their power at that time? Are you aware of times when you have asserted or at least attempted to assert yourself in such bids for power as described in the text?

_____
_____
_____
_____
_____
_____
_____
_____
_____
_____
_____
_____

3. Consider the four skills used to promote successful norming in the second phase of the transition period: *supporting, empathizing, facilitating* and *self-disclosure*. Be particularly observant in whatever group experiences you are currently involved with and take note of any of these four skills in action. Who demonstrates them, leader or member? What is the apparent member response to the process? Do you identify more closely with any one of these skills over the others? Discuss your observations and perceptions with others in class or small group.

_____
_____
_____
_____
_____
_____
_____
_____
_____
_____
_____

**Prompts for Group Members**

1. What does storming feel like? What did you notice as you entered this phase in transition? How did your group leader work with the storming? Did the storming last longer, or maybe shorter, than you anticipated? Any speculations as to why?


2. As you and members of the group move through the storming phase into the norming phase of the group's transition and into the working stage, what do you notice? How would you characterize the interpersonal relations of the members during norming?

## Journal and Reflection

Space for journaling about your group work experiences is provided below. Use this space to reflect on your reading about group work, your classroom presentations and activities, the group dynamics of your classes themselves, and any simulations or actual group participation opportunities you may have. Comment here thoughtfully. Be sure to carefully honor your ethical commitment to uphold the confidentiality of others in your group. Reflections are yours and are not to reveal anyone else's information. Recording your thoughts and feelings will provide a written history of this phase of your group work education. (Attach additional sheets of paper if desired.)

_Entry date_ _____

# THE WORKING STAGE IN A GROUP: PERFORMING

**Outcome Objectives**

1. I am able to describe and to discuss the stages encountered during the working stage in groups including performing.
2. I understand and can explain the following:
     a. Peer relationships
     b. Task processes during the working stage
     c. Teamwork and team building during the working stage
3. I am aware of potential problems during the working stage of groups including racial and gender issues and group collusion.
4. I comprehend and am able to describe the working stage of the groups.
5. I am able to describe strategies for assisting groups during the working stage, including:
     a. Modeling by the leader
     b. Exercises
     c. Group observing group
     d. Brainstorming
     e. Nominal-group technique
     f. Synectics
     g. Written projections
     h. Group processing
     i. Teaching of skills
6. I understand and am able to describe outcomes of the working stage.

## Chapter Overview

This chapter examines the working stage of group process. The working stage in the life of a group is generally the time when task, educational, or personal issues are resolved, and is most often remembered fondly by group members. A group that is successful during the working stage can then move forward onto the termination process.

## Chapter Highlights

The working stage focuses on the achievement of individual and group goals and the movement of the group itself into a more unified and productive system (Maples, 1988).

The working stage is also labeled the "performing stage" (Tuckman & Jensen, 1977) and the "action stage" (George & Dustin, 1988).

The working stage is a time of problem solving that usually lasts longer than any of the other group stages.

The working stage is often regarded as the most productive stage in group development and is characterized by its constructive nature and the achievement of results.

During this stage, group leaders and members feel more freedom and comfort in trying out new behaviors and strategies because the group is settled and issues, such as power and control, have been worked through enough for members to trust each other (Hansen, Warner, & Smith, 1980).

A healthy group, regardless of its purpose, displays a great amount of intimacy, self-disclosure, feedback, teamwork, confrontation, and humor.

## PEER RELATIONSHIPS

There appears to be genuine concern on a deep, personal level by members for each other in the working stage of most groups. Feelings of empathy, compassion, and care abound, and groups gradually grow closer emotionally.

This interpersonal bonding or **cohesiveness** usually increases, even in task/work groups, as group members interact and understand each other better.

Along with positive feelings about the group and the constructive behaviors of its members comes a greater willingness to self-disclose (i.e., reveal information about oneself to the group). It involves listening and receiving feedback as well as speaking.

The *Johari Window* illustrates how appropriate self-disclosure develops during the life of the group (Luft, 1984).

In the working stage of the group, members become increasingly aware of individual participants and the world of each person.

## TASK PROCESSES DURING THE WORKING STAGE

The major emphasis in the working stage is productivity. Group members focus on improving themselves and/or achieving specific individual and group goals.

One way productivity may be increased is by encouraging equal member airtime through making the **rounds** (Yalom, 1995).

A second way tasks are accomplished at the working stage is through **role playing**. In role plays, members are given a chance to assume an identity that differs widely from their present behavior.

Another task process that is prevalent in the working stage is **homework**, or working outside the group itself (Gazda, 1989).

A final dimension that must be considered in the working stage of the group is **incorporation** (i.e., a personal awareness and appreciation of what the group has accomplished on both an individual and collective level).

Incorporation prepares members to move on to the termination stage.

## TEAMWORK AND TEAM BUILDING DURING THE WORKING STAGE

Teamwork and team building are vital in the working stage of groups (Kline, 2001; Ward, 1997).

Groups sometimes function as teams whether planned or not. However, selecting members of a group who will function best in a team environment ensures the best possible results.

## PROBLEMS IN THE WORKING STAGE OF GROUPS

Among the specific problems that arise during the working stage are fear and resistance, challenges to leaders, and a lack of focus on achieving individual and group goals.

Problems are expressed in numerous ways, such as intense emotionality in members, projection or scapegoating of a member, and lack of constructive participation.

Focusing on issues outside the group, such as gender/race or turning inward as a group to be protective (collusion), are also problematic.

### Racial and Gender Issues

Some groups may struggle and/or engage in high conflict because of racial prejudices among members. Other groups deal with racial issues through denial (Lanier & Robertiello, 1977).

Contact with others from different cultures in a group context often helps members become more aware of their racial feelings.

The same dysfunctional/functional and nonproductive/productive dynamic of prejudice and stereotypes may occur in regard to gender, too (Sullivan, 1983).

The issue of gender is highly visible and dealt with constructively by group leaders and members as part of larger issues in the working stage.

### Group Collusion

**Group collusion** involves cooperating with others unconsciously or consciously "to reinforce prevailing attitudes, values, behaviors, or norms" (Butler, 1987, p. 1).

The purpose of such behavior is self-protection. Its effect is to maintain the status quo in the group.

To prevent group collusion from occurring to any great extent, group membership should be diversified. In addition, open discussion should be promoted, and goals and purposes should be continuously clarified.

## GROUPS THAT WORK

Just as there is a difference in the dynamics that underlie the working stage of a group's development, there is also a difference in working and nonworking groups.

Corey and Corey (2001) have identified some 20 characteristics that compare working and nonworking groups.

## STRATEGIES FOR ASSISTING GROUPS IN THE WORKING STAGE

When groups are not doing well in the working stage, several approaches can rectify the situation, including the following:

**Modeling** by the leader is used to teach group members complex behaviors in a relatively short period of time by copying/imitating.

**Exercises** involve less direct showing and more experiential integration.

**Group observing group (fishbowl procedure)** requires that the group break up into two smaller groups in any way the leader directs and that each observe the other function (as outsiders) for about 10 minutes each (Cohen & Smith, 1976).

**Brainstorming**, a way to stimulate divergent thinking, requires an initial generating of ideas in a nonjudgmental manner (Osborn, 1957). The premise of this approach is that critical evaluation of ideas and actions often holds back creativity and member participation.

**Nominal-Group Technique** (Delbecq, Van de Ven, & Gustafson, 1975) is quite useful in getting group members to think and to work on problematic situations, especially in task/work groups but it is less public than brainstorming.

**Synectics** theory applies to the integration of diverse individuals into "a problem-stating, problem-solving group" (Gordon, 1961, p. 1).

In **written projections**, members are asked to see themselves or their groups in the future having been successful and to describe what the experience was like.

**Group processing** can be defined as capitalizing on significant happenings in the here-and-now interactions of the group to help members reflect on the meaning of their experience; better understand their own thoughts, feelings, and actions; and generalize what is learned to their life outside the group" (Stockton, Morran, & Nitza, 2000, p. 345).

The importance of processing is that it helps those involved in the group make or find meaning in their experiences and thus leads to growth.

Sometimes group members are not successful because they do not know how to relate well to others, such as giving and receiving interpersonal feedback (Toth & Erwin, 1998). By teaching members skills, group functioning improves.

## OUTCOMES OF THE WORKING STAGE

The end result of the working stage on a group is usually tangible. Goals have been worked on and achieved.

One of the most productive aspects of the group in the working stage is the learning and sharing of ideas and information between members.

Group participants can gain insight and become more cognitively aware of themselves and their options during this stage through such means.

Expressing negative emotions without cognitive restructuring only reinforces such feelings.

Group members seem to genuinely care how others perceive their behaviors in the working stage. The focus is on the present, and it may include confrontation.

**Feedback** is sharing relevant information with other people, such as how they are perceived, so they can decide whether to change. Information should be given in a clear, concrete, succinct, and appropriate manner.

The **corrective emotional experience** is another benefit that can come in the working stage of the group.

In addition to increased intimacy, openness, and feedback, another quality that is useful, important, and likely to be helpful during the working stage is **humor** — the ability to laugh at oneself or a situation in a therapeutic and nondefensive manner (Watzlawick, 1983).

## Key Concepts

*Can you define and describe each of the following terms? Be able to offer a brief example or relevant context for these concepts.*

blind quadrant
brainstorming
cognitively restructure
cohesiveness
confrontation
corrective emotional experience
culturally encapsulated
devil's advocate procedure
excursions
exercises
feedback
fishbowl procedure
group collusion
group observing group
group processing
groupthink
hidden quadrant
homework
humor
icebreaking exercises
incorporation
Johari Awareness Model
modeling
nominal-group technique (NGT)
open quadrant
process observer
processing
role playing
rounds
self-disclose
synectics
team
team building
Team Player Inventory (TPI)
teamwork
therapeutic fairy tales
unknown quadrant
working stage
written projections

### Group Experience –Parallels and Reflections

1. Describe several incidents of the interpersonal bonding—cohesiveness—that is emerging as your group transitions fully into the *working stage* of the small group experience.

2. Utilizing the Johari Awareness Model, can you recall one or more examples of your self-disclosure that can be illustrative of this model? Is there a sense that your "hidden quadrant" is indeed shrinking during the working stage of the group? Ask yourself similar questions regarding both the *blind quadrant* and the *unknown quadrant*?

3. Consult the list on page 163 and 164 of working versus nonworking groups. Cite examples (be careful to ensure anonymity) from each column. Overall, comment on the working stage of your group.

4. Nine strategies for assisting groups in the working stage are examined in your text. Of them, what are you observing your group leader(s) employing? What strategy or intervention, do you believe, would enhance the work that you and your group members are accomplishing?

5. How are you with *feedback*? What are you aware of in relation to this group experience regarding your "receiving feedback"? Do you notice any personal changes comparing your experience of giving and receiving feedback today and your self-perceptions of a year ago? Explain.

### Self Assessment Questions

### True or False Statements

The following statements check your comprehension of terms and identification of individuals (knowledge and comprehension level); your ability to apply that knowledge to solve more challenging questions (application level), and your ability to evaluate given information (analysis and evaluation level).

Indicate whether each statement is true or false. If you believe a statement is false, identify the error in the space provided. When necessary, refer to your text, *Group Work: A Counseling Specialty* (4th ed.). An answer key appears at the end of this book.

1. In groups of all types, approximately 30-70% of the total group time will be spent in the working stage.

_____

_____

_____

2. If group members can identify socially with others and have successfully worked through their struggles together, the result is usually growth in emotional closeness.

_____

_____

_____

3.  Through incorporation, during the working stage, group members come to realize the value of the group in their lives and become prepared to move on to the termination stage.

    _____
    _____
    _____

4.  In nominal-group technique, an "excursion" is an enhancing technique for members during the working stage.

    _____
    _____
    _____

5.  Revealing information about oneself to the group is known as self-disclosure.

    _____
    _____
    _____

6.  The Johari Awareness Model is a model of what happens in the arenas of empathy and reflection during the working stage.

    _____
    _____
    _____

7.  Rounds can be used to increase members' equal air-time.

    _____
    _____
    _____

8.  Establishing a personal awareness and appreciation of the group is known as groupthink.

    _____
    _____
    _____

9.  Cultural encapsulation labels individuals who hold stereotypical views about race and gender issues.

    _____
    _____
    _____

10. The concept of "cognitive restructuring" might help explain the tragedy of Jonestown, Guyana, or that of the Branch Davidians in Waco, Texas.

    _____
    _____
    _____

11. Feedback is the process of sharing relevant information with other group members, such as how they are perceived, so they can decide whether to change or not.

    _____
    _____
    _____

12. Group collusion involves cooperating with others unconsciously or consciously to strengthen existing attitudes, values, behaviors, or norms.

_____

_____

_____

13. Self-disclosure is a multi-dimensional activity that includes talking about oneself and listening and receiving feedback.

_____

_____

_____

14. Brainstorming is a way to stimulate divergent thinking that allows group members to generate ideas in a nonjudgmental fashion.

_____

_____

_____

**Multiple Choice Questions**

1. The concept of the "culturally encapsulated" describes individuals who _____.
   a. hold their own cultural beliefs
   b. hold stereotyped view and act accordingly
   c. espouse racist attitudes and ideologies
   d. (none of the above)

2. One strategy for assisting groups during the working stage is a procedure in which the leader gives multiple steps, beginning with problem/issue, individual solutions, shared solutions, clarification dialogue, and so on. This procedure is called_____.
   a. written projections
   b. nominal-group technique
   c. synectics
   d. brainstorming

3. A result of the successful working stage in groups is _____.
   a. goals have been achieved
   b. emotional catharsis
   c. increased intermember exchanges
   d. (all of the above)

**Written Exercises**
Respond in writing to several of the following questions, prompts, and inquiries, designed to deepen your comprehension of the text. Student responses can lead to self-reflection and interesting discussions with others. You are encouraged to flex your imagination and make your understanding of group work as presented in these chapters come to life.

## Questions & Prompts for Written Reflection and Discussion

### Chapter 7

1. Recreate the *Johari Window* (see p. 156). Attempt to fill in each of the four quadrants with information about yourself. Throughout the course return to this graphic and add information as it is revealed. Write only what you are comfortable writing. Use this opportunity to consider how new information for quadrants III and IV became known to you. What value do you see in conceptualizing self-disclosure in this way during the working stage of a group?

_____
_____
_____
_____
_____
_____
_____
_____
_____
_____
_____
_____
_____

2. Methods of increasing productivity of members during the working stage in groups are the use of *rounds, role-playing,* and *homework.* How would you respond to each of these processes? What types of groups do you think these methods would be most beneficial for? Discuss your answers in small groups. Notice how these methods are utilized in your classrooms; what effect do they have?

_____
_____
_____
_____
_____
_____
_____
_____
_____
_____
_____
_____
_____

3. Describe an incident of group collusion either from your personal experiences or hypothetically. As you recall, what was the motivation for collusion? Did the leader(s) or members of the group attempt to intervene? And if so, in what way(s)? What was the outcome? On a continuum of beneficial to catastrophic, where does your example fit best? Discuss these experiences.

_____
_____
_____
_____
_____
_____
_____
_____
_____
_____
_____
_____

4. Have you ever been in a "group observing group" experience? If you have, describe what the experience was like for you. Perhaps the course instructor uses this fishbowl procedure. Pay attention to what you become aware of as you are in the outer circle. Thoughts? What is your perception of the "audience" when you are in the middle circle? Overall, what does this process afford members, in your opinion?

_____
_____
_____
_____
_____
_____
_____
_____
_____
_____
_____
_____

5. Throughout the working stage of many groups, the use of feedback is prevalent. Explore your responses and reactions to feedback in a variety of group situations. Consider harsh or punitive (inappropriate) "feedback." What are your defenses? How do others perceive your ability to hear feedback of any type? How well do you hear positive feedback? To extend this exercise further, purposefully observe others and their responses to feedback.

_____
_____
_____
_____
_____
_____
_____
_____
_____
_____
_____
_____


**Prompts for Group Members**

1. What strategies has the leader applied to the working stage of your group? How have these strategies moved your group experience forward?


2. Has the leader of your group utilized any "preplanned" exercises during the working stage of your group? What was your reaction to these exercises?

**Journal and Reflection**

Space for journaling about your group work experiences is provided below. Use this space to reflect on your reading about group work, your classroom presentations and activities, the group dynamics of your classes themselves, and any simulations or actual group participation opportunities you may have. Comment here thoughtfully. Be sure to carefully honor your ethical commitment to uphold the confidentiality of others in your group. Reflections are yours and are not to reveal anyone else's information. Recording your thoughts and feelings will provide a written history of this phase of your group work education. (Attach additional sheets of paper if desired.)

_____
_____
_____
_____
_____
_____
_____
_____
_____
_____
_____
_____
_____
_____
_____
_____
_____
_____
_____
_____
_____
_____
_____
_____
_____
_____
_____
_____
_____
_____
_____

*Entry date* _____

CHAPTER 8

# TERMINATION OF A GROUP

**Outcome Objectives**

1.  I comprehend the importance of and the tasks involved in the termination stage of a group, including:
    a.  Preparing for termination
    b.  Effects of termination on individuals
    c.  Premature termination
    d.  Premature termination of the group as a whole
    e.  Premature termination initiated by group members
2.  I understand the use of the following skills utilized during termination of group sessions:
    a.  Member summarization
    b.  Leader summarization
    c.  Rounds
    d.  Dyads
    e.  Written reactions
    f.  Rating sheets
    g.  Homework
3.  I understand the use of capping skills utilized during termination of a group.
4.  I comprehend and can describe the following problems often encountered in terminations, including:
    a.  Denial
    b.  Transference
    c.  Countertransference
    d.  Handling terminations correctly
5.  I can discuss the use of follow-up sessions.

## Chapter Overview
Termination is a crucial stage in group development both for members and the group leader. The group leader has the responsibility of ensuring that each session of group ends on time as well as helping each member deal with his or her unfinished business before the group ends. Group leaders may utilize structured exercises such as journal keeping or questionnaires to assure that termination is a positive experience for members.

## Chapter Highlights

Prior to the 1970s, many believed that ending a group experience on any level was a natural phenomenon and that most leaders and members knew how.

Termination is filled with thoughts and feelings that tend to influence individuals long after the group experience is just a memory (Stein, 1993).

During the initial forming stage of a group, members get to know one another better; during the termination stage, they come to know themselves on a deeper level.

If properly understood and managed, termination can be an important force in promoting change in individuals (Yalom, 1995).

Primary activities of group members in termination are to (a) reflect on their past experiences, (b) process memories, (c) evaluate what was learned, (d) acknowledge ambivalent feelings, and (e) engage in cognitive decision making (Wagenheim & Gemmill, 1994).

Termination provides group members an opportunity to clarify the meaning of their experiences, consolidate the gains they have made, and make decisions about the new behaviors they want to carry away from the group and apply to their everyday lives.

Within termination are many issues and processes including **emotional ambivalence,** transference, countertransference, and unfinished business.

## PREPARING FOR TERMINATION

Proper preparation for ending a group begins in the planning stage. Leaders should have in mind not only what type of group they wish to conduct but also how long it will meet and how it will end.

To ensure proper group procedures from start to termination, leaders must establish appropriate boundaries. **Boundaries** are physical and psychological parameters under which a group operates.

Termination occurs on two levels in groups: at the end of each session, and at the end of a certain number of group sessions. Both types of termination have step processes within them that are predictable.

One of the best guidelines for making plans to terminate is based on a model for ending family therapy sessions, whose main idea is that regardless of theory, termination entails four steps: (a) orientation, (b) summarization, (c) discussion of goals, and (d) follow-up (Epstein & Bishop, 1981).

In closing a group session, a leader should inform members that the group is ending about 5 to 30 minutes before its conclusion. This orientation to the end makes it possible for the group members to summarize, set goals, and plan for follow-up if they wish.

In ending a total group experience, the orientation to termination involves a planned number of sessions that are devoted to the topic of closure.

## EFFECTS OF TERMINATION ON INDIVIDUALS

Termination's impact on individuals depends on many factors including whether the group was opened-ended or closed-ended, whether members were prepared in advance for its ending, and whether the speed and intensity of work within sessions was at an appropriate level to allow participants to properly identify and resolve concerns or problems (Tudor, 1999).

The behavior of group members during termination of the group indicates how members think and feel as well as what they have experienced (Luft, 1984; Shulman, 1999).

Group leaders may have to focus special attention on the issue of separation with some people more than others (Corey, Corey, Callanan, & Russell, 1992).

A few group members may require more beyond termination. Three options are productive: individual counseling, referral, and recycling.

## PREMATURE TERMINATION

There are guidelines (e.g., ASGW, 1998) to follow in premature termination cases regardless of the reason for the action or the group leader's theoretical persuasion.

Three types of premature termination must be dealt with: the termination of the group as a whole, the termination of a successful group member, and the termination of an unsuccessful group member (Yalom, 1995).

Premature termination of the whole group may occur because of a group leader or group member action. Premature termination can be appropriate or inappropriate.

To handle either type of premature termination properly, leaders need to have at least one group session to say good-bye to the group as a whole, or they need to be able to contact group members directly. The logistics of making such arrangements is sometimes difficult.

For individual members, premature termination may be due to appropriate or inappropriate reasons, and the ending experience may be successful or unsuccessful.

Yalom (1995) lists a number of reasons that are often given by individuals who leave psychotherapy and counseling groups prematurely.

Sometimes steps can be taken to prevent premature termination and its potential negative impact.

When premature termination is unpreventable, the first action is for the leader or members to inform the group as soon as possible about their departure from the group.

When faced with a member wanting to leave prematurely, the group leader can discuss thoroughly the ramifications of such a move with the member and the group in a safe, protected atmosphere (Corey & Corey, 2002).

In cases of premature termination, members should be helped to realize what they have gained from the group and what positive steps they can take in the future to build on these achievements.

## TERMINATION OF GROUP SESSIONS

Among the most effective formats for closing a session are having the members summarize, having the leader summarize, using a round, using dyads, and getting written reactions (Jacobs, Masson, & Harvill, 2002).

Rating sheets and homework are also recommended (Wagenheim & Gemmill, 1994).

In member summarization, one or more members of the group summarize what has transpired during the session, describing what has happened to them individually and how they have gained from the particular session.

In leader summarization, leaders give a personal reaction to what they perceive to have occurred in the group.

The exercise of **rounds** (sometimes called **go-rounds**) is a variation on member summarization, except in this procedure every group member comments briefly (usually in a sentence or two) about highlights of the group session.

Having members form into groups of two, or **dyads**, at the end of a session, the group leaders make sure all members are involved in termination, and at the same time, the group is energized.

Writing is often used in the termination of group sessions. It is an aid to promoting reflection because of the time and structure group members have to devote to it.

Another way of closing a group and obtaining an accurate picture of how the group assessed the session is by having the leader distribute a **rating sheet** to members that they fill out and return before they leave.

## TERMINATION OF A GROUP

The termination of a group is filled with a mixture of emotions and tasks. It is a time when members' behavior undergoes noticeable changes (Davies & Kuypers, 1985).

Although members of all groups realize the group will end, it is the leader who provides the type of guidance that will make this process positive and productive.

A number of capping (i.e., closure) skills enable the group to close appropriately.

**Reviewing and summarizing** the group experience is a procedure having members recall and share special moments they remember from the group.

Assessing, finishing business, applying change to everyday life, sharing homework, providing feedback, expressing farewells, and developing a specific plan for continuing each member's progress are ways of enhancing group termination.

## PROBLEMS IN TERMINATIONS

Sometimes group members (and occasionally group leaders) have difficulty with termination. Four possible problem areas are denial, transference, countertransference, and the way issues of closure and transition are handled.

Overall, termination is a gradual process, and group leaders who handle it properly "give it time" to evolve (Hansen et al., 1980).

"Embedded in the process of termination are issues of the individual's separateness, autonomy, and independence from the group" (Ohlsen, et al., 1988, p. 93).

## FOLLOW-UP SESSIONS

Follow-up is the procedure of reconnecting with group members after they have had enough time to process what they experienced in the group and work on their goals/objectives.

Usually follow-up is planned for 3 to 6 months after a group ends, either with the group as a whole or with the leader and a group member. Techniques include private interviews, a reunion, an evaluation questionnaire, and reading member journals.

## Key Concepts

*Can you define and describe each of the following terms? Be able to offer a brief example or relevant context for these concepts.*

assessing members' growth and change
boundaries
capping
countertransference
denial
dyads
emotional ambivalence
evaluation questionnaire
farewell-party syndrome
follow-up
go-rounds
homework
journal letters
journals/logs
pat on the back
planning for continued problem resolution
premature termination
projecting the future
rating sheet
recycling
rehearsal
reviewing and summarizing the group experience
rounds
saying goodbye
summarization
summarizing
termination
time limit for the group
transference
unfinished business

### Group Experience –Parallels and Reflections

1. As your small group experience comes to an end, describe what you are feeling. Are you aware of regrets, wishes, or desires that you are currently experiencing? What do you intend to do?

2. It is likely that you have observed numerous examples of termination through each and every group session. Describe the leader's use of exercises to assist in the process of termination in small group work.

3. As the group ends entirely, what do you notice? What are you most aware of as you reflect back on your participation in the group?

4. Of what value would a follow-up session later in the year be? Do you feel that the leader is offering you feedback that you are unable to hear at this point in your professional and personal development?

## Self Assessment Questions

### True or False Statements

The following statements check your comprehension of terms and identification of individuals (knowledge and comprehension level); your ability to apply that knowledge to solve more challenging questions (application level), and your ability to evaluate given information (analysis and evaluation level).

Indicate whether each statement is true or false. If you believe a statement is false, identify the error in the space provided. When necessary, refer to your text, *Group Work: A Counseling Specialty* (4th ed.). An answer key appears at the end of this book.

1. Boundaries are physical and psychological parameters under which the group operates.

_____
_____
_____

2. *Best Practice Guidelines* (Association for Specialists in Group Work, 1995), suggests that when a group member drops out, the group leader should avoid contacting him or her to discuss the benefits and liabilities of staying in the group.

_____
_____
_____

3. A positive reason for utilizing rounds in termination, according to Trotzer (1999), is to ensure that each member feels involved in the group.

_____
_____
_____

4. "Capping" is a skill that group members use to recall and reflect on significant events or experiences in the group at its end.

_____
_____
_____

5. Projecting the future is a skill that can be used to aid in the closure, when appropriate, during termination.

_____
_____
_____

6. Repression phenomenon in members repeatedly triggers many unexplained feelings for many group leaders.

_____

_____

_____

7. Acknowledging ambivalent feelings is a primary activity of group members during the termination stage.

_____

_____

_____

8. The subject of termination should first be addressed during orientation of a group.

_____

_____

_____

9. Individuals quitting a group early or a group ending due to the actions of a leader are both examples of recycling.

_____

_____

_____

10. "Unfinished business" is where group members are asked to imagine what changes they would like to make through the group experience.

_____

_____

_____

11. Countertransference is usually thought of as the leader's emotional responses to members that are a result of the leader's own needs or unresolved issues.

_____

_____

_____

12. The total number of sessions devoted to the termination process should be two to four sessions.

_____

_____

_____

13. Transference allows individuals to repeat a similar group experience a second time to learn lessons missed the first time.

_____

_____

_____

14. In member summarization individuals are allowed to discuss what occurred during a session, what occurred for them individually, and how they gained from a particular session.

_____
_____
_____

15. Denial is acting as if the experience of the group will never end.

_____
_____
_____

16. Follow-up is the procedure of reconnecting with group members after they have had enough time to process what they experienced in group.

_____
_____
_____

## Multiple Choice Questions

1. At termination, when members' experiences of loss, sadness, and separation are mingled with feelings of hope, joy, and accomplishment, the result is called _____.
    a. farewell syndrome           c. recycling
    b. premature termination     d. emotional ambivalence

2. If *member summarization* is utilized regularly over the life of a group, results will likely include all of the following EXCEPT_____.
    a. how members have gained from the session
    b. a challenge to members to consider what they give and get
    c. what objectives each member has for the following session
    d. a summary of what has occurred during this session

3. One method of closing a group session and obtaining an accurate picture of how the group members assess the session is through using _____.
    a. homework              c. rounds
    b. rating sheets        d. unfinished business

4. A particular challenge often noticed during termination occurs when members attempt to relate to other persons in ways inappropriate for that situation. This is called _____.
    a. transference          c. denial
    b. countertransference    d. projecting the future.

**Written Exercises**

Respond in writing to several of the following questions, prompts, and inquiries, designed to deepen your comprehension of the text. Student responses can lead to self-reflection and interesting discussions with others. You are encouraged to flex your imagination and make your understanding of group work as presented in these chapters come to life.

## Questions & Prompts for Written Reflection and Discussion

### Chapter 8

1. How accurately does the following statement apply, based on your life experiences with endings? "When one door closes, another opens." What are several memorable closings in your life? Write about them. Imagine how your experiences with endings might influence your membership or eventual leadership of groups. Share your reflections with others in class.

_____
_____
_____
_____
_____
_____
_____
_____
_____
_____
_____
_____
_____
_____

2. Thinking of groups in which you have been a member, what experiences have you had with terminations? Do you recall premature "departures" of members? What effect did such attrition have on the group? What have leaders (e.g., teachers, coaches, professors) that you have observed done to prevent termination? How closely do those interventions align with those in your text (Gladding, p. 184)?

_____
_____
_____
_____
_____
_____
_____
_____
_____
_____
_____
_____
_____

3. Describe the process of "capping" (p. 190). In role-play or in some other appropriate small group experience, practice your emerging capping skills. To extend this vital learning, observe in your real group experiences both in and outside of class how the leader utilizes these capping skills at the end of group sessions. Pay close attention to how you felt and what you were thinking as a result.

_____
_____
_____
_____
_____
_____
_____
_____
_____
_____
_____
_____
_____

4. Select one or more references (e.g., journal articles, texts) that cover the phenomenon of either *transference* or *countertransference* (especially with respect to group counseling and psychotherapy). As you read the material, can you envision a time when you were aware of either phenomenon? Describe your experience(s) with others in your class. What was the experience like for you? Try not to limit your response and discussion to what you think; what did this transference feel like?

_____
_____
_____
_____
_____
_____
_____
_____
_____
_____
_____
_____
_____

**Prompts for Group Members**

1. What mood characterizes termination for your group work experience? Describe what you are feeling and write about how you are dealing with whatever it is you feel.

2. What has been the overall effect of this group experience for you? What have you noticed about the member relationships, the role of the leader, your role and function in the group?

3. How did the formality (if it seemed formal) of "ending" matter to your overall experience?

**Journal and Reflection**

Space for journaling about your group work experiences is provided below. Use this space to reflect on your reading about group work, your classroom presentations and activities, the group dynamics of your classes themselves, and any simulations or actual group participation opportunities you may have. Comment here thoughtfully. Be sure to carefully honor your ethical commitment to uphold the confidentiality of others in your group. Reflections are yours and are not to reveal anyone else's information. Recording your thoughts and feelings will provide a written history of this phase of your group work education. (Attach additional sheets of paper if desired.)

_____
_____
_____
_____
_____
_____
_____
_____
_____
_____
_____
_____
_____
_____
_____
_____
_____
_____
_____
_____
_____
_____
_____
_____
_____
_____
_____
_____
_____
_____
_____
_____
_____

*Entry date* _____

# GROUP WORK WITH CULTURALLY DIVERSE POPULATIONS

**Outcome Objectives**

1. I comprehend the importance of and the responsibilities inherent in group work with culturally diverse populations.
2. I understanding the historical overview of cultural diversity in groups including:
   a. Challenges of culturally diverse groups
   b. Myths about multicultural groups
   c. The goals of multicultural groups
   d. Assessing cultural diversity in a group
   e. Leadership in culturally diverse groups
3. I can describe both my awareness and understanding of working with different cultural populations in groups, including:
   a. African Americans
   b. Hispanic/Latino Americans
   c. Asian and Asian-Pacific Americans
   d. Native Americans
   e. European Americans
   f. Groups for gay, lesbian, and bisexual people

## Chapter Overview

Multicultural issues in the realm of group work are extremely important to examine and understand. In leading a multicultural group, the leader cannot ignore the presence of different cultures. Leaders need to expand their cultural awareness and develop specific skills in order to be effective in their leadership.

## Chapter Highlights

In a complex, pluralistic society like the United States that is composed of people who differ widely in regard to their lifestyles and worldviews, group leaders must be skilled and aware of cultural significance.

When individuals in groups feel threatened by differences, they become defensive and withdraw from interactions from those with whom they are uncomfortable.

By working collaboratively in groups of all types with persons who differ from oneself, group members can not only achieve common goals but in the process can (a) bridge the gap of differences, (b) become more creative in their problem solving, (c) grow in their cognitive and moral reasoning, and (d) learn to view matters from a new perspective (Johnson, 2000).

### A HISTORICAL OVERVIEW OF CULTURAL DIVERSITY IN GROUPS

In 1996 the Association for Specialists in Group Work (ASGW) set up a task force to incorporate multicultural competencies into its standards.

In 1997 the ASGW endorsed the *Multicultural Counseling Competencies and Standards* of the American Multicultural Counseling and Development Association (Sue, Arredondo, & McDavis, 1992).

In 1998, the ASGW adopted its own *Principles for Diversity-Competent Group Workers* (Haley-Banez, Brown, & Molina, 1999) but did not operationalize this document with articles.

Reports from group leaders imply that the cultural backgrounds of group members often have a powerful impact on interpersonal relationships and the work that the group does (Conyne et al., 2000; Rose, 2001).

## CHALLENGES OF CULTURALLY DIVERSE GROUPS

To work effectively with culturally diverse populations in a group context, group leaders must make three modifications in regard to traditional ways of working in a group.

First, group leaders must understand what a culture is. Since many different groups of people live in the United States and other pluralistic nations, *most group work is multicultural in nature.*

Second, group theory and technique must be modified and applied to different cultures in ways that are congruent with the beliefs and behaviors of those cultures (DeLucia-Waack, 1996b, p. 218).

Third, for group work to be multicultural, group theory and techniques that "acknowledge, explore, and use group member differences to facilitate change and growth" must be developed (DeLucia-Waack, 1996b, p. 218).

This last change, which stresses the use of differences to enhance group effectiveness, has been slow to emerge; almost all group approaches are based on European-American models.

Multiculturalism as a movement has been defined traditionally in terms of cultural, ethnic, and racial differences.

## MYTHS ABOUT MULTICULTURAL GROUPS

DeLucia-Waack (1996b, pp. 219-221) has articulated four myths that need to be dispelled if diverse groups are going to be productive.

*Myth 1: "Discussion of racial or cultural differences will offend group members."*

*Myth 2: "Groups can be truly homogeneous."*

*Myth 3: "Group member differences do not affect the process and outcome of task and psychoeducational groups."*

*Myth 4: "Group work theory is appropriate for all clients."*

## GOALS OF MULTICULTURAL GROUPS

Like all successful forms of group work, multicultural groups are goal directed.

A primary challenge of conducting multicultural groups relates to the different views, values, and interpersonal style that members display and how these forces are not only managed but also highlighted in productive ways.

According to DeLucia-Waack (1996a), multicultural groups, regardless of their emphasis, have three common goals: (a) to understand the situation that brought the person to the group from a cultural perspective, (b) "to approach all events and behavior in the group from a functional perspective" (p. 171), and (c) to help members make sense of "new behaviors, beliefs, and skills within a cultural context" (p. 171).

## ASSESSING CULTURAL DIVERSITY IN A GROUP

It is imperative that group workers understand the cultural backgrounds of their clients before attempting to work with them and that they have a broad and culture-centered perspective.

For most cultural groups, core group skills and principles will work on some level. However, for other groups, depending on their specific composition, there is a need to develop culture-specific strategies (Sue, 1992).

## LEADERSHIP IN CULTURALLY DIVERSE GROUPS

Before beginning a group, it is important that leaders examine their own thoughts and feelings about people who are culturally or otherwise distinct from them.

When thoughts and emotions about culturally different groups of people are not dealt with before a group begins, they may well play themselves out detrimentally within the group itself (Allport, 1958; Donigian & Malnati, 1997).

In conducting groups that include members who are culturally distinct, leaders must sensitize themselves continually to cultural variables and individual differences in order that they may become more aware of the issues of culture that influence their own backgrounds.

Increasing the awareness and abilities of group leaders in culturally diverse groups may be done in multiple ways.

Group leaders might also examine their family as the place where they learned about their culture and relationships with others (Ivey, 1999).

A final strategy is the employment of both didactic and experiential education.

## WORKING WITH DIFFERENT CULTURAL POPULATIONS IN GROUPS

Group workers from the majority culture in the United States (i.e., European American) need to increase their knowledge about cultural variables.

Among the most important pieces of knowledge group workers will need regarding diversity in groups is information about group process in naturally occurring groups.

While acquiring process knowledge, group workers should attune themselves to the nonverbal behaviors of group members.

In conducting any group, cultural heritage will influence levels of comfort and patterns of interaction for better or worse depending on the knowledge of group leaders and other group members.

Group workers can never assume that persons from certain backgrounds will behave in a set way. In fact, to make such an assumption is to stereotype and act with prejudice.

## African Americans

African Americans are quite diverse, and within-group differences are great.

Collectively, African Americans share a common bond that is the result of the legacy of slavery and bondage that prevailed in the United States from 1619 to 1865.

The history of discrimination that followed their freedom from slavery has influenced most members of this group in significant ways.

Group work is appropriate for counseling African Americans, especially a homogeneous group, "grounded in the African American worldview" (Williams et al., 1999, p. 260).

The "'safety in numbers' principle makes it easier" for some African Americans to disclose before a group rather than an individual professional helper (Merta, 1995, p. 574).

"In addition, group counseling experiences may help African Americans increase their sense of hope and optimism, decrease their feelings of alienation, develop more effective coping techniques, and acquire more effective socialization skills" (Ford, 1997, p. 103).

In working with African Americans in counseling and therapeutic settings, group leaders have found the creative arts, "especially music, poetry, literature, folklore and graphic expression," to be useful aids in promoting group interaction (Brinson & Lee, 1997, p. 52).

## Hispanic/Latino Americans

Like other ethnic and cultural groups, there is considerable variety in populations that are characterized as Hispanic/Latino.

Group workers need to be aware of the overlaps and distinctions found in these groups if they are going to be effective in leading them (Altarriba & Bauer, 1998).

In groups for Hispanics/Latinos, group counselors need to be active, validating, and supportive (Baca & Koss-Chioino, 1997).

Recommendations have been made regarding language, especially in groups in which members' first language is Spanish. Espin (1987) recommends that leaders of such groups be bilingual because for many members of Hispanic/Latino groups, Spanish is the language of emotions since it was in Spanish that affective meanings were originally encoded.

In working with Hispanic/Latino groups, sex-role socialization issues and cultural identity may impact the process.

Considerable anecdotal information is available about the effectiveness of group work with Hispanics/Latinos in such areas as academic skills, value clarification, problem solving, self-esteem, and pride in one's cultural identity (Merta, 1995).

## Asian and Asian-Pacific Americans

Asians and Pacific Islander Americans are often clumped into one main category; however, there are wide intergroup and intragroup differences that may make it difficult for group workers to deal effectively with unique issues of particular individuals (Chen & Han, 2001).

The myth that members of this population are the "model minority" and have no serious problems is exactly that — a myth.

"Asians in the U.S. not only face many of the same problems as other minorities, such as racism and stereotyping, but the very press coverage which extols their virtues often complicates and exacerbates those problems, especially for those Asians who for many reasons, cannot meet the expectations raised" (Cheng, 1995, p. 8).

Members of this population must be understood and worked with beyond the myths that surround them.

One issue that needs to be addressed in working with Asian and Asian-Pacific American culture groups is the disparity "between group work values (e.g., openness, expression of feelings, directness) and the cultural values of Asian Americans (e.g., verbal nonassertiveness, reluctance to display strong emotions in front of strangers, and unwillingness to disclose personal problems to strangers)" (Merta, 1995, p. 574).

One way to work with groups of Asian Americans, especially college students, is to offer "groups which focus on practical concerns to them rather than on forums which focus on more personal concerns" (Cheng, 1996, p. 10).

Another successful way of conducting groups with Asian Americans is a stage-specific interactive approach (Chen & Han, 2001).

## Native Americans

"Native Americans are a group-oriented people who consider the whole greater than the sum of its parts" (Garrett & Osborne, 1995, p. 34).

Native Americans generally share some common values, such as an emphasis on cooperation, health, holism, sharing, spirituality, healing, and an extended family orientation (Colmani & Merta, 1999; Dufrene & Coleman, 1992).

In work with Native Americans, groups have been found to be more appropriate than individual counseling (Appleton & Dykeman, 1996).

Numerous group approaches to working with Native Americans that seem to work well have been identified.

## European Americans

People descended from European ancestors compose the largest number of people in the United States and make up what is known as the majority culture who share some similarities, with the most obvious being their white skin color.

This similarity has both positive and negative attributes.

"White Americans often have difficulty perceiving themselves as members of a cultural group and often refer to themselves and others as 'American,' or 'a person' without regard to race" (Brown, Parham, & Yonker, 1996, p. 510).

Regardless of skin color or identity, European Americans differ dramatically among themselves, just as in other cultural groups. Their values, religious traditions, and customs vary.

As a group, people of European origin in North America "have been in a position of social and cultural dominance with respect to other groups" (Lee, 1997, p. 19).

European Americans who understand their worldview, cultural values, and racial identity are more likely than not to have a positive influence on others in groups who both differ from and are similar to them.

## Groups for Gay, Lesbian, and Bisexual People

As a group, gays, lesbians, and bisexuals (GLB) comprise approximately 10% to 15% of the overall population (Dorland & Fischer, 2001).

GLB individuals have distinct concerns about sexism and homophobia as well as other matters including career and life development.

Lifestyles of GLBs vary from being invisible, to coming out, to openly acknowledging their sexual orientations. Groups devoted specifically to working with members of each group, who often have more in common than not, have proven useful and productive at least according to anecdotal reports.

Mixed groups, whose members have heterosexual, homosexual, and bisexual identities, have also been successful (Firestein, 1999).

In working with GLBs in groups, it is important to remember that they represent a diverse population. There are large within-group differences as well as between-group differences in members.

The matter of confidentiality is often of uppermost importance in groups for GLBs regardless of age.

## Key Concepts

*Can you define and describe each of the following terms? Be able to offer a brief example or relevant context for these concepts.*

> Chicanas
> inner circle/outer circle approach
> sweat lodge ceremony
> talking circle

## Group Experience –Parallels and Reflections

1.  What diversity have you become aware of in your small group? What issues of diversity appear to be present? Where do you fit in terms of the minority or the majority culture present in your group? What cultural phenomena have you seem play out in your group experience so far?

2.  How are issues of cultural diversity addressed by your group leader? What, if any, unique interventions have you observed? How have the group members responded to any such intervention around cultural differences?

3.  Consider the six cultural populations written about in your text. Are members from any of these six populations present in your small group? What have you been able to learn about yourself, your beliefs, biases, or expectations regarding these cultural groups by being a member in this small group experience?

## Self Assessment Questions

### True or False Statements

The following statements check your comprehension of terms and identification of individuals (knowledge and comprehension level); your ability to apply that knowledge to solve more challenging questions (application level), and your ability to evaluate given information (analysis and evaluation level).

Indicate whether each statement is true or false. If you believe a statement is false, identify the error in the space provided. When necessary, refer to your text, *Group Work: A Counseling Specialty* (4th ed.). An answer key appears at the end of this book.

1.  The notion that "Group work is appropriate for all clients without specific regard to their backgrounds," has been well supported in the professional literature.

_____
_____
_____

2.  Brinson and Lee (1997) claim that culturally responsive group leaders must be aware of their *cultural values*, *assumptions* and *biases* in order to understand how they might have impact upon the group process.

_____
_____
_____

3.  Chiu (1997) advocates increasing the awareness and abilities of group leaders of culturally diverse groups through group coleadership.

_____
_____
_____

4. When grounded in the African American worldview, many African Americans may especially favor heterogeneous group work (Williams et al., 1999).

 

 

 

5. Working with African Americans in counseling and psychotherapy groups, Brinson and Lee (1997) found the use of creative arts to aid in promoting group interaction.

 

 

 

6. Cuban Americans, Mexican Americans and Puerto Ricans are the three major Hispanic/Latino subgroups in America.

 

 

 

7. Because many Hispanic/Latino group members originally learned to express their emotions in their first language of Spanish, a *bilingual group leader* is recommended.

 

 

 

8. Asian and Pacific Islander Americans represent a large but relatively homogeneous cultural group.

 

 

 

9. Group work values such as openness, expression of feelings, and directness mirror Asian and Pacific Islander Americans' cultural values.

 

 

 

10. Native American healers often treat individuals in isolation from their family, friends, and neighbors.

 

 

 

11. Specific attention to nonverbal communication as a means of increasing the Native American's self-disclosure may benefit working with Native Americans in heterogeneous groups.

 

 

 

12. The most obvious similarity shared by members of the majority culture in America is common values.

_____
_____
_____

13. According to Lee (1997), people of European origin in North America hold a position of cultural dominance with respect to other cultural groups.

_____
_____
_____

14. The professional literature on group work with European Americans as a specific group has been nonexistent until recently.

_____
_____
_____

15. Social issues such as homophobia and sexism are significant and often are areas of attention by members of the gay, lesbian, and bisexual communities in group work.

_____
_____
_____

16. Group leaders working with gay, lesbian and bisexual clients have special concerns regarding issues of informed consent.

_____
_____
_____

17. Quite simply, culture is the values and behaviors shared by a group of people.

_____
_____
_____

18. Members of the majority culture (European Americans) in most group settings are not affected by cultural difference.

_____
_____
_____

19. Working with African Americans in counseling groups has been found to be more appropriate than individual counseling.

_____
_____
_____

**Multiple Choice Questions**

1. A conclusion made as a result of the fact that many different groups of people live in the United States and other pluralistic nations is that _____.
    a.  most groups are multicultural in nature
    b.  leaders must familiarize themselves with different cultures
    c.  group theory must be modified for multicultural application
    d.  (all of the above)

2. Different views, values, and interpersonal styles refer to the _____ of conducting multicultural groups.
    a. primary challenge          c. common experience
    b. largest hurdle to rise above    d. (none of the above)

3. Which of the following is NOT a recommended strategy for increasing the awareness and abilities of group leaders in culturally diverse groups?
    a.  group coleadership with minority counselors
    b.  participation in cultural immersion experiences
    c.  volunteerism in culturally different communities
    d.  language training when possible

**Written Exercises**
Respond in writing to several of the following questions, prompts, and inquiries, designed to deepen your comprehension of the text. Student responses can lead to self-reflection and interesting discussions with others. You are encouraged to flex your imagination and make your understanding of group work as presented in these chapters come to life.

## Questions & Prompts for Written Reflection and Discussion

### Chapter 9

1. Consider the "multicultural myths" (pp. 205-206) described in your text. Were you surprised as you read any of these four myths? To some degree, perhaps, you believed one or more of them were true. What do you believe contributes to their believability? What social stereotypes are perpetuated by these myths, and what do you think are some ways of challenging group members to debunk these myths?

_____
_____
_____
_____
_____
_____
_____
_____
_____
_____
_____

2. Group workers are expected to assess multiple factors in order to maximize the effectiveness of members in the groups they lead. Consider both screening/selection and pretraining functions. How do you believe a group leader can effectively gather information regarding cultural variables during these processes? Discuss your strategies with other members of your class.

_____
_____
_____
_____
_____
_____
_____
_____
_____
_____

3. Consider your own ethnic and cultural heritage. What do you "take for granted" as your worldview? Can you identify biases and stereotypes that might befall you as a member in a group? What potential conflicts may arise with members of other cultural groups given your beliefs, traditions, and culture? Share aspects of these responses with members of your class. How do others react to you? How do you react to them and their disclosures?

_____
_____
_____
_____
_____
_____
_____
_____
_____
_____

4. At this point in your journey toward a specialty in group work, what do you identify as the most challenging aspects of working in groups with members from different cultural groups? As you search, do you become aware of any areas that require some careful self-exploration? What is your initial reaction when you locate your biases or beliefs that will likely affect your leadership? Share what you propose to do about these findings with others in your class.

_____
_____
_____
_____
_____
_____
_____
_____
_____
_____

## Prompts for Group Members

1. What issues of diversity are you aware of in your group?

2. How have diversity issues played themselves out during the development of your group?

3. Where do you struggle in this area? What particular biases are you most aware of at this moment?

## Journal and Reflection

Space for journaling about your group work experiences is provided below. Use this space to reflect on your reading about group work, your classroom presentations and activities, the group dynamics of your classes themselves, and any simulations or actual group participation opportunities you may have. Comment here thoughtfully. Be sure to carefully honor your ethical commitment to uphold the confidentiality of others in your group. Reflections are yours and are not to reveal anyone else's information. Recording your thoughts and feelings will provide a written history of this phase of your group work education. (Attach additional sheets of paper if desired.)

_Entry date_ _____

# ETHICAL AND LEGAL ASPECTS OF GROUP WORK

**Outcome Objectives**

1.  I understand the ethical and legal aspects of group work.
2.  I can describe the nature of ethics and ethical codes.
3.  I am able to demonstrate an understanding of the major ethical issues in group work, including:
    a.  Training of group leaders
    b.  Screening of potential group members
    c.  The rights of group members
    d.  Confidentiality
    e.  Personal relationships between group members and leaders
    f.  Dual relationships
    g.  Personal relationships among group members
    h.  Uses of group techniques
    i.  Leaders' values
    j.  Referrals
    k.  Records
    l.  Termination and follow-up
4.  I can describe and demonstrate the skills involved in making ethical decisions.
5.  I comprehend how to promote ethical principles in group work, including the training, the continuing education and peer supervision of group leaders.
6.  I can discuss how to respond to alleged complaints of unethical behavior.
7.  I am able to define legal issues in group work, including community, state, and national standards and legal actions.

## Chapter Overview

Ethical and legal issues abound in the specialty area of group work. In order to be a responsible counselor, each group leader must be familiar with the ethical codes and professional standards designed to assist leaders and groups. Group workers must also be familiar with legal issues.

## Chapter Highlights

Group leaders are constantly making decisions guided by the ethical guidelines of the professional organizations to which they belong and the legal codes of local, state, and federal governments (Remley & Herlihy, 2001).

*Ethics* and the *law* are not one and the same. Rather, "they can probably be best conceptualized as two over-lapping circles which share a common intersection" (Kitchener, 1984a, p. 16).

Knowledge in and of itself does not guarantee proper ethical behavior (Baldick, 1980; Welfel & Lipsitz, 1984).

Ethical and legal decision-making is a dynamic activity that needs careful attention if group leaders are to stay current and act in the best interest of their group members.

## THE NATURE OF ETHICS AND ETHICAL CODES

**Ethics** may best be defined as "suggested standards of conduct based on a set of professional values" (George & Dustin, 1988, p. 124). To behave in an ethical way is to act in a professionally acceptable manner based on these values (Hayes, 1991).

Dominant values underlying the practice of ethics are based on the virtues of autonomy, beneficence, nonmaleficence, justice (i.e., fairness), fidelity, and veracity (truthfulness) (Kitchener, 1984b; Meara, Schmidt, & Day, 1996).

A **code of ethics** is a set of standards and principles that organizations create to provide guidelines for their members to follow in working with the public and each other.

Codes of ethics are constantly evolving and do not refer to all possible situations.

One document that specifically addresses ethical issues in group work is the *Best Practices Guidelines* of the Association for Specialists in Group Work (1998).

The more general *Codes of Ethics and Standards of Practice* of the American Counseling Association (1995) provides direction for group workers in ethically interacting with members of their groups.

The ASGW *Professional Standards for the Training of Group Workers* (2000) and the ASGW *Principles for Diversity-Competent Group Work* (1999) are important sources of ethical information. They outline the qualifications of group leaders in different types of groups and ways of working with diverse groups.

## MAJOR ETHICAL ISSUES IN GROUP WORK

Among the most important issues regarding ethics are those involving training of group leaders, screening of potential group members, the rights of group members, confidentiality, personal relationships between group members and leaders, dual relationships, personal relationships among group members, uses of group techniques, leader's values, referral, records, and termination and follow-up.

### Training of Group Leaders
It is the responsibility of professional education programs, such as those accredited by the Council for the Accreditation of Counseling and Related Educational Programs (CACREP), to be sure that persons whom they graduate are personally integrated and have received the experiences and possibly therapy they need to work out biases and utilize strengths (Yalom, 1995).

The training of group leaders involves selected course work and experience in core group skills, such as being able to identify the basic principles of group dynamics (ASGW, 2000).

It is important for trainees to be involved in different types of group experiences, both as participants and as leaders or coleaders (Corey et al., 1998; Yalom, 1995).

Both the ASGW and the AGPA recommend personal-growth experiences as part of the total program for aspiring group leaders.

One way for beginning group leaders to gain clarity and experience, in addition to those ideas mentioned previously, is to join a **training group** (Corey & Corey, 2002).

## Screening of Potential Group Members

**Screening** is actually a three-part process: leaders formulate the type of group they would like, and are qualified, to lead; in recruitment, leaders must be sure not to misrepresent the type of group that is to be conducted; and leaders screen applicants on a one-to-one or small-group basis.

The potential group member ultimately must decide in collaboration with the group leader(s) whether to join the group. He or she needs as much information as possible about the benefits and liabilities of such action.

It is advisable at the end of the screening process, and before accepting a member into the group, that the leader obtains a member's signature on an **informed consent statement** (Welfel, 2002).

## Rights of Group Members

Group members have rights that must be respected and protected if the group is going to work well. Specific guidelines pertaining to rights and risks in particular group situations should be covered, too (Remley & Herlihy, 2001).

Basically, group members have the right to know as realistically as possible what type of group procedures will be used and what the risks are in their participation.

## Confidentiality

**Confidentiality** is the right of group members to reveal personal thoughts, feelings, and information to the leader and other members of the group and expect that information to not be disclosed to others outside the group.

It should be stressed to potential group members that confidentiality is expected of everyone in the group to promote trust, cohesiveness, and growth (Corey et al., 1998; Cottone & Tarvydas, 1998).

The leader must acknowledge that he or she cannot guarantee confidentiality and that there may be certain cases in which ethical and/or legal considerations may force the leader to break confidentiality (Welfel, 2002).

## Personal Relationships Between Group Members and Leaders

The amount and kind of relationship between group members and leaders will vary from group to group.

It is more likely that relationships between group members and leaders will be detrimental to the group as a whole if they are not carefully handled.

Usually, outside personal contact between group leaders and members in therapeutic or counseling groups is discouraged or prohibited.

## Dual Relationships

**Dual relationships** occur when group leaders find themselves in two potentially conflicting roles with their group members (Donigian, 1993).

"Although certain dual relationships may seem unavoidable and may even seem harmless. . . all dual relationships carry the potential for harm because of the inherent vulnerability of the client and the imbalance of power between counselor and client" (Neukrug, Milliken, & Walden, 2001).

In academic settings, Remley and Reeves (1989) advise counselor educators to avoid "dual relationships" such as requiring or allowing students to participate in a group experience led by them as a part of a course, since such situations involve a conflict of interest.

## Personal Relationships Among Group Members

Most group leaders do not make hard and fast rules about personal relationships among group members because this type of rule is impossible to enforce (Jacobs, Masson, & Harvill, 2002).

In most counseling and psychotherapy groups, member-to-member contact outside the group results in the formation of subgroups or hidden agendas, that are detrimental. Therefore, discouraging socialization in these types of groups is probably a prudent policy (Remley & Herlihy, 2001).

## Uses of Group Techniques

**Group techniques** or exercises are structured ways of getting members to interact with one another. They can have a powerful impact on group members and positively affect how people work together or change.

When leaders misuse them, exercises can inhibit the natural ebb and flow of a group (Carroll & Wiggins, 1997).

Group leaders face ethical problems when they lack the skill or sensitivity to use exercises properly or when they "deskill" group members by making them overly dependent on the leader and less likely to help each other (Jacobs et al., 2002; Yalom, 1995).

Using techniques isolated from relationships and theories amounts to the employment of "gimmicks," which is an unprofessional and unethical way to work (Patterson, 1985).

Whenever an exercise is used in a group, it should be processed so that it allows group members to become better informed about themselves and the group.

## Leaders' Values

Group leaders have values, and, for better or worse, values influence the goals, methods, and ultimately the success of group work and counseling (Corey et al., 1998; Mitchell, 1993; Patterson, 1958; Williamson, 1958).

Leaders must be careful not to impose their values on group members. Such action short-circuits members' exploration, especially in counseling and psychotherapy groups, and results in confusion and chaos.

If group leaders and members have conflicts about values, leaders are responsible for making referrals (Corey et al., 1998). Leaders must stay attuned and be aware of the impact of values in a group of any kind.

## Referrals

**Referrals** (i.e., transfers of members to another group) are made when group leaders realize they cannot help certain members achieve designated goals or when a conflict between leaders and members prove unresolvable.

Group leaders should maintain an extensive and current list of referral sources.

The referral process itself involves four steps: "(1) identifying the need to refer; (2) evaluating potential referral sources; (3) preparing the client for the referral; and (4) coordinating the transfer" (Cormier & Hackney, 1996, p. 294).

## Records

When conducting groups for counseling or therapeutic purposes, it is important that group workers keep records. Documentation helps the group worker concretely review what happened in the group, when it occurred, and who was involved.

Written records should be kept in locked files in a secured area that is also locked and has limited access.

## Termination and Follow-up

The ethical issue in follow-up usually centers on its neglect rather than its inclusion.

Group leaders should make themselves available to group members for consultation as well as follow-up meetings after the termination of the group.

Besides providing for the welfare of group members, follow-up after termination also has the added benefit of helping group leaders evaluate the effectiveness of what they did in the group and improve their group leadership styles.

## MAKING ETHICAL DECISIONS

Since group leaders face such a wide variety of issues, it is crucial that they know beforehand how they will make ethical decisions.

**Principle ethics** are ethics based on obligations. Codes of ethics are based on principle ethics (i.e., actions stemming from obligations).

**Virtue ethics** focus on "the character traits of the counselor [or group worker] and nonobligatory ideals to which professionals aspire rather than on solving specific ethical dilemmas" (Corey, Corey, & Callanan, 1998, p. 10).

One way of making ethical decisions is to use specific steps as a guideline: for example, the **A-B-C-D-E Worksheet** (Sileo & Kopala, 1993) or the Hill, Glaser, and Harden (1995) seven-step model.

## PROMOTING ETHICAL PRINCIPLES IN GROUP WORK

The promotion and implementation of ethical conduct in groups occur on two levels: training and practice.

## Training Group Leaders

The training of group leaders to address ethical issues is a multidimensional process.

Kitchener (1986) points out the training of potential group leaders requires sensitizing them to ethical standards and issues, helping them learn to reason about ethical situations, developing within them a sense of being morally responsible in their actions, and teaching them tolerance of ambiguity in ethical decision making.

To become familiar with ethical codes, best practices, and standards in group work is initially as simple as reading pertinent documents and articles. However, reading does not teach trainees that ethics are normative rather than factual (Gladding, Remley, & Huber, 2001).

Ethical training requires individuals to examine and understand their own personal codes of ethics (Van Hoose & Kottler, 1977; Van Hoose & Paradise, 1979).

Prospective group leaders can gain a greater exposure to dealing with ethical dilemmas from a practical viewpoint through role plays in simulated groups and direct participation in practitioner training groups (Conyne, Wilson, & Ward, 1997).

Individuals who aspire to be group leaders need to be exposed to developmental theories of ethical reasoning so they can gauge their own professional growth (Welfel, 2002).

## Continuing Education and Peer Supervision
For practitioners already in the field of group work, the matter of keeping up with ethical codes and growing as an ethically based professional can be met by taking continuing education courses and by undergoing peer supervision.

Almost all professional associations offer programs on ethics at their national, regional, and state conventions.

Continuing education can be supplemented with **peer supervision**, in which practitioners meet regularly to consult with each other about particularly difficult group situations (Ohlsen et al., 1988).

## RESPONDING TO ALLEGED UNETHICAL COMPLAINTS

It is unusual for a group member to file an unethical complaint against a group leader.

If a complaint is made against a group leader, two essential actions are to notify his or her professional liability insurance carrier and to "ensure that an attorney is promptly retained" (Chauvin & Remley, 1996, p. 564).

## LEGAL ISSUES IN GROUP WORK

Ethics and the law are separate but sometimes overlap (Remley, 1996).

*Law* refers to a body of "agreed-upon rules of a society that set forth the basic principles for living together as a group" (Remley & Herlihy, 2001, p. 3).

When persons feel wronged by professional helpers, the helpers' actions will be judged according to the standards of the group with which their services are most identified (Woody, Hansen, & Rossberg, 1989).

The conduct of group leaders, for example, would likely be compared with the type of behavior considered appropriate in the ASGW's *Best Practices Guidelines* (ASGW, 1998) or a similar definitive document.

## Community, State, and National Standards

Group leaders who function successfully are aware of "community standards, legal limitations to work, and state laws" governing the practice of groups, especially those that directly affect counseling or psychotherapy (Ohlsen et al., 1988, p. 391).

The best procedure to employ in preventing legal difficulties is to do one's professional "homework" beforehand.

## Legal Action

Legal action is most likely to be taken against a group worker, especially in a psychotherapy or counseling group, if members think they have suffered physical harm, emotional trauma, or psychological/financial damage as a result of participating in a group experience (Shaffer & Galinsky, 1989; Swenson, 1997).

This legal action usually is in the form of a **malpractice suit** that implies the group leader has failed to render proper service because of either negligence or ignorance.

There are numerous specific practices that are most likely to prevent lawsuits (see Corey et al., 1998; Anderson & Hopkins, 1996; Hummel et al., 1985; Paradise & Kirby, 1990; Van Hoose & Kottler, 1985).

In suits charging that the group leader's conduct fell below minimum standards, the measure usually used in such cases is what other practitioners in the same geographical area would do under similar circumstances (Gladding et al., 2001).

Group workers who are in contact with and in line with other practitioners in their area are less likely to be affected by this criterion, although local standards are increasingly being replaced with those on the national level.

Most malpractice suits in group work will center on **unintentional civil liability** (i.e., a lack of intent to cause injury).

In all cases, group specialists, especially those who work in psychotherapeutic or counseling groups, are advised to study their professional standards and codes of ethics carefully. Professionals who work with groups should carry **professional liability insurance** (i.e., insurance designed specifically to protect a group worker from financial loss in case of a civil suit).

## Key Concepts

*Can you define and describe each of the following terms? Be able to offer a brief example or relevant context for these concepts.*

A-B-C-D-E Worksheet
autonomy
beneficience
code of ethics
confidentiality
continuing education units (CEUs)
dual relationships
ethics
fidelity
group techniques
informed consent statement
intentional civil liability
justice
malpractice
malpractice suit
nonmaleficence
peer supervision
principle ethics
professional liability insurance
referrals
screening
training group
unintentional civil liability
veracity
virtue ethics

## Group Experience –Parallels and Reflections

1. In your small group experience, how did your leader/facilitator introduce the topic of ethical behavior, if at all? What mention of ethics was there during your screening, selection, or pregroup training?

2. How has the concern for confidentiality been addressed in your small group? Note, through various stages of your group experience, how issues of confidentiality reappear and how they are handled.

**115**

### Self Assessment Questions

**True or False Statements**

The following statements check your comprehension of terms and identification of individuals (knowledge and comprehension level); your ability to apply that knowledge to solve more challenging questions (application level), and your ability to evaluate given information (analysis and evaluation level).

Indicate whether each statement is true or false. If you believe a statement is false, identify the error in the space provided. When necessary, refer to your text, *Group Work: A Counseling Specialty* (4th ed.). An answer key appears at the end of this book.

1. Group leaders who keep well informed by numerous information sources make the best and wisest ethical and legal decisions.

   _____
   _____
   _____

2. Beneficence refers to the promotion of self-determination, the power to choose one's own direction in life.

   _____
   _____
   _____

3. Veracity in group work has to do with both interpersonal and intrapersonal honesty.

   _____
   _____
   _____

4. An important source for ethical information for group work specialists is the Association for Specialists in Group Work's *Principles for Diversity Competent Group Workers* (1999).

   _____
   _____
   _____

5. To decide whether or not to join a group, potential group members must receive as much information as possible regarding the benefits and liabilities of group membership.

   _____
   _____
   _____

6. To maximize group members' participation during every group session, ethical group leaders hold on to breaches of confidentiality until the termination stage.

   _____
   _____
   _____

7. The code of ethics and standards of practice that govern group counselors' ethical behavior is by *Chi Sigma Iota* (International Academic and Professional Counseling Honor Society).

_____

_____

_____

8. To lessen legal liability, group leaders should keep minimal written records when conducting group counseling and psychotherapy.

_____

_____

_____

9. The stage of ethical behavior called Institutional Orientation (Van Hoose and Paradise, 1979) could be termed "agency loyalty."

_____

_____

_____

10. Valuable sources in assessing community, state, and national standards include professional state counseling boards, state departments of education, local attorneys, and civic, religious, and business leaders.

_____

_____

_____

11. Criminal action is most often taken against group workers if one or more group members have suffered psychological or financial damages.

_____

_____

_____

12. "Virtue ethics" are ethics based on obligations.

_____

_____

_____

13. When an ethics complaint is filed against you as a group leader, you should immediately contact the individual who filed the complaint.

_____

_____

_____

14. Unintentional civil liability cases include occurrences of sexual impropriety.

_____

_____

_____

15. It is suggested that beginning group leaders join a support group in order to learn more about personal and professional issues surrounding group work.

_____

_____

_____

## Multiple Choice Questions

1. The dominant values underlying the practice of ethics are based on certain virtues. Of them, *nonmaleficence* is best described by which of the following?
    a. to do no harm          c. loyalty and duty
    b. truthfulness            d. promoting the good of others

2. The Association for Specialists in Group Work and the American Group Psychotherapy Association recommends _____ for group work leaders-in-training.
    a. selected course work        c. personal-growth experiences
    b. experience with core group skills    d. (all of the above)

3. _____ occur when group leaders find themselves two or more potentially conflicting roles with their group members.
    a. Legal liabilities           c. Dual relationships
    b. Mutual benefits          d. (all of the above)

4. *Confidentiality* is a particularly challenging issue in group counseling and therapy because the group leader can assure members that he or she will maintain confidences but cannot assure them that other members will be trustworthy. The standard of practice for group leaders is to _____ .
    a. inform members of this inherent risk
    b. inform and remind members of their obligation to uphold each others' confidences
    c. (both a and b)
    d. (neither a nor b)

5. The group worker who asks herself, "Am I doing the right thing in this particular situation?" is practicing from a _____ ethic.
    a. virtue               c. dominant
    b. principle           d. legal

6. Methods used by group workers to maintain their ethical postures include all of the following EXCEPT _____ .
    a. continuing education       c. maintain licensure
    b. peer supervision         d. hold liability insurance

## Written Exercises

Respond in writing to several of the following questions, prompts, and inquiries, designed to deepen your comprehension of the text. Student responses can lead to self-reflection and interesting discussions with others. You are encouraged to flex your imagination and make your understanding of group work as presented in these chapters come to life.

## Questions & Prompts for Written Reflection and Discussion

### Chapter 10

1.  Name what you believe are the two or three most prominent "professional values" inherent in group work upon which our ethical standards are built. Describe your conclusions with others in class.

_____
_____
_____
_____
_____
_____
_____
_____
_____
_____
_____
_____
_____
_____

2.  What practical difficulties can you imagine might arise from adherence to ethical standards? What do you envision will be the most challenging group leadership ethical responsibility you will encounter? Support your contention by creating a scenario or two to bring the difficulty to life. Discuss these with class members in small groups.

_____
_____
_____
_____
_____
_____
_____
_____
_____
_____
_____
_____
_____
_____

3.  Write a sample "informed consent" based on some aspect of group work that fits your professional track and aspirations (e.g., school counselor, community mental health, student affairs in higher education). What do you want to ensure that members in this hypothetical group understand, and why? As an alternate, if you recently signed an informed consent for membership in a group experience, recall what signing it entailed. What does signing such a document mean to you as a group member?

_____
_____
_____
_____
_____

4. With regard to the training of group leaders, consider your personal growth and readiness for ethical group leadership by evaluating your development on Van Hoose and Paradise's (1979) model (p. 238). Where do you assess yourself to be currently? Discuss your self-perceptions with others in class.

5. Describe what is involved in *unintentional civil liability*. Consider your professional aspirations. What ethical and legal safeguards will maximize your protection from liability? What claims might you foresee in your eventual career that a plaintiff in such legal action could make? Discuss your risks with others. Name several concrete steps that you will take to ensure this type of suit will never affect you.

## Journal and Reflection

Space for journaling about your group work experiences is provided below. Use this space to reflect on your reading about group work, your classroom presentations and activities, the group dynamics of your classes themselves, and any simulations or actual group participation opportunities you may have. Comment here thoughtfully. Be sure to carefully honor your ethical commitment to uphold the confidentiality of others in your group. Reflections are yours and are not to reveal anyone else's information. Recording your thoughts and feelings will provide a written history of this phase of your group work education. (Attach additional sheets of paper if desired.)

_____
_____
_____
_____
_____
_____
_____
_____
_____
_____
_____
_____
_____
_____
_____
_____
_____
_____
_____
_____
_____
_____
_____
_____
_____
_____
_____
_____
_____
_____
_____
_____
_____

*Entry date*

# GROUPS FOR CHILDREN

## Outcome Objectives

1.  I have explored types of groups for children, including:
    a.  Group guidance for elementary/middle school children
    b.  Group guidance in the schools
    c.  Group guidance and counseling in community settings
2.  I comprehend how to set up appropriate groups for children with specific understanding of:
    a.  Nonverbal versus verbal communication with children
    b.  Group structure and materials
    c.  Recruiting members and screening
    d.  Group session length and number in group
    e.  Gender and age issues
3.  I understand and can discuss the roles of the leader in children's groups.
4.  I am able to cite relevant studies on the outcome of children's groups.
5.  I am aware of and can discuss strengths and limitations of using groups with children.

## Chapter Overview

Group work with children under the age of 14 requires group leaders to be knowledgeable in areas of group dynamics, group process, and child development. Crucial issues in group work with children include the structure of the group, including time, size and diversity of the members as well as other unique requirements. The role of the leader varies according to the purpose of the group and the age/maturity of the group members.

## Chapter Highlights

Group workers must be attuned to children's issues and needs in a distinct way if they are going to be helpful to them. Group specialists must adapt their approaches accordingly to the social, emotional, physical, and intellectual levels of this population (Johnson & Kottman, 1992).

When children face natural age and stage developmental tasks together (e.g., learning how to work cooperatively, learning how to express emotions appropriately), they frequently master more than the specifically targeted skills.

Timing as well as content in children's groups is crucial, and learning occurs best at what Havighurst (1972) describes as a **teachable moment**, a time when children are ready and able to learn.

Since the late 1960s, small-group work, especially in school settings, has proven its efficacy and has become a major model by which children are helped (Bowman, 1987; Stamm & Nissman, 1979).

Small groups give students the opportunity to "explore and work through their social and emotional challenges with others who are experiencing similar feelings" (Campbell & Bowman, 1993, p. 173).

Overall, the key to working with children in groups is readiness on the part of both the leader and the children.

## TYPES OF GROUPS FOR CHILDREN

Developmental and nondevelopmental factors determine what types of groups are set up for children.

Groups for children generally take the form of guidance and psychoeducation (i.e., learning a new skill or experience) or counseling and psychotherapy (i.e., rectifying or resolving problematic behaviors, assumptions, or situations).

Guidance and psychoeducation groups usually involve the group worker in the role of an information giver with a large group of children. In such situations, the group worker functions as a teacher and may work directly with teachers.

Psychoeducation groups can be an effective way to help children unlearn inappropriate behaviors and learn new ways of relating more easily through interaction and feedback in a safe practice situation with their peers (Thompson & Rudolph, 2000).

Group counseling and psychotherapy are remediation based and deal with such personal and interpersonal concerns as "self-concept, social skills, interpersonal relationships, problem solving, academic skills, communication skills, and values" (Franks, 1983, p. 201).

Greater personal risks are taken in group counseling and psychotherapy, and the environment is less structured than is found in group guidance and psychoeducation (Myrick, 1993).

Learning is more cognitively based in guidance and psychoeducational groups, whereas it is more emotionally based in counseling and psychotherapeutic groups.

### Group Guidance for Elementary/Middle School Children
Group guidance for children of elementary and middle school age may be conducted in school, community agencies, or both (Corey & Corey, 2002).

Because group guidance in the schools is a preventive approach, counselors usually act as group leaders.

Traditionally, group leaders have presented their lessons to groups of children within a regular classroom environment.

Career development and self-exploration are two particularly proactive topics often explored (DeLucia-Waack, 2000).

Group guidance works best when counselors know what they want the group to achieve. One model for reaching this goal is known as SIPA (structure, involvement, process, and awareness) (Tyra, 1979).

Many psychoeducational groups revolve around activities and are subsequently called **activity group guidance (AGG)** (Hillman & Reunion, 1978). These activities are developmental in nature and typically include coordinated guidance topics.

In guidance and psychoeducational groups, a variety of techniques work well; group workers should move developmentally from more simple activities to those that are more complex.

A relatively new model for offering group guidance and psychoeducational material in middle schools is for counselors to train teachers to provide this service.

## Group Counseling Within the Schools

Psychoeducational and counseling groups, "where a counselor works with a group of 6 to 8 students, greatly increases the number of students who can benefit from working with a school counselor" (DeLucia-Waack, 2000, p. 131).

Group counseling usually takes one of three approaches in dealing with persons and problems: (a) crisis centered, (b) problem centered, and (c) growth centered (Myrick, 1993).

## Group Guidance and Counseling in Community Settings

The basic dynamics of group guidance and counseling for children in settings outside school environments do not differ substantially from those conducted within.

A major difference between schools and community agencies is the populations of children served. Community organizations will usually have more homogeneous groups than will schools.

By forming clubs instead of guidance or counseling groups, children avoid any stigmas attached to mental health activities. In the process, they can become more involved in the group and, thereby, get more from the experience.

## SETTING UP GROUPS FOR CHILDREN

In designing group experiences, group workers must consider the maturity of the children with whom they are working and the purpose of the group.

Decisions about what groups might be offered can be made when counselors conduct needs assessments with students, teachers, parents, and other related school personnel or when counselors hear several students voicing similar concerns over a short period of time.

## Nonverbal versus Verbal Communication

Many experts believe that children under 12 years of age should participate primarily in groups that involve play and action, using techniques such as sociodrama, child drama, and psychodrama.

Those experts opposed to this **action-centered view of groups** are theorists who believe that children can be taught the proper ways to express themselves verbally and that verbal-oriented groups are viable with even very young children.

Those who advocate verbal interaction believe the interplay of words and roles will "change the cognitive map and action patterns of a group member," whereas those who are activity oriented "believe that personality modifications occur through activity" (Kaczkowski, 1979, p. 45).

## Group Structure and Materials

**Highly structured groups** have a "predetermined goal and a plan designed to enable each group member to reach this identified goal with minimum frustration" (Drum & Knott, 1977, p. 14).

Such groups are usually used for teaching skills that may be transferred to a wide range of life events.

Unstructured groups are used in more experientially based situations in which process is emphasized rather than product. It is rare for a children's group of any kind to be totally unstructured.

Group workers must decide how materials will be employed in the groups (Leland & Smith, 1965).

If the emphasis of the group is on completing a project (e.g., drawing a figure) as opposed to experiencing a feeling (e.g., freehand drawing), the materials that are distributed and instructions given should reflect this.

The key to making the group a productive vehicle for helping children is for the group worker to use a leadership style that will enable him or her to blend meaningful materials with an appropriate degree of verbalization and activity (Kaczkowski, 1979, pp. 50–51).

## Recruiting Members and Screening

One of the best ways to recruit members is to provide parents, teachers, and students with an **information statement** that describes what the group is about and what is expected of its members (Ritchie & Huss, 2000).

Not all children who volunteer or who are referred are appropriate for a group. Therefore, a pregroup screening process must be used.

With children's groups, prescreening has special importance because of the ethical and legal responsibilities involved in conducting groups for minors (Ritchie & Huss, 2000).

One way to screen potential participants is through pregroup assessment methods. These methods may be informal or formal. An informal method is having a child write out what he or she wishes to get from a group.

Selection is crucial to the group's success, because group member satisfaction and identity with the group will influence group cohesion and ultimately affect personal outcomes.

Group work with children is more difficult to set up than group work with adults because of the many considerations involved in protecting children's rights (Corey, Corey, & Callanan, 1998).

## Group Session Length and Number in Group

Opinions vary on how long the group sessions should last and how many children should be included. One general guideline is the younger the children, the shorter the session and the smaller the group (Myrick, 1993; Vinson, 1992).

Most counselors "think in terms of 25 to 30 students in large-group guidance activities. This enables the group to be conveniently subdivided into five or six small working teams with about five or six students each" (Myrick, 1987, p. 282).

In group counseling, numbers are of concern. "Group size should always be determined after examining the purpose of the counseling group, the developmental needs of the students, and the time available" (Gumaer, 1986).

### Gender and Age Issues

A final consideration in setting up a group is a decision regarding the sex and age range of the participants. On the issue of gender, there is considerable disagreement (George & Dustin, 1988).

In regard to age, a general rule of thumb is to group children with those who are within about one chronological year of one another (Gazda, 1989).

## ROLE OF THE LEADER IN CHILDREN'S GROUPS

In group guidance, the leader is a teaching facilitator who encourages self-exploration.

Guidance lessons are planned in cooperation, and often participation, with classroom teachers. Sometimes a counselor and teacher will colead a group and map out their developmental curriculum far in advance.

Many group guidance leaders operate from an atheoretical base in regard to the process of change. They stress developmental learning.

Leaders of children's guidance and psychoeducational groups influence what happens in the groups by the way they arrange chairs, for instance: row formation, circle, semicircle arrangement, in and out circles (the fishbowl), or discussion teams.

In group counseling, leaders have more of a tendency than in group guidance to have a theoretical orientation and act accordingly (Long, 1988).

The group counselor [leader] must adapt his or her techniques to the clients' social, emotional, and intellectual development, as well as their ability to communicate verbally" (George & Dustin, 1988, p. 136).

### Studies on the Outcome of Children's Groups

Because psychoeducational and counseling groups have been conducted with elementary and middle school children for years, numerous studies have been conducted on their effectiveness.

One of the most promising research studies on groups with children is a replication study conducted by Lee (1993) of classroom guidance on student achievement.

Some studies are now investigating the strengths and weaknesses of specific packaged group guidance kits, such as DUSO-R, to help counselors maximize the effectiveness of these tools in working with children (Morse, Bockoven, & Bettesworth, 1988).

Overall, research is making strides in informing potential group workers with children about what types of groups and experiences are effective with certain populations and when.

## STRENGTHS AND LIMITATIONS OF USING GROUPS WITH CHILDREN

How successful a particular group will be depends on many variables, such as how well prepared the leader and members are, the composition of members, the amount of time allotted, and the group's focus.

Children who profit most from group counseling and psychotherapy share the following characteristics:  they volunteer, are committed to discussing what genuinely concerns them, are committed to learning new behaviors, are interested in helping other group members learn new behaviors, and believe that their counselor/group leader, parents (and even teachers) have confidence in their ability to learn and implement new behaviors (Ohlsen et al., 1988).

## Key Concepts

*Can you define and describe each of the following terms? Be able to offer a brief example or relevant context for these concepts.*

action-centered view of groups
activity group guidance (AGG)
BASIC-ID
circle
crisis-centered groups
Developing Understanding of Self and Others- Revised (DUSO-R)
developmental factors
discussion teams
fishbowl
growth-centered groups
HELPING
highly structured groups
in and out circles
information statement
non-developmental factors
preadolescents
preschool and early school-aged children
problem-centered groups
row formation
semicircle arrangement
SIPA
succeeding in school lessons
teachable moment
timely teaching
transient children
universalization

## Self Assessment Questions

### True or False Statements

The following statements check your comprehension of terms and identification of individuals (knowledge and comprehension level); your ability to apply that knowledge to solve more challenging questions (application level), and your ability to evaluate given information (analysis and evaluation level).

Indicate whether each statement is true or false. If you believe a statement is false, identify the error in the space provided. When necessary, refer to your text, *Group Work: A Counseling Specialty* (4<sup>th</sup> ed.). An answer key appears at the end of this book.

1. Tasks/work groups are where individuals could focus on improving his interpersonal awareness and skills.

   _____

   _____

   _____

2. Crisis-centered, problem-centered, and growth-centered group counseling are three approaches for working with children in groups (Myrick, 1993).

   _____

   _____

   _____

3. According to many experts, talk-centered counseling should NOT be a primary tool in group work with children prior to the age of 10.

   _____

   _____

   _____

4. Negative labeling of children in groups, according to Ritchie and Huss (2000), might put school counselors at risk for legal liability group work with minor clients.

   _____

   _____

   _____

5. Semicircle seating arrangements are appropriate for managing large groups of children in school counseling programs (Myrick, 1997).

   _____

   _____

   _____

6. Activity-centered groups are formed in response to a conflict between student groups.

   _____

   _____

   _____

7. A child's interest is the major difference between groups for children held in community settings and groups held in educational settings.

   _____

   _____

   _____

8. In setting up groups for children, group workers must be particularly sensitive to the families of the clients.

   _____

   _____

   _____

9.  Groups that involve group discussion are generally regarded as most beneficial for children under the age of 12.

_____
_____
_____

10. Children should generally be grouped with others who are in the same grade regardless of age.

_____
_____
_____

11. In group counseling with children, confidentiality issues become a major challenge; breach of confidentiality is always a potential risk.

_____
_____
_____

12. Group guidance in schools is often considered preventative in its approach, with counselors generally acting as group leaders.

_____
_____
_____

13. Children who become involved in a group often feel a sense of universalization, realizing that they are not the only ones facing certain problems.

_____
_____
_____

**Multiple Choice Questions**

1. Group work is essential to school counselors. Groups in school provide which of the following?
   a.  an efficient service delivery
   b.  a forum where affective and cognitive domains are explored
   c.  a way for problems to lead to prevention efforts
   d.  (all of the above)

2. Group work with children requires special considerations. Which of the following is the MOST likely issue that group leaders who work with children will need to address in planning a group?
   a.  How long will group sessions be?
   b.  What medium will be most used in group communication?
   c.  What will the gender mix be?
   d.  How will group members be recruited and screened?

3. HELPING (acronym) represents a multimodal format for structuring group work with children. "E", "L", and "G" stand for:
   a. entertainment, learning, and gender
   b. education, letting go, and guidance
   c. emotions, learning, and guidance
   d. education, learning, and gender

## Written Exercises

Respond in writing to several of the following questions, prompts, and inquiries, designed to deepen your comprehension of the text. Student responses can lead to self-reflection and interesting discussions with others. You are encouraged to flex your imagination and make your understanding of group work as presented in these chapters come to life.

## Questions & Prompts for Written Reflection and Discussion

### Chapter 11

1. Think about the many variations of group work with children across professional settings. What are some of the differences between working with children in groups in a school setting versus a community counseling setting? What advantages and disadvantages do you see inherent in working with children in either setting?

_____
_____
_____
_____
_____
_____
_____
_____
_____
_____
_____
_____
_____
_____

2. Describe the continuum of *nonverbal to verbal* group work with children. Describe what you think draws a demarcation between the two polarities. What challenges do you anticipate in working with young, relatively nonverbal children in groups? On the other hand, what unique difficulties would you anticipate working with children and relying on verbal interactions?

_____
_____
_____
_____
_____
_____
_____
_____
_____
_____

3.  Review some current group-related literature regarding work with children. What assumptions or ideologies (i.e., verbal, nonverbal) can you detect as you read this professional literature? How do you see these articles promoting effective group work with children? Discuss your readings with others in you class. Do any consistent themes emerge through your discussions?

_____
_____
_____
_____
_____
_____
_____
_____
_____
_____
_____
_____
_____
_____

4.  If you were given an assignment to lead a group (in whatever professional arena that suits you personally), describe the type of group you envision it being (e.g., counseling, psychoeducation, task/work group). What is entailed in *setting up* this group for children and what do you determine your role to be in leading/facilitating this group? Talk about your reply with others. How do responses from those present in class differ?

_____
_____
_____
_____
_____
_____
_____
_____
_____
_____
_____
_____
_____

## Journal and Reflection

Space for journaling about your group work experiences is provided below. Use this space to reflect on your reading about group work, your classroom presentations and activities, the group dynamics of your classes themselves, and any simulations or actual group participation opportunities you may have. Comment here thoughtfully. Be sure to carefully honor your ethical commitment to uphold the confidentiality of others in your group. Reflections are yours and are not to reveal anyone else's information. Recording your thoughts and feelings will provide a written history of this phase of your group work education. (Attach additional sheets of paper if desired.)

*Entry date* _____

# GROUPS FOR ADOLESCENTS

## Outcome Objectives

1. I can discuss types of groups appropriate for adolescents, including:
   a. Developmental psychoeducational/guidance groups
   b. Nondevelopmental counseling and psychotherapy groups
2. I can demonstrate setting up groups for adolescents, specifically with skills associated with:
   a. Nonverbal versus verbal communication
   b. Group structure and materials
   c. Recruiting members and screening
   d. Group session length and number in group
   e. Gender and age issues
3. I comprehend the role of the leader in adolescents' groups.
4. I can demonstrate an understanding of working with problems in adolescents' groups, including:
   a. Outright disruptiveness
   b. Hesitancy to engage with others
   c. Polarizations
   d. Monopolizing
   e. Inappropriate risk taking
   f. Overactivity or giddiness
5. I understand and can discuss relevant studies on the outcome of groups for adolescents.
6. I am able to discuss and describe both strengths and limitations of using groups with adolescents.

## Chapter Overview

Leaders of groups for adolescents face vast challenges, including making the group attractive to members, taking maturity levels into consideration, and even legal and ethical issues. Adolescent group work is important, and both the positive and negative aspects must be acknowledged.

## Chapter Highlights

**Adolescence** is a difficult period in the life of many young people. It is a time of both continuity and discontinuity marked by extensive personal changes (Graber & Brooks-Gunn, 1996; Hamburg & Takanishi, 1989).

Often, adolescents "seem to have to wait for circumstances to make their decisions for them, because they are not really free to decide for themselves" (Harris, 1967, p. 176). At other times, adolescents are pressured into adult roles too soon (Elkind, 1991).

Fads in clothing, music, language, and dance, while isolating some adolescents from general society, unite them with peers and in many cases help them constructively break away from their families of origin and establish a sense of individuation from others (Santrock, 2000).

Overall, *adolescence* (a term originated by G. Stanley Hall) is a time of rapid changes. It is characterized by some or all of the following: "storm and stress" (Hall, 1904), heightened emotionality (Gesell, Ilg, & Ames, 1956), experimentation (McCandless, 1970), and a desire for independence (Ohlsen, Horne, & Lawe, 1988).

Groups of all kinds can be helpful to adolescents in making a successful transition from childhood to adulthood. They can provide support, facilitate new learning, help ease internal and external pressures, and offer hope and models for change (Malekoff, 1997).

In a group setting, adolescents can safely experiment with reality, test their limits, express themselves, and  be heard.

Within groups, adolescents often find "genuine acceptance and encouragement" from peers and "a trustworthy adult who seems to trust and respect" them (George & Dustin, 1988, p. 142).

## TYPES OF GROUPS FOR ADOLESCENTS

Two main types of groups to which adolescents may belong and to which adults may have input include the developmental psychoeducational group, which is primarily voluntary and self-focused, and the nondevelopmental counseling or psychotherapy group, which can be voluntary or nonvoluntary and focuses on either oneself or oneself with others.

### Developmental Psychoeducational Groups
**Developmental psychoeducational groups** usually focus on common concerns of young people such as identity, sexuality, parents, peer relationships, career goals, and educational/institutional problems. Developmental psychoeducational groups tend to focus on life skill issues for adolescents.

Such groups are conducted in community agencies, school settings, or both (Berube & Berube, 1997). Traditionally, they have an adult leader.

Within the schools, group topics for adolescents include career, college plans, communication skills and peer helping, decision making, study skills, and self-concept.

Most of the school counselors surveyed by Bowman (1987) believed that small-group psychodeducational and counseling services are "vital and practical to implement in their programs" (p. 261).

The actual and potential results for employing developmental psychoeducational groups with adolescents are great.

### Nondevelopmental Counseling/Psychotherapy Groups
**Nondevelopmental counseling and psychotherapy groups** tend to concentrate more on concerns adolescents have with adults and society, such as drug/alcohol use, school problems (e.g., poor grades, truancy), or deviant behavior.

Usually, schools, agencies, or courts establish these groups, and troubled adolescents may either volunteer or be forced to attend (Jacobs, Masson, & Harvill, 2002).

Morganett's *Skills for Living* (1990) covers topics pertinent to the needs of this age population, such as developing self-esteem, managing stress, making friends, and coping with grief and loss.

An exemplary program in helping volunteer adolescents who experience high levels of stress and a lack of support is "Teachers as Counselors" (TAC), designed and implemented by the Spring Independent School District (Houston, Texas) (Wasielewski et al., 1997).

When potential members are not given a choice of participating, the result is usually resistance and reluctance to participate.

Some of the hostility of involuntary members may be overcome prior to the beginning of the group by talking to the participants and inviting them to share their thoughts and feelings. Leaders of such groups face an uphill battle to create cohesion.

Listening to the adolescents' complaints about having been referred to the group is a good place to begin such groups. After such feelings have been ventilated, members and leaders can begin to talk about common concerns and goals (O'Hanlon & Weiner-Davis, 1989).

Several constructive ways of handling participants' negative feelings and resistance are suggested by Corey and Corey (2002).

Overall, developmental psychoeducational and nondevelopmental counseling/psychotherapy groups are two of the primary ways adolescents receive constructive help from adults and each other.

Developmental psychoeducational groups are almost always choice oriented, whereas developmental counseling/psychotherapy groups are usually geared toward both choice and change.

## SETTING UP GROUPS FOR ADOLESCENTS

Determining how a group will be set up is based on the type of group to be led. Cultural, situational, and developmental aspects of group content and context must always be kept in mind.

Group leaders need to be careful in selecting group members. They must make sure that adolescents who are chosen are mature and motivated enough to benefit from the group and be of benefit to the group.

Various factors that must be considered in working with adolescents in groups include the use of verbal versus nonverbal behavior, group structure and materials, recruiting members and screening, group session length, number of members, and gender and age issues.

### Nonverbal versus Verbal Communication

Attention to adolescents' nonverbal communications in groups is vital.

In groups for adolescents, just as in groups for adults, members should be free to decide whether to talk, but the leader should work at setting up conditions that promote positive exchanges. Sometimes these conditions involve teaching basic communication skills in a structured manner (Goldstein, Sprafkin, Gershaw, & Klein, 1980; Leaman, 1983).

## Group Structure and Materials

Many adolescent groups work best when they are structured around themes. **Themes** center around the genuine interests of participants. They hold group members' interests and invite their participation.

The materials needed in a group for adolescents vary according to the type of group to be led and the personalities of the members and leaders.

**Structured activities** (i.e., group exercises) and associated materials will generate discussion and participation, help the group focus, promote experiential learning, provide the group leader with useful information, increase group comfort, and facilitate fun and relaxation (Jacobs et al., 2002).

Regardless of how materials are used, it is crucial that groups for adolescents do not focus on the materials to the exclusion of the meaningful process.

## Recruiting Members and Screening

In voluntary groups for adolescents, recruitment is of major importance.

Public relations is a very crucial part of the recruitment process (Huey, 1983). Potential members and referral sources must be courted and sold on the idea that what the group is designed to do can be effective, if properly supported.

Leaders must develop systems that help them screen potential candidates in a minimum amount of time and yet promote two-way interaction so that the potential group members become more informed about the leader and structure of the group.

Ohlsen et al. (1988) state that attraction is a key component to the final selection of adolescents for a group. **Attractiveness** is a multidimensional concept, but basically it refers to members positively identifying with others in the group.

## Group Session Length and Number in Group

Sessions with adolescents usually last between 1 and 2 hours (Gazda, 1989; Jacobs et al., 2002). They may be extended, however, and even include minimarathons lasting all day (Corey & Corey, 2002).

In educational settings, the number of group sessions is usually dictated by divisional times in the school year, such as quarters or semesters. For instance, if a semester lasts 16 weeks, a psychoeducational group might be geared toward a similar timetable, such as 14 weeks.

If group members have major problems or deficits, the group sessions may last longer and be more frequent. Psychotherapeutic groups may especially benefit from these enlarged parameters.

The number in a group ultimately affects its outcome and rate of progress. Small groups of 5 to 10 members may be ideal in working with adolescents.

## Gender and Age Issues

Whether to include both males and females in a group for adolescents depends on its purpose. Sometimes one-gender groups will be more appropriate.

In one-gender groups, a key to the success of the group is the identity associated with gender and the topic. This type of identity comes through early socialization patterns.

Adolescent boys, as compared with adolescent girls, are usually less comfortable, less involved, and less likely to achieve as positive an outcome in groups that emphasize interpersonal relationships.

Adolescent girls are more interested as a group in social relationships and are more at ease in sharing.

It appears that older adolescents are less affected by age differences than are younger adolescents.

## ROLE OF THE LEADER IN ADOLESCENTS' GROUPS

The role of leaders in groups for adolescents is multidimensional.

Group leaders must be willing and courageous enough to explore, and perhaps relive, much of their own adolescent experience so that it will not interfere with their work and result in countertransference.

Adolescents respond well to leaders who are open with them, enthusiastic, and caring. These types of leaders are true to themselves first and are good role models for those whom they lead.

In general, group leaders for adolescents in high school are active. Both activity level and structure are related to the group's maturity.

Leaders can promote group cohesiveness and the acquisition of skills in adolescent groups through modeling the types of behaviors they wish to encourage.

Peer leaders in adolescent groups are usually more persuasive than adult leaders in bringing about change (Bates et al., 1982; Frank, Ferdinand, & Bailey, 1975).

Adult group leaders may work well by training mature adolescents to lead groups and then supervising the adolescent leaders.

It is the leader's responsibility to stress the importance of confidentiality. Adolescents may use personal information gathered in a group for gossip or simply to be vindictive (Jacobs et al., 2002).

Leaders of groups for adolescents face a number of challenges, including being understanding, yet firm; facilitative, yet controlling; and active, yet trusting of the group process.

Myrick (1987, p. 153) states that six basic responses make leaders more effective facilitators: using feeling-focused responses, clarifying or summarizing responses, using open-ended questions, giving facilitative feedback, acknowledging others' comments, and linking.

Leaders of adolescent groups must avoid what Myrick (1987, p. 168) describes as **low facilitative responses**: advice/evaluation, analyzing/interpreting, and reassuring/supportive.

## PROBLEMS IN ADOLESCENTS' GROUPS

Among the possible problems (McMurray, 1992) are outright disruptiveness, a hesitancy or reluctance to engage with others, polarization, attempting to monopolize, inappropriate risk taking, and overactivity.

Overall, adolescent groups have unique problem behaviors that those who work with such groups need to know about to be effective. A good adolescent group leader will use the power of the group as well as his or her skills.

## STUDIES ON THE OUTCOME OF GROUPS FOR ADOLESCENTS

Groups have a powerful potential for helping many adolescents change and develop new social and academic skills. Studies with these groups need to use control groups more and refine their research methods.

The use of groups with adolescents in preventive and remedial ways is promising, especially in the schools.

## STRENGTHS AND LIMITATIONS OF USING GROUPS WITH ADOLESCENTS

### Strengths

Groups are a "natural" environment in which adolescents can learn because adolescents spend a great deal of their time everyday in groups (Carroll et al., 1997; Trotzer, 1980).

In groups, a sense of belonging is created, and adolescents are given opportunities to learn through direct interaction or observation (Trotzer, 1999). Often this learning is carried over (**generalization**) from the group experience to the adolescent's daily life.

Groups provide for multiple feedback that can help adolescents in their personal growth and development. In addition to having the advantage of the leader's input, adolescents in groups also receive peer feedback (Myrick, 1987).

Groups provide members the opportunity to help one another (Trotzer, 1980; Yalom, 1995). It is often through helping others that an individual's own self-esteem and self-confidence are increased.

### Limitations

Many adolescents deny they have any type of problem and believe there is a stigma in discussing problems with others. Adolescent boys, especially, may feel this way (LeCroy, 1986).

Peer group pressure is extremely strong in the adolescent years and may be misused in a group of adolescents unless carefully monitored (Corey & Corey, 2002; Ohlsen et al., 1988).

Individuals within the groups may not be given enough attention.

Poor group communication and interaction may result if the group is not screened carefully. To work with minors, group leaders almost always have to obtain parental consent. In addition, if leaders want their groups to succeed, they must get the consent of the adolescent as well.

## Key Concepts

*Can you define and describe each of the following terms? Be able to offer a brief example or relevant context for these concepts.*

action-oriented group techniques
adolescence
advice/evaluation
analyzing/interpreting
attractiveness
developmental psychoeducational/guidance groups
facilitative feedback
generalization
linking
low facilitative responses
mixed-gender groups
non-developmental counseling and psychotherapy groups
nonverbal cues
open-ended questions
polarization
reassuring/supportive
structured activities
themes

## Self Assessment Questions

### True or False Statements

The following statements check your comprehension of terms and identification of individuals (knowledge and comprehension level); your ability to apply that knowledge to solve more challenging questions (application level), and your ability to evaluate given information (analysis and evaluation level).

Indicate whether each statement is true or false. If you believe a statement is false, identify the error in the space provided. When necessary, refer to your text, *Group Work: A Counseling Specialty* (4th ed.). An answer key appears at the end of this book.

1. Adolescent boys typically have less difficult adjustments in adolescence than do adolescent girls.

_____

_____

_____


2. Malekoff (1997) suggests that groups of all kinds can be helpful to adolescents in making the transition from childhood to adulthood.

_____

_____

_____

3. Common experiences, concerns and topics of self-interest are usually the focus "nondevelopmental groups" with adolescents.

_____

_____

_____

4. By leaders meeting first individually with members and by learning to respond to adolescent sarcasm with caring statements, Corey and Corey (2002) suggest leaders may lessen the negative feelings and resistance of adolescents required to participate in the group.

_____

_____

_____

5. "Flexible theme format" in groups allows group leaders to rely upon adolescents' interest and willingness to talk about what they feel is valuable.

_____

_____

_____

6. Typically, group sessions with adolescents often last between 2½ and 3 hours.

_____

_____

_____

7. Considering developmental issues, Kymissis (1993) cautions against "mixing" boys and girls in group counseling.

_____

_____

_____

8. Advice giving, interpretation, and reassurance are important skills for leaders of adolescent groups, according to Myrick (1987).

_____

_____

_____

9. According to Donigian and Malnati (1997), dropping a disruptive member from an adolescent group risks decreasing the trusting feelings of the rest of the group.

_____

_____

_____

10. In an attempt to win leader favor, adolescent group members often share information too soon or even reveal inappropriate information about themselves.

_____

_____

_____

11. Adolescents tend to strongly identify with the values generated by primary peer groups.

_____
_____
_____

12. Developmental psychoeducational/guidance groups usually focus on a concern such as deviant behavior.

_____
_____
_____

13. When dealing with adolescents required to participate in group work, the leader should <u>avoid</u> listening to the members' complaints about being there.

_____
_____
_____

14. A group session lasting longer than an hour and a half for adolescents will likely be unproductive.

_____
_____
_____

15. Polarization is a term used to describe the conflict between group facilitator and group members.

_____
_____
_____


**Multiple Choice Questions**

1. Which of the following is NOT included on the list of how groups can be helpful to adolescents in making a successful transition from childhood to adulthood?
    a. facilitate new learning
    b. help ease internal and external pressures
    c. explore career decisions
    d. offer models for change

2. Working with adolescents in *nondevelopmental counseling and psychotherapy groups* may be more challenging than group work with adolescents in developmental psychoeducational groups because nondevelopmental groups _____.
    a. work with involuntary group members
    b. concentrate on specific adolescent concerns
    c. may deal with a more difficult membership
    d. (all of the above)

3. The relationship between group session length and the number of adolescents in the group is optimum if duration_____.
    a. is short, with fewer members    c. is short, with more members
    b. is long, with more members    d. is long, with fewer members

**Written Exercises**

Respond in writing to several of the following questions, prompts, and inquiries, designed to deepen your comprehension of the text. Student responses can lead to self-reflection and interesting discussions with others. You are encouraged to flex your imagination and make your understanding of group work as presented in these chapters come to life.

## Questions & Prompts for Written Reflection and Discussion

### Chapter 12

1. Consider the many psychological, social, and biological developmental issues young people encounter in adolescence. How do you see group work as a natural extension of "common" adolescent experience? What pitfalls do you imagine are inherent in working with adolescents in groups?

_____
_____
_____
_____
_____
_____
_____
_____
_____
_____
_____
_____
_____

2. Thinking back on your own adolescence, what are some of the most enduring memories? What "group work" experiences do you recall? Imagine working with adolescents in a group appropriate to your professional interest. What issues might be triggered for you as a result of your personal development? How might your adolescent experiences benefit and detract from your group leadership with young adults?

_____
_____
_____
_____
_____
_____
_____
_____
_____
_____
_____
_____

3. Review some additional professional literature regarding *nondevelopmental* (involuntary) group work with adolescents. What strategies and suggestions appear frequently? Discuss your findings with others in your class. What consensus emerges within your class about working with this population?

_____
_____
_____
_____
_____
_____
_____
_____
_____
_____
_____

4. Refer to the list of six *problems in adolescents' groups* (pp. 289-291). Write an illustrative vignette for each. Share these with your class members and either discuss or role-play appropriate interventions for your challenging task of leading these hypothetical groups. Discuss the responses as to what you believe would work and what you believe would fail. Why? Support your positions.

_____
_____
_____
_____
_____
_____
_____
_____
_____
_____
_____

## Journal and Reflection

Space for journaling about your group work experiences is provided below. Use this space to reflect on your reading about group work, your classroom presentations and activities, the group dynamics of your classes themselves, and any simulations or actual group participation opportunities you may have. Comment here thoughtfully. Be sure to carefully honor your ethical commitment to uphold the confidentiality of others in your group. Reflections are yours and are not to reveal anyone else's information. Recording your thoughts and feelings will provide a written history of this phase of your group work education. (Attach additional sheets of paper if desired.)

_Entry date_ _____

# GROUPS FOR ADULTS

## Outcome Objectives

1. I can describe various types of groups commonly available for adults.
2. I can describe the role of the leader in groups for adults and the steps in setting up such groups.
3. I am familiar with studies on outcomes of groups for adults, including specialty groups for:
   a. College students and young adults
   b. Adults in midlife
   c. Men and women
   d. Couples, families, the divorced, and the widowed
   e. Adult offenders
   f. Persons with life-threatening illnesses
4. I can discuss and describe strengths and limitations of using groups with adults.

## Chapter Overview

Groups for adults (people in their early twenties to mid-sixties) are as varied as the concerns that may be discussed. Adult groups might focus on one issue, be a self-help group, be single sex, or even serve as marriage enrichment. Groups can be effective for adults regardless of age, gender, or relationship status, but the group leader must take into account these issues in order to provide a healthy environment whether for psychoeducation, counseling, task/work, or psychotherapy.

## Chapter Highlights

**Adulthood** implies that a person has reached physical, mental, social, and emotional maturity.

Numerous researchers note that adulthood is a multidimensional stage of growth often characterized by a certain unevenness and unpredictability (Neugarten, 1979; Santrock, 2000). There is little uniformity to it.

Conceptualized as the age period between 20 and 65 years, adulthood includes individuals in **young adulthood** (20 to 40 years), in which identity and intimacy are two intense primary issues, as well as adults in **midlife** (40 to 65 years), in which needs related to generativity become the main focus (Erikson, 1963).

Men and women experience this stage of life differently (Santrock, 2000), as do individuals with special needs and developmental concerns.

As Nichols (1986) points out, the **aging process** is as much a mental process of considering one's self older, as it is a biological phenomenon composed of physiological changes.

## TYPES OF GROUPS FOR ADULTS

There are probably more types of groups available and run for adults than for any other age or stage population.

Work and task groups are a primary type of group conducted in adulthood because many adults work outside the home and many more are involved in volunteer civic and community activities (Hulse-Killacky, Killacky, & Donigian, 2001).

Counseling groups are used for exploring personal issues in adulthood and for helping adults deal "with transitions relevant to their life-cycle changes" (Ohlsen, Horne, & Lawe, 1988, p. 301).

Group psychotherapy is utilized in mental health facilities for adults whether on an inpatient or outpatient basis (Yalom, 1995).

## SETTING UP GROUPS FOR ADULTS

While it is artificial to divide adult groups based on simply the obvious characteristics of the populations involved, such as those connected with age, gender, status, or specific concerns, it is sometimes helpful or necessary to form adult groups on the basis of such dominant factors.

Themes are important criteria used in establishing groups. Many groups for adults center on issues related to particular interests or concerns in life (i.e., themes).

A second guideline for establishing groups for adults focuses on needs.

Overall, in setting up groups for adults, the purpose of the group should be made clear, potential participants should be screened, rules governing the life of the group should be explained, member's rights as well as expectations should be noted, and the leader's qualifications should be communicated.

## ROLE OF THE LEADER IN GROUPS FOR ADULTS

As with other age span groups, the role of the leader in adult groups varies according to type, membership, and format (open-ended or close-ended) of the group.

Leaders within psychoeducational/prevention groups must plan carefully what they are going to do and must have a solid rationale behind their actions. Their goal is to instruct and help members learn new skills.

In counseling and psychotherapy groups, theory is a driving force behind the behavior of leaders. What they do and how they do it comes from both a philosophical and research base connected with the theory they embrace.

Task/work groups usually do not have clear expectations of the leader except that he or she will focus on both the process and outcome of the group (Hulse-Killacky et al., 2001).

## STUDIES ON THE OUTCOMES OF GROUPS FOR ADULTS

There are more studies on groups for adults than on any other type of group.

### Groups for College Students
One specific way groups are used in higher education environments that is both preventive and remedial is to help young people separate from their families and become independent adults.

Psychoeducational groups may help college students become more aware of what careers they wish to pursue and more decisive about an occupation (Cooper, 1986; McWhirter, Nichols, & Banks, 1984).

Psychoeducational groups may help college students find information and resources about academic life, obtain emotional support from peers, interact socially, and meet developmental and remedial needs (Wilcoxon, Wilcoxon, & Tingle, 1989).

A structured counseling group for excessively self-critical university and college students has been reported to work well by Phelps and Luke (1995).

A group for college students who are shy, advertised as a "clinic" to minimize any implication of psychopathology, has been found to be effective.

For students with test anxiety, groups may be used to help them manage their fears (Stevens, Pfost, & Bruyere, 1983). These psychotherapeutic groups concentrate on helping students reduce somatic tension and modify disruptive cognitions.

A psychotherapeutic type of group for college students that is useful is for adult children of alcoholics (Harman & Withers, 1992).

To assess the needs of all persons in campus communities, college officials may use a *nominal-group process* (a structured small-group technique).

## Groups for Adults in Midlife

Many types of groups are available for adults in midlife (ages 40 to 65).

In the area of psychoeducation and prevention, Parker (1975) reports on the use of systematic desensitization within a leadership group for the purpose of helping adult members become less anxious about public speaking

Bisio and Crisan (1984) used a one-day group workshop with adults to focus on nuclear anxiety and hidden stress in life. They emphasized principles of Frankl's (1962) logotherapy and helped participants create a renewed sense of hope and purpose in life.

An interesting, interdisciplinary, positive-wellness model of group work for self-selected adults that is more long term (16 weeks) is the **jogging group** (Childers & Burcky, 1984).

A common developmental and situational reality for adults in all walks of life is loss and grief. In working through loss, adults must accomplish four tasks related to the mourning process.

For adults who have grown up in families in which at least one parent abused alcohol, heterogeneous groups based on Yalom's (1995) therapeutic factors, especially altruism, imitative behavior, and corrective recapitulation of the family dynamic, can be empowering (Corazzini, Williams, & Harris, 1987; Harris, 1996).

Groups may also be used to help adults who were abused as children (Courtois & Leehan, 1982).

**Group for survivors of suicide** (Moore & Freeman, 1995) helps adults break out of isolation and resolve grief issues.

Two types of trauma groups are **critical incident stress debriefing (CISD) groups** (Mitchell & Everly, 1993) and **solution-focused debriefing (SFD) groups** (Juhnke & Osborne, 1997).

Three types of groups for adults in midlife that are psychoeducational and psychotherapeutic in nature include the career change group (Zimpfer & Carr, 1989), the career support group (Giordano, 1995), and the job support group (Riordan & Kahnweiler, 1996).

## Groups for Men and Women

Socialization patterns dramatically influence the ways men and women perceive themselves and how they function in society. Therefore, a gender-specific group approach may give men and women a "safe place to explore new frontiers of their personal, economic, and social development" (Gonzalez-Lopez & Taylor, 1997, p. 20).

### *Groups for Men*

Groups can help men in identifying personal and general concerns of being male and ways of constructively dealing with issues and problems they face.

Getting men to participate in groups, although usually beneficial, is often difficult because traditional sex-role stereotypes hinder many males from even thinking they could benefit from a group experience (Washington, 1979; Wilcox & Forrest, 1992).

Many times men particpate in groups through telling stories; group leaders may need to encourage some men to tell their stories in order to get them to interact with others (A. Horne, 1999).

The men's movement, exemplified in the mythopoetic approach of Bly (1990), can be a power adjunct to traditional therapeutic groups for men.

### *Groups for Women*

"Women's groups are becoming an increasingly popular therapeutic avenue to help women with issues that confront them" (McManus, Redford, & Hughes, 1997, p. 22).

There are some issues, such as dealing with chemical dependency, in which women do better in women-only treatment groups (Kauffman, Dore, & Nelson-Zlupko, 1995).

There is evidence that group psychotherapy is effective in improving the quality of life among women with disorders most commonly found in women, such as breast cancer (Gore-Felton & Spiegel, 1999).

Support groups for women who have particular concerns, such as working mothers, may also be beneficial (Morgan & Hensley, 1998).

While women's groups have dealt with topics as diverse as spirituality and community change, some of the most focused issues in groups for women center around sexual abuse, relationships, healthy self-concepts, anger, and work.

## Groups for Couples, Families, the Divorced, and the Widowed

Couples, families, and those who are divorced or widowed face many stresses. Therefore, psychoeducational, counseling, and psychotherapy groups are especially popular for persons in these circumstances.

### *Parent Education Groups*

To help parents acquire knowledge and evaluate their beliefs and attitudes, **parent education groups** were organized beginning in the late 1800s by the Child Study Association of America (Resnick, 1981).

Parent education groups are now considered "a form of consultation in which the consultant (leader) is assisting the consultee (parent) by teaching effective child-rearing techniques" (White & Riordan, 1990, p. 201).

Literally dozens of parenting programs operate across the United States, in which single parents or couples work in groups to develop healthy strategies for dealing with each other and their children as the family develops.

Overall, parents are best served in parenting groups when they are listened to, helped to sort through their options, and newly empowered to make decisions regarding their children.

### *Couple and Family Group Therapy*

**Multiple-family group therapy (MFGT)** involves treating several families together at the same time with the explicit focus on problems or concerns shared by all families in attendance (Baltimore, 1997; Homrich & Horne, 1997). It is probably the most demanding form of group work and requires its leaders to have a solid, working knowledge of both group and family theories.

This approach has many of the same advantages that couples group therapy has, including the fact that families can often serve as cotherapists for each other (Piercy et al., 1996).

### *Groups for the Divorced and Widowed*

In groups, the divorced and widowed can share experiences with one another, as well as obtain emotional support, receive feedback on one's perceptions and behaviors, gain advice and information on dealing with problems, and get tangible assistance (Addington, 1992; DiGiulio, 1992).

Outside of structured groups offered by professionals, most *groups for the divorced and widowed* tend to be of a psychoeducational or self-help nature.

### Adult Offenders Groups

Potential problematic areas in working with adult offenders are their low level of trust and high level of anger, frustration, and sense of deprivation.

Among the specific types of adult offenders targeted for treatment in groups have been those found guilty of sex offenses, people driving while intoxicated, shoplifters, domestic violence perpetrators, and crack cocaine users.

### Groups for Persons with Life-Threatening Illnesses

Psychotherapeutic groups have been employed as a way of treating persons with life-threatening diseases.

In a review of the literature on groups for cancer patients, Harman (1991) notes that groups are a preferred method of working with cancer patients and their families. Such groups offer education, support, and release from the stress and emotion that have built up.

Some forms of group work, specifically existential groups, can assist individuals with life-threatening illnesses in better coping with their diagnosis and living more fully in the time they have left (Spira, 1997).

## STRENGTHS AND LIMITATIONS OF USING GROUPS WITH ADULTS

### Strengths
One strength of using groups with adults is cost savings.

Many adults have similar concerns, and it is more effective to address these common matters in a group setting than individually.

Effectiveness is another positive connected with groups for adults.

Adults in groups may be highly motivated to work on concerns with others and may also have an idea of outcomes they would like to achieve.

### Limitations
A limitation of doing group work for adults is scheduling. Setting up a group for adults takes organizational skill and patience.

A second limitation of conducting groups with adults is resistance to participating in a group by some members.

A third drawback to doing groups with adults is screening and assembling group members who have a common focus.

Group work with adults may be difficult because of past beliefs and behavioral patterns of adults. Adults have had longer to practice certain interactions and may take longer to change them or learn new ways of behaving.

### Key Concepts

*Can you define and describe each of the following terms? Be able to offer a brief example or relevant context for these concepts.*

> Adlerian parent education
> adult children of alcoholics
> adulthood
> aging process
> career awareness and self-exploration groups
> career change groups
> career support groups
> C group
> consciousness-raising groups (C-R groups)
> couples group therapy
> critical incident stress debriefing (CISD groups)
> eating disorders groups
> emotional impact of separation
> emotional response of separation
> families in high-risk environments

generativity
genogram
group for survivors of suicide
groups for victims of abuse
high-risk families
imago relationship therapy
job support groups
jogging group
marriage enrichment
midlife
multiple family group therapy (MFGT)
mythopoetic
parent education groups
Parent Effectiveness Training (PET)
Parents Without Partners (PWP)
polarities
rape survivors' group
relationship groups
self-actualization
solution-focused debriefing groups (SFD groups)
sophistry
study groups
systematic training for effective parenting
theme groups
young adulthood

## Self Assessment Questions

### True or False Statements

The following statements check your comprehension of terms and identification of individuals (knowledge and comprehension level); your ability to apply that knowledge to solve more challenging questions (application level), and your ability to evaluate given information (analysis and evaluation level).

Indicate whether each statement is true or false. If you believe a statement is false, identify the error in the space provided. When necessary, refer to your text, *Group Work: A Counseling Specialty* (4<sup>th</sup> ed.). An answer key appears at the end of this book.

1.  Midlife is thought to begin around age 50.

    _____
    _____
    _____


2.  Group leaders working with adults often use activities in a sequential pattern because it is developmental and logical.

    _____
    _____
    _____

3. Genograms can help adult group members better understand the complex dynamics affecting their life development.

_____
_____
_____

4. Groups on college campuses advertised as "clinics" minimize any implication of psychopathology.

_____
_____
_____

5. There is remarkable similarity between men and women in their experience of midlife, as well as for individuals with developmental concerns.

_____
_____
_____

6. Price and colleagues (1995), following their sixteen-week, closed-ended, grief and loss psychotherapy group with adults, identified *universality* as the most therapeutic factor.

_____
_____
_____

7. Members in *solution-focused debriefing* groups (Juhnke & Osborne, 1997) share in common that each has witnessed the same traumatic event.

_____
_____
_____

8. Mythopoetic groups with adult men use ritual processes such as drumming, physical movement, and imagery exercises as powerful adjuncts to traditional therapeutic processes.

_____
_____
_____

9. "Relationship groups" for adult women primarily focus on learning new ways of relating to women.

_____
_____
_____

10. In preparation for women with eating disorders to have successful group experiences, members must deal with their disordered body image prior to group.

_____
_____
_____

11. According to Sayger (1996), high-functioning families are the best candidates for multiple-family group therapy (MFGT).

_____

_____

_____

12. Taking time for evaluating, deciding, and making adjustments in one's life is a process known as midlife transition.

_____

_____

_____

13. "Displaced homemakers" describes those who have lost their source of economic support and have been "forced" back into the work force after a long absence.

_____

_____

_____

14. Job support groups were one of the first types of groups set up specifically for men in the early 1970s.

_____

_____

_____

15. *Imago relationship therapy* includes elements of psychoanalysis, transactional analysis, Gestalt, cognitive therapy, and systems theory.

_____

_____

_____

16. Parents Without Partners is probably the best known group nationally for the divorced and widowed.

_____

_____

_____

**Multiple Choice Questions**

1. Which of the following types of groups usually does NOT have clear expectations of the leaders beyond her or his focus on process and the outcome of the group?
    a. psychoeducation                c. psychotherapy
    b. counseling                     d. task/work

2. Group work with students in higher education (e.g., college student personnel) views the task of assisting young adults in separating from their families and in becoming independent adults as both _____ and _____.

    a. cost-efficient / timely          c. remedial / timely
    b. cost-efficient / preventative    d. remedial / preventative

3. An example of an interdisciplinary wellness model of group work for self-selected, long-term membership is _____.
    a. a book club                   c. psychoanalytic psychotherapy
    b. a jogging group             d. an adult children of alcoholics group

### Written Exercises
Respond in writing to several of the following questions, prompts, and inquiries, designed to deepen your comprehension of the text. Student responses can lead to self-reflection and interesting discussions with others. You are encouraged to flex your imagination and make your understanding of group work as presented in these chapters come to life.

## Questions & Prompts for Written Reflection and Discussion

### Chapter 13

1. What are your thoughts about the subgrouping of *adulthood* (i.e., young adulthood and midlife)? Given your own personal experiences, in what ways do you think that these subgroups are appropriate? Inappropriate? Support your argument. What is gained by looking at adulthood in this fashion?

_____
_____
_____
_____
_____
_____
_____
_____
_____
_____
_____
_____
_____

2. Review some current professional literature that addresses working with adult men and women in groups. Upon broad survey (e.g., subject search, abstract search), do any themes stand out for you? What is your personal reaction to the characterization of adults portrayed in this literature?

_____
_____
_____
_____
_____
_____
_____
_____
_____
_____
_____
_____
_____

3. The trend of *parent education groups* is well documented in the literature. Consider social variables that likely exert new or pronounced challenges for parenting adults. What do you believe would be effective parenting education? Review parent education models. What stands out as particularly relevant to the times?

_____
_____
_____
_____
_____
_____
_____
_____
_____
_____
_____
_____
_____

## Journal and Reflection

Space for journaling about your group work experiences is provided below. Use this space to reflect on your reading about group work, your classroom presentations and activities, the group dynamics of your classes themselves, and any simulations or actual group participation opportunities you may have. Comment here thoughtfully. Be sure to carefully honor your ethical commitment to uphold the confidentiality of others in your group. Reflections are yours and are not to reveal anyone else's information. Recording your thoughts and feelings will provide a written history of this phase of your group work education. (Attach additional sheets of paper if desired.)

_Entry date_ _____

# GROUPS FOR THE ELDERLY

## Outcome Objectives

1. I can describe various types of groups commonly available for the elderly.
2. I can describe the role of the leader in groups for the elderly and the steps in setting up such groups.
3. I am familiar with studies on the outcomes of groups for the elderly.
4. I can describe the design and function of groups for caretakers of the elderly
5. I can describe and discuss strengths and limitations of groups for the elderly

## Chapter Overview

Although the prominence of group work with elderly clients is relatively new, the use of groups has shown to be effective. Six major types of groups used with the elderly are described in this chapter. They include: *reality orientation, remotivation therapy, reminiscing, psychotherapy and counseling, topic-specific,* and *member specific.* Group work with older clients is helpful for a variety of reasons, but three specific benefits provided by groups are help in integrating their lives, support, and a sense of universality.

## Chapter Highlights

Late adulthood begins in the 60s and extends up to approximately 120 years of age, thus making it the longest span of any period of human development — 50 to 60 years (Santrock, 2000).

The percentage of those over age 65 continues to grow and is now about 12%, with one out of every 14 people in the United States being a woman over the age of 65 (Burnside, 1993; Myers, 1989; Williams & Lair, 1988).

In the year 2000, the number of Americans over the age of 65 was about 35 million; by the year 2050, the number is projected to be around 64 million.

Although older adults (age 65 and up) are of interest to mental health professionals, existing services for this population have not kept up with demand (Knight, 1996).

One reason the elderly are underserved is that mental health services have traditionally been geared towards those in middle age and younger.

Limitations some helpers place on themselves and older adults by accepting many of the myths, misconceptions, and stereotypes about the aged represents a bias known as **ageism** (Butler, 1975).

Benefits and liabilities come with any age, and growing old is no exception. On the positive side are a high quality of life, many years to live, "**wisdom**," "**integrity**," increased marital satisfaction and intimacy, an increase in religious and spiritual life, and a sense of well-being and meaningfulness.

Approximately 70% of persons over age 65 are grandparents; they often find enrichment and pleasure through interacting with their grandchildren (Mead, 1972; Streib & Beck, 1981).

A significant percentage of the elderly (95%) maintain their own households and seem to value their independence.

Up to age 75, the majority of individuals in this age group are, as a rule, relatively free from disabling physical impairments, view themselves as basically middle-aged, and generally enjoy a variety of physical exercises and activities. Persons in this age range are known as the **young-old.**

Individuals over the age of 75 are considered the **old** and over 85 are viewed as the **old-old**.

Collectively, this group is more likely than others to experience declines in health and overall functioning and eventually to have chronic health problems that require increased attention (Myers, 1989; Walsh, 1988).

Numerous individuals, especially older men, have difficulty adapting to retirement and mourn the loss of meaningful roles outside the household. Sometimes this adjustment can lead to conflict and dysfunctioning.

The poor and those who are cultural minorities usually have more trouble in old age, too—a continuation of discrimination and need they have suffered through their lives for the most part (Himes, Hogan, & Eggebeen, 1996).

Widowhood is another downside to aging. Because women traditionally marry older men and live longer than men, this possibility is of special concern to them (Neugarten, 1970).

The inevitable end of life is an event some individuals in old age have difficulty accepting.

Changes required of most individuals at the older stages of life include making adjustments for declining physical strength, retirement, death of friends and/or spouse, and declines in income and health (Cox, 2001; Havighurst, 1972; Santrock, 2000).

Many of the problems associated with living over 65 years "are the result of limited socialization and interpersonal activities; others involve damaged self-image and self-esteem" (Vander Kolk, 1985, p. 286). Almost all of these difficulties can be constructively addressed through some form of group work.

## TYPES OF GROUPS FOR THE ELDERLY

On the psychoeducational and task/work side of groups are two advocacy groups for the elderly: the Gray Panthers and American Association of Retired Persons (AARP).

Counseling and psychotherapy groups for this population include six major types of groups: (a) reality-oriented, (b) remotivation therapy, (c) reminiscing, (d) psychotherapy and counseling, (e) topic-specific, and (f) member-specific (Beaver, 1983; Burnside, 1984; Capuzzi & Gross, 1980; Wellman & McCormack, 1984).

**Reality-oriented groups** are set up for older individuals who have become disoriented to their surroundings. These groups, while educationally focused, are therapeutically based in that they emphasize helping group members become more aware of their present surroundings in terms of time, place, and people (Burnside, 1984).

**Remotivation therapy groups** are aimed at helping older clients become more invested in the present and future. Their membership is composed of individuals who have "lost interest" in any time frame of life except the past.

**Reminiscing groups**, which originated in the 1960s, are based on the importance of "life review" (Butler, 1961; Ebersole, 1978). These groups help individuals who are at the older life stage to comprehend and appreciate more fully who they are and where they have been. They are aimed at increasing life satisfaction rather than improving social skills (Kennedy & Tanenbaum, 2000).

A major therapeutic value of the reminiscing group process lies in the sense of affiliation it creates among its members. Reminiscing groups provide "an opportunity for social intimacy with others" (Singer, Tracz, & Dworkin, 1991, p. 167).

Further beneficial aspects include a more positive mood among members, increased self-esteem, enhanced life satisfaction, and uncovered meaning from the past (Goldwasser, Auerbach, & Harkins, 1987; Thomas & Martin, 1997).

**Psychotherapy and counseling groups** for the elderly are geared toward the remediation of specific problems this population faces, such as role changes, social isolation, physical decline, and fear of the future (Altholz, 1978; Weisman & Schwartz, 1989).

**Topic-specific groups** are centered around a particular topic, such as widowhood, bibliotherapy, sexuality, health, parenting grandchildren, or the arts.

They are psychoeducational in nature and "are designed ultimately to improve the quality of daily living for older people" (Beaver, 1983, p. 241).

Membership is voluntary, and improved self-esteem, skills, and encouragement through significant social interaction often result from such experiences (Burnside, 1984; Capuzzi & Gross, 1980; Vacha-Haase, Ness, Dannison, & Smith, 2000).

**Member-specific groups** focus on particular transitional concerns of individual members, such as grief, hospitalization, or institutionalized day care.

## SETTING UP GROUPS FOR THE ELDERLY

Older adults generally need a clear, organized explanation of the specific purpose of a group and why they can benefit from it.

The establishment of any group for the elderly involves pregroup screening, especially if the group is counseling or therapeutically oriented.

Regardless of the setting or the focus, certain procedures should be followed when preparing to work with a group of individuals aged 65 and older, including considering the physical environment, scheduling, and consideration for the physical ability of group members,

## ROLE OF THE LEADER IN GROUPS FOR THE ELDERLY

The role of the leader in groups for the elderly depends on his or her knowledge of theory, the type of group to be led, the leader's previous experience and abilities, and the level of readiness of participants.

Overall, group leaders for the elderly must be verbally and nonverbally active, personally and professionally concerned, as well as clear and direct. By performing in such a fashion, leaders can help move their groups away from a self-centeredness to a healthy group-centeredness (Hendrix & Sedgwick, 1989).

Group leader alertness to certain key issues, such as religion, economics, intergenerational conflict, or loss, is usually greater than would be the case in other age groups.

A major issue that most group workers face in dealing with the elderly is their inexperience in knowing what that stage of life is like. Therefore, they must accept this reality and be open to being a learner, as well as a facilitator, within these groups.

### STUDIES ON THE OUTCOMES OF GROUPS FOR THE ELDERLY

Studying groups for the elderly is complicated at times because along with the inclusion of a group experience, some individuals, especially in counseling and psychotherapy groups, receive individual and medical treatments that have an impact on how they function.

There are some clear-cut studies that indicate the effectiveness of groups for the elderly.

### GROUPS FOR CARETAKERS OF THE ELDERLY

Caregivers are crucial in the daily care and well being of older adults who may not be able to completely take care of themselves.

With today's increased life span, middle-aged adults, the children of the elderly, often find themselves as caretakers of this population with limited information and few role models.

As a group they "experience problems with confinement, infringement on lifestyle, restricted social life, work and family conflicts, and emotional and physical stress" (Thomas & Martin, 1997, p. 44).

The result is often frustration, resentment, and physical/emotional strain. To address these concerns, groups for caretakers have been formed.

Overall, groups for caretakers are preventive in nature. They affirm, support, and educate. They help link caretakers with others who can help them handle unique and universal problems (Myers et al., 1991).

### STRENGTHS AND LIMITATIONS OF GROUPS FOR THE ELDERLY

Being a member of a group has numerous benefits for older people. The strengths are related to both the quantity and quality of interpersonal relationships that older adults have (Horswill, 1993).

### Strengths
Group members become more aware of their needs, commonalities, uniquenesses, and possibilities through sharing in a group. They are also able to find support and resolutions.

Belonging to a group, especially with people who are around the same age, helps participants realize they are not alone in their focus on "body image, physical ailments, and fear of mental deterioration" (Hawkins, 1983, p. 187).

Groups for the elderly give their members an opportunity to try out different responses and initiate new behaviors. Older persons often engage in **growing times** when fresh learning occurs on an individual and interpersonal level (Wrenn, 1989).

A popular movement in the United States since the 1970s is the **elder hostel**, in which older individuals live and study together for a period of time, often on a college campus (Ganikos & Benedict, 1982).

Through groups, the elderly can be helped to focus on some of the advantages of growing old.

Groups for the elderly provide a series of checks and balances for those who participate in them. They shift responsibility for growth and development from caretakers or relatives to the persons in the group (Mardoyan & Weis, 1981).

## Limitations

One limitation of groups for the elderly is they are labor intensive. Finding a room environment that is suitable and setting it up in a way that is conducive to good communication takes time and effort.

A drawback to groups for older adults is that they require specialized skills of their leaders that may be anxiety producing at best.

In groups for the elderly, especially the old-old, group members and leaders have to face real loss. The death of a member may occur during the group or shortly thereafter.

A limitation of groups for the elderly is that they often have more lmited goals than other groups, and members are more limited in carrying them out.

## Key Concepts

*Can you define and describe each of the following terms? Be able to offer a brief example or relevant context for these concepts.*

American Association of Retired Persons (AARP)
ageism
density of time
elder hostel
Gray Panthers
growing times
hypokenesis
integrity
member-specific groups
multimodal method
old
old-old
psychotherapy and counseling groups for the elderly

reality-oriented groups
reminiscing groups
remotivation therapy groups
topic-specific groups
wisdom
young-old

## Self Assessment Questions

### True or False Statements

The following statements check your comprehension of terms and identification of individuals (knowledge and comprehension level); your ability to apply that knowledge to solve more challenging questions (application level), and your ability to evaluate given information (analysis and evaluation level).

Indicate whether each statement is true or false. If you believe a statement is false, identify the error in the space provided. When necessary, refer to your text, *Group Work: A Counseling Specialty* (4th ed.). An answer key appears at the end of this book.

1. "Wisdom," according to Erikson (1963), refers to the ability to make effective choices among alternatives.

   _____
   _____
   _____

2. Approximately 75% of elderly (those age 65 years or older) maintain their own households.

   _____
   _____
   _____

3. The Gray Panthers and the American Association of Retired Persons (AARP) are examples of task/work and psychoeducational groups serving those age 65 and over.

   _____
   _____
   _____

4. Reality-oriented groups are designed to help older persons become more cognitively organized and to increase their socialization skills through interpersonal interaction.

   _____
   _____
   _____

5. Counseling groups for the elderly differ in several ways from those designed for other age groups; one such unique distinction is screening for group membership.

   _____
   _____
   _____

6. Members of young-old groups, according to Thomas and Martin (1997) identify problems with physical and emotional stress as common features.

_____
_____
_____

7. Since the 1970s, elder hostels have grown as popular group experiences for older persons where they gather together to study, often on college campuses.

_____
_____
_____

8. The percentage of people in the United States over the age of 65 is approximately 25%.

_____
_____
_____

9. Reminiscing groups are designed for individuals who have "lost interest" with the present and future and tend to focus only on the past.

_____
_____
_____

10. Topic-specific groups with the elderly are counseling groups in nature.

_____
_____
_____

11. Self-disclosure by the group leaders is usually a benefit in working with elderly group members.

_____
_____
_____

12. Socializing outside of the group is encouraged in groups composed of elderly members.

_____
_____
_____

13. Information and support are primary group objectives for caretakers of the elderly.

_____
_____
_____

14. Several major theoretical approaches prove to work better with elderly clients than others.

_____
_____
_____

**Multiple Choice Questions**

1. Unlike adolescents, older individuals often have more time to make transitions gradually. _____ seem(s) to lessen with age.

    a. Hope for the future           c. Personal responsibilities

    b. The density of time           d. (all of the above)

2. One significant difference that defines groups for the elderly from groups for other aged individuals is that elderly members are_____.

    a.   often encouraged to socialize outside of group meetings

    b.   often cognitively diminished

    c.   seldom under significant stress

    d.   rarely benefited by group psychotherapy

3. Tasks of affirmation, support, education, linking with others, and renewal are often the goals of group work with _____.

    a. young-old               c. old-old

    b. old                    d. caretakers

### Written Exercises

Respond in writing to several of the following questions, prompts, and inquiries, designed to deepen your comprehension of the text. Student responses can lead to self-reflection and interesting discussions with others. You are encouraged to flex your imagination and make your understanding of group work as presented in these chapters come to life.

### Questions & Prompts for Written Reflection and Discussion

#### Chapter 14

1. What do you consider *ageism*? How do you think group work with older persons would put unique demands on you as a group leader? What advantages do you think working with older people in groups would provide members? Share your positions with others in class. What themes emerge from your conversations? What special training do you suppose would benefit specialists in group work who choose to work with the aging?

_____
_____
_____
_____
_____
_____
_____
_____
_____
_____
_____
_____
_____
_____

2. Consider both *reminiscing groups* and *remotivation therapy groups*. What specific tasks do each present the therapy group leader? How do you see yourself as a leader of these unique group opportunities? Discuss your thoughts with others in class. Identify common perceptions of working with the elderly in these therapy groups.

_____
_____
_____
_____
_____
_____
_____
_____
_____
_____
_____
_____
_____

3. What distinctive tasks can you identify in setting up groups for the elderly? In particular, how would this task differ between working with young-old, old, and old-old group members?

_____
_____
_____
_____
_____
_____
_____
_____
_____
_____
_____
_____
_____

4. Reflect on the issues common for caretakers of the elderly. How do you see group psychoeducation and counseling benefiting members who are caregivers? Review very current professional literature on this topic. Share results of your reviews with others in class. Describe some of your feelings as you read the new material. What are some of the shared concerns about caregivers, and working with the elderly in general, among your class members?

_____
_____
_____
_____
_____
_____
_____
_____
_____
_____
_____
_____

## Journal and Reflection

Space for journaling about your group work experiences is provided below. Use this space to reflect on your reading about group work, your classroom presentations and activities, the group dynamics of your classes themselves, and any simulations or actual group participation opportunities you may have. Comment here thoughtfully. Be sure to carefully honor your ethical commitment to uphold the confidentiality of others in your group. Reflections are yours and are not to reveal anyone else's information. Recording your thoughts and feelings will provide a written history of this phase of your group work education. (Attach additional sheets of paper if desired.)

_Entry date_ _____

# PSYCHOANALYTIC AND TRANSACTIONAL ANALYSIS GROUPS

## Outcome Objectives

1. I understand and can describe psychoanalytic groups, including:
    a. the premises upon which psychoanalytic groups are built;
    b. the application of psychoanalytic theory in a group;
    c. the role of the psychoanalytically oriented group leader; and
    d. the desired outcome of psychoanalytic groups.
2. I understand and can describe transactional analysis groups, including:
    a. the premises upon which transactional analysis groups are built;
    b. the application of transactional analysis theory in a group;
    c. the role of the transactional analysis group leader; and
    d. the desired outcome of transactional analysis groups.

## Chapter Overview

Psychoanalytic and transactional analysis groups have uniquely different and effective ways to help individuals grow in the group setting. Psychoanalytic groups concentrate on helping individuals resolve unconscious thoughts and problematic psychosexual development. Transactional analysis groups emphasize understanding intrapersonal and interpersonal dynamics and participatory learning. TA groups focus on the ego states (Parent, Adult or Child) of group members. Both theoretical perspectives have very specific theoretical underpinnings and accompanying techniques associated with them.

## Chapter Highlights

### PSYCHOANALYTIC GROUPS

Psychoanalytic theory assumes that in-depth change takes years to produce. Therefore, it is usually oriented toward individuals with deep underlying psychological problems.

Freud (1959), although never interested in conducting groups, applied his psychoanalytic theory to groups in 1922 in his book *Group Psychology and the Analysis of the Ego*.

Freud stressed the importance of ego development within a group context and the reconstruction of the family unit among group members.

Not until 1938 was a psychoanalytic model of group work implemented on a sustained basis.

Alexander Wolf, a psychiatrist and psychoanalyst, is generally credited with being the first to apply psychoanalytic principles and techniques systematically to groups (Corey, 2000; Ruitenbeek, 1970).

Another early contributor to the psychoanalytic group work model was Samuel Slavson, who formed activity groups for children ages 8 to 15 based on psychoanalytic principles.

At least two models for conducting psychoanalytic groups have developed.

Alexander Wolf created a model that stresses **psychoanalysis in groups**. In this model, the focus is on the individual in the group.

George Bach (1954) and W. R. Bion (1959) developed **group psychoanalysis**. These models emphasize that the whole group is the client and that group dynamics are an essential feature to analyze.

Bion's point of view is similar to general systems theory (Bertalanffy, 1968), whereas Bach's view is based on field theory (Lewin, 1951).

The most practiced form of psychoanalytically oriented group work emphasizes individual therapy in a group context (i.e., psychoanalysis in groups) (Seligman, 1982).

### Premises of Psychoanalytically Oriented Groups

Regardless of the model, common denominators deal with the major tenets of classic psychoanalytic theory, as well as the belief that psychoanalysis is possible in a group setting.

The importance of freeing unconscious thoughts, making the unconscious more conscious, and using specific techniques to do so (e.g., free association, transference, interpretation) are universally emphasized.

The major assumptions of classic psychoanalytic theory are premised on the importance of the interaction among the id, ego, and superego.

Classic psychoanalytic theory hypothesizes that individuals pass through **four stages of psychosexual development** during the first 20 years of life: oral, anal, phallic, and genital, with a period of latency between the phallic and genital stages.

Failure to resolve the development tasks associated with these stages by being overindulged or excessively frustrated results in **fixation.** The main task of classic psychoanalysis is to undo fixation and to help people gain insight.

**Defense mechanisms** (ways of protecting a person from being overwhelmed by anxiety), such as repression or denial, are over-utilized when a person is not coping adequately.

Group psychoanalysis, as well as psychoanalysis in a group, is more a modification of individual analysis than a distinct school of thought (Slavson, 1964).

Group psychoanalysis and psychoanalysis in a group differ from Freud's original opinions about group members.

Basically, psychoanalytically oriented groups can be practiced on either a regressive-reconstructive or a repressive-constructive basis.

Both approaches emphasize that a major change in personality is the goal of the group, which comes about only if there is sufficient regression followed by reconstruction.

## Practice of Psychoanalytic Theory in a Group

Because psychoanalytic theory emphasizes regression and resolution of previously unresolved stages of psychosexual development, membership in the group is usually restricted to either psychiatric patients or analytically oriented individuals.

Most psychoanalytic groups are heterogeneous by design; such groups are more reflective of the world at large and promote transference and interaction while discouraging conformity (Wolf & Schwartz, 1962).

The most important techniques used in the psychoanalytic approaches to groups parallel those employed in individual analysis.

***Free Association*** - In a group, free association works as a type of "free-floating discussion" (Foulkes & Anthony, 1965) in which group members report their feelings or impressions immediately.

***Dream Analysis*** - Through sharing dreams, group members get to know each other better and, at the same time, are able to be more concrete in handling their feelings associated with the dream and in managing themselves in general.

Dream content is manifest (conscious) and latent (hidden). Manifest content is the obvious and recallable features of the dream. Latent content is the symbol features of the dream that escape first analysis.

Dreams work on an interpersonal as well as an intrapersonal level in group psychotherapy (Kolb, 1983).

***Interpretation*** focuses on helping clients gain insights into their past or present behavior.

There are generally three levels of interpretation: thematical, constructional, and situational (Clark, 1993).

Using interpretation in group settings has several drawbacks and thus should be employed with caution.

***Resistance*** works in overt and covert ways to keep the group from making progress. Overtly, it may take the form of rebellion by group members against the leader (Saravay, 1978). Covertly, it is demonstrated when group members get bogged down in details and become preoccupied with the unimportant (Corey, 2000).

Psychoanalytically oriented group work is an especially good approach to use with very resistant clients.

***Transference*** is the projection of inappropriate emotions onto the leader or group members. It usually occurs when members have come to know each other fairly well.

In psychoanalysis, transference is encouraged, and clients are helped to work through unresolved experiences of the past and gain insight into their present patterns of interaction.

Participants in groups that are psychoanalytically oriented are helped to see patterns of transference when the group leader directs their attention to present interactions and invites them to examine how much they are investing in relationships with each other and the leader.

***Projective identification*** is one of the most complex and potentially disruptive behaviors that can occur in a group.

The result is that group development is arrested and in place of trust, feelings of shame, hostility, and aggression surface.

## Role of the Psychoanalytically Oriented Group Leader

The role of the psychoanalytically oriented group leader varies with the characteristics and emphases of the groups he or she is leading.

As a rule, psychoanalytic group leaders should be objective, warm, and relatively anonymous. They should strive to conceal, rather than reveal, information about themselves, while at the same time attempt to foster transference.

The psychoanalytic group leader is of necessity not a member of the group, but at the same time, he or she must avoid taking a dictatorial attitude toward group members.

Group leaders should recognize each participant's potential to contribute to the good of the group and recognize the potential power of the group as a whole.

## Desired Outcome of Psychoanalytically Oriented Groups

Psychoanalytic group theory emphasizes stages of development of individual members in the group rather than of the group as a whole.

**Stages of psychoanalytically oriented groups** are as follows: (1) preliminary individual analysis, (2) establishment of rapport, (3) analysis of resistance, (4) analysis of transference, (5) working through, and (6) reorientation and social integration.

## Evaluation of Psychoanalytically Oriented Groups
### *Strengths and Contributions*

Psychoanalytically oriented groups have a major advantage when compared with individual psychoanalysis in that group members can experience transference feelings with others in the group as well as with the group leaders (Esman, 1990).

Members have an opportunity to work with others in the group to resolve current as well as past problems.

Group members realize that they each experience and express a wide range of feelings. In a successful group, members develop "their capacities to contain, express, and integrate a full range of positive and negative affective components" even if some of these emotions have historically been overwhelming (Nusbaum, 2000, p. 300-301).

A strength of this type of group is its emphasis on long-term personality change through the group process (Moreno, 1998).

### *Limitations*

One contention is that free association is not possible in a group setting. Group members tend to be interrupted in groups and may be unable to link their thoughts.

Too often those within the "psychoanalytic establishment" only read and absorb their own papers and thoughts (Ruitenbeek, 1970). This type of inbreeding prevents more creative thinking and innovations.

The theory on which psychoanalytically oriented groups are based is deterministic, biologically biased, and oriented toward a pathological view of the human nature.

Psychoanalytically oriented groups and the theory of psychoanalysis are criticized for a lack of openness to rigorous scientific investigations.

## TRANSACTIONAL ANALYSIS GROUPS

In transactional analysis (TA) groups, the emphasis is on understanding intrapersonal and interpersonal dynamics and participatory learning through interaction and homework assignments.

Eric Berne believed that groups are more efficient in helping individuals understand their personal life scripts than individual counseling or psychotherapy (Barnes, 1977; Berne, 1966).

Individuals must learn basic TA concepts, such as "ego state," "stroke," and "script" before they can participate in a TA group. Members must be willing to work on past experiences in a present context.

The emphasis of TA groups is on both interpersonal (i.e., the classic model) and intrapersonal (i.e., the cathexis and redecision models) (Barnes, 1977).

### Premises of Transactional Analysis Groups

The basic concepts of TA revolve around the development and interaction of what Berne (1964) called an **ego state** — "a system of feelings accompanied by a related set of behavior patterns" (p. 23).

Three basic ego states — Parent, Adult, and Child — exist and operate within every individual and can be observed in the dynamic interactions of individuals with each other (Rath, 1993).

There are four basic ways to identify which ego state individuals are in at a particular moment — behavioral, social, historical, and phenomenological (Woollams, Brown, & Huige, 1977).

Knowledge of their own ego states empowers individuals and those working with them to assess what types of transactions they are most likely to have and to take corrective measures, if needed.

Information regarding ego states helps persons avoid playing "**games**," which Berne (1964) defined as "an ongoing series of complementary ulterior transactions progressing to a well-defined, predictable outcome" (p. 48).

People who play games operate from three distinct positions: the *victim*, the *persecutor*, and the *rescuer*.

Several other TA beliefs about human nature are that individuals structure their time to obtain **strokes**; that over their life span, people gradually develop **scripts**, or habitual patterns of behavior, that influence how they spend their time; and that scripts include **transactions**.

## Practice of Transactional Analysis in a Group
Transactional analysis is preferably used in groups.

"Groups serve as a setting in which people can become more aware of themselves, the structure of their individual personality, the transactions they have with others, the games they play, and the scripts they act out." (James & Jongeward, 1971, p. 11)

According to Berne (1966), the objective in group treatment settings is to "fight the past in the present in order to assure the future" (p. 250).

### *Therapeutic Contracts*
All TA groups are based on the participants' ability and willingness to make and work on **therapeutic contracts** (Dusay & Dusay, 1989).

Contracts are specific, measurable, concrete statements of what participants intend to accomplish during the group.

Contracts can be made in all types of groups: psychoeducational, counseling, psychotherapeutic, and task/work.

The contract establishes the departure point for group activity. Well-written contracts make it clear that participants are getting what they want from the group (Dusay, 1983).

### *Classic Contracts*
Classic school contracts are carried out with an emphasis on one or more of the following: (a) structural analysis, (b) transactional analysis, (c) game analysis, and (d) life script analysis (Berne, 1961).

"In order to achieve the most complete treatment, all four need to be accomplished, and since each one is built upon the previous level, it is necessary that they be accomplished in order" (Donigian & Hulse-Killacky, 1999, p. 75).

### *Redecision Contracts*
A special form of TA, **redecision theory**, helps clients make redecisions while they are in their child ego state (Goulding & Goulding, 1979; McCormick, 1995).

This task is accomplished by having these individuals reexperience a past event as if it were now present.

## Role of the Transactional Analysis Group Leader
Transactional analysis group leaders are "primarily listeners, observers, diagnosticians, and analysts — and, secondarily, process facilitators" (Donigian & Hulse-Killacky, 1999, p. 115).

TA groups are leader centered, and although member–member transactions occur, they do not have the same effect as a leader–member interaction.

It is vital that TA group leaders understand themselves well from a TA perspective and that they adopt an "I'm OK" life position because they are teachers within the group.

The leader has four specific roles within the TA group (Corey, 2000; Grimes, 1988), which are protection, permission, potency, and operations.

## Desired Outcome of Transactional Analysis Groups

Group members will learn about themselves through their analysis of structures, transactions, games, and scripts. The knowledge they acquire from this process will enable them to think, feel, and behave differently if they so choose.

Woollams and Brown (1978) view the process that leads to desired outcomes in TA groups as going through seven steps: (a) trust in the other, (b) trust in self, (c) moving into group, (d) work, (e) redecision, (f) integration, and (g) termination.

## Evaluation of Transactional Analysis Groups

### *Strengths and Contributions*

The cognitive clarity of the language used to explain TA concepts is a strength (Grimes, 1988; Yalom, 1995).

One strength of TA is its simplicity (O'Hearne, 1977). TA concepts can be readily grasped and the theory can be used in its most elementary form in just a few hours.

Individuals "move faster toward getting well" in TA groups (Harris, 1967, p. 204). Group members who make progress toward achieving their goals reinforce others in the group to do the same.

TA in groups can be used in task/work, psychoeducational, counseling, and psychotherapy settings and combined effectively with other more action-centered approaches such as Gestalt, to produce a dynamic method of change (Goulding & Goulding, 1979; James & Jongeward, 1971; Tyler, 1995).

### *Limitations*

A major drawback of TA is its restrictive interpretation of the complexities of human nature by categorizing them into a limited number of games, ego states, and scripts (Yalom, 1995).

A limitation of TA in groups is that the strong emphasis on understanding can make analysis become an intellectual exercise.

TA in groups doesn't emphasize group process (Yalom, 1995). Transactional analysis centers largely on member–leader interaction and does not effectively use other group dynamics such as interpersonal learning, cohesiveness, and universality.

A limitation of the use of TA in groups is the lack of empirical evidence to support its effectiveness.

## Key Concepts

*Can you define and describe each of the following terms? Be able to offer a brief example or relevant context for these concepts.*

adult ego state
cathexis (TA school)
child ego state
classic (TA school)
conductors
defense mechanisms
denial
displacement
dream analysis
ego
egogram
ego state
fixation
four stages of psychosexual development
free association
game analysis
games
group analysis
group psychoanalysis
id
identification
injunctions
interpretation
major transactions
minor transactions
multiple transferences
life script analyses
operations
parent ego state
permission
potency
primal horde
projection
projective identification
protection
psychoanalysis in groups
rationalization
reaction formation
redecision school of TA
redecision theory
regression
regressive-reconstructive model
repression
repressive-constructive model
resistance
scripts

situational therapy
stages of psychoanalytically oriented groups
strokes
superego
therapeutic contracts
transactional analysis
transactions
transference

## Key Personalities

*Can you identify and discuss the contributions of the following experts?*

Bach, George
Berne, Eric
Bion, W.R.
Burrow, Trigant
Freud, Sigmund
Goulding, M.
Goulding, R.
Lazell, E. W.
Schilder, Paul
Slavson, Samuel
Wender, Louis
Wolf, Alexander

## In-Class or Small-Group Discussion Prompts and Activities:

A. What are your initial reactions to psychoanalytic and transactional analysis theoretical approaches to working with groups? What in particular feeds this reaction? Be specific in order to support your position to others in the group.

- After sharing your reaction and hearing what others think and feel, how has your initial reaction changed, if at all? What elements of others' reactions are you drawn to? How did others' positions affect your own?

- Do you notice any subgroups forming within your class or study group arising from your unique positions? Talk about the potential detrimental effect that such a subgroup might have in your discussion group.

_____
_____
_____
_____
_____
_____
_____
_____
_____

B. These theories share some things in common that allow them to be paired even if only for such academic purposes as the organization of chapters in your group work text. What do psychoanalytic and Transactional Analysis theories share? Consider answering this question in two ways: What do they share in a very academic way? What do they share in a more affective/felt way? How are these theories uniquely different?

_____
_____
_____
_____
_____
_____
_____
_____

C. What elements (e.g., terms, concepts, procedures, techniques) from these theoretical approaches to group work are you unsure of or confused by? Discuss them; help one another to better understand. Analyze your questions. Do you conclude anything about either theory as a result?

_____
_____
_____
_____
_____
_____
_____
_____

**Activity:** For a moment, imagine yourself to be a group leader practicing from this theory, this approach.

1. Imagine yourself leading this group from either the psychoanalytic or Transactional Analysis theoretical vantage point. What fits you best from this vantage? And what does not fit? Why? Which of your personality features (states or traits) do you become aware of while leading this imaginary group?

_____
_____
_____
_____
_____
_____
_____

2. Who in your small discussion group do you picture most able to lead a group from this theoretical orientation? Why? What do you see in him or her that forms your opinion? What does that individual think and feel about your "nomination" as a psychoanalytic or Transactional Analysis group leader? Who is the member "least" aligned with this approach, in your opinion? Why? What is her or his reaction?

_____
_____
_____
_____
_____
_____
_____
_____
_____

3. Envision your group members, each carefully screened as appropriate for the group you are leading. What are they like? How does "seeing" them through this theoretical lens affect "who" you see? What about these imaginary group members is distinctive to the theory that you are adhering to for this group?

- How does your understanding of this theory influence your member selection? What do you see as advantages or disadvantages to leadership from Psychoanalytic or Transactional Analysis with underrepresented group members (e.g., a Native American member, a lesbian client, a physically challenged member)?

_____
_____
_____
_____
_____
_____
_____
_____
_____

4. Divide your class or small group into two (or three) "theory teams" and discuss one of the following prompts for a few moments. Then, if you wish, switch "teams" and try again. Following this activity, discuss your reactions—remember to include what you felt, not just what you thought.

- The way "we" conceptualize and implement our task as group leaders affords "us" the best opportunity to reach our intended goals. Members are best served by this approach to leadership.

- Members in "our" groups are at an advantage over "your" members because "our" members" are/have/will/can _____ *(list several advantages)* _____.

_____
_____
_____
_____
_____
_____
_____
_____
_____

5. Consider the chapters on working with children, adolescents, adults, and the elderly in groups. Identify and share in your small group elements from these two theoretical perspectives that you believe would appeal to members from each of these four developmental groups. Is there anything that you agree would disadvantage one or more of these age groups by adhering to either of these two theories?

_____

_____

_____

_____

_____

_____

_____

_____

**Activity:** Without exception the ten theories covered in the Gladding text and here in this workbook are left wanting for empirical support of their approach. Theorists and practitioners alike would greatly value sound research that would show one theory as superior over others (although, perhaps thankfully, such a claim is unlikely to ever emerge).

For the psychoanalytic and Transactional Analysis theories of group work and practice covered in this chapter, design one or more research projects to learn more about one of these theories.
1.  What are the questions that you would like to investigate through your research? Knowing what you do about research design (and keeping in mind ethical practice) how might you go about testing your hypotheses?
2.  What do you see as dependent and independent variables in your research?
3.  Are you drawn toward any particular research design? Are either quantitative or qualitative methods more appealing to you for asking and answering questions about these theories?
4.  What are the complexities and challenges that you encounter in your design?
5.  Extend this activity if you wish by reviewing the professional literature. Look for actual empirical research that attempts to accomplish what you and your group member colleagues have proposed.

_____

_____

_____

_____

_____

_____

_____

_____

**Activity:** Individually locate one or two texts written by recognized authors who claim allegiance to either psychoanalytic or Transactional Analysis group theory. After skimming (or reading if time permits) these original sources, prepare a short statement (one page) that you will read to your class or to study group members "selling" your theoretical perspective! How do others receive your statement? What reactions do they have? Discuss either as a class or in small groups.

## Self Assessment Questions

### True or False Statements

The following statements check your comprehension of terms and identification of individuals (knowledge and comprehension level); your ability to apply that knowledge to solve more challenging questions (application level), and your ability to evaluate given information (analysis and evaluation level).

Indicate whether each statement is true or false. If you believe a statement is false, identify the error in the space provided. When necessary, refer to your text, *Group Work: A Counseling Specialty* (4th ed.). An answer key appears at the end of this book.

1. Key to psychoanalytic theory is the premise that when facing overwhelming anxiety an individual relies on healthy or unhealthy "defense mechanisms."

   _____
   _____
   _____

2. Responding to conflict by behaving in ways that make others think everything is absolutely fine is called displacement.

   _____
   _____
   _____

3. Membership in psychoanalytic group therapy is typically heterogeneous in order to decrease member conformity.

   _____
   _____
   _____

4. In psychoanalytic group therapy, thematic interpretation is based upon an individual's immediate interactions with members within the group.

   _____
   _____
   _____

5. In psychoanalytic group therapy, the most acceptable intervention with highly resistant clients is to passively ignore the resistant member's behavior.

   _____
   _____
   _____

6. A member's projective identification can result in the arrest of the group's development as shame, hostility, and aggression arise.

   _____
   _____
   _____

7. According to transactional analysis, groups are superior to individual counseling or psychotherapy in helping clients understand their personal life scripts,.

_____
_____
_____

8. Free association in groups is a technique used to promote spontaneity, interaction, and a feeling of unity in the group.

_____
_____
_____

9. In transactional analysis, an ego state is the system of feelings that accompany a pattern of behaviors for an individual.

_____
_____
_____

10. Therapeutic contracts in transactional analysis hold group members responsible for all aspects of their change process.

_____
_____
_____

11. Injunctions are a TA group leader role which consists of employing interrogation, confrontation, and illustration.

_____
_____
_____

12. Leaders of psychoanalytically oriented groups should discourage transference.

_____
_____
_____

13. In TA, the parent ego state functions much like a computer.

_____
_____
_____

14. Habitual patterns of behavior that influence how time is spent are known in TA as scripts.

_____
_____
_____

15. The primary attention of transactional analysis is between the leader and the group members.

_____
_____
_____

16. A major disadvantage of TA group theory is its simplicity.

_____
_____
_____

17. Defense mechanisms are ways a person protects the self from becoming overwhelmed by the anxieties in his or her life.

_____
_____
_____

18. Redecision TA helps clients by having them reexperience a past event as if it were now present.

_____
_____
_____

**Multiple Choice Questions**

1. Defense mechanisms are internal processes that are employed to protect a person from being overwhelmed by anxiety. Which of the following is an example of *displacement*?
    a. Cathryn obviously is under enormous pressure balancing multiple demands on her time. To the amazement of others in the group, she admits to feeling no stress or strain.
    b. Alfred actually stuck his 40-year-old tongue out at Barb in group today when she challenged his opinion.
    c. Marty seems to blame his struggles at work on his partner's failure to pay any attention to him anymore.
    d. Zipora has so much anger at her daughter, but she seems to take her feelings out on her son. He seems to absorb the blow better than her daughter would.

2. "George's behavior with Alan (the leader) is so adolescent-like in group. He seems to treat the group leader like a military officer. 'Yes sir, no sir!' Where does that all come from?" This is an illustration of what phenomenon in psychoanalytic group therapy?
    a. transference               c. projective identification
    b. countertransference     d. interpretation

3. In transactional analysis the *parent ego state* is dualistic. The two parts that make up this dualism include the _____ parent and the _____ parent.
    a. critical / nurturing          c. classic / cathexic
    b. adult / child               d. protective / permissive

4. In TA, major transactions represent, _____ interactions, and minor transactions represent _____ interactions.
    a.   leader-member / member-member
    b.   script-member / script-leader
    c.   member-games / leader-games
    d.   member-ego / leader-ego

**Group Work Scenario**

Barry has had moderate to severe depression for many years, beginning around age 14 and lasting intermittently until now. He is 33 years old. His primary care physician, in consultation with a psychiatrist, has referred him to a psychoanalytic (or transactional, student's choice) group psychotherapist for treatment.

1. Imagine yourself in the role of group therapist. During Barry's initial screening interview, he says, "I've been to counseling before. How is this group psychotherapy going to be any different?" Write several points that you would include in your reply.

_____
_____
_____
_____
_____
_____

2. Barry has no "reasons" for his depression, although he tells group members that he came from a very "tense and rigid home situation." Using either psychoanalytic theory of group work or transactional analysis, write down key points, and group interventions that might be used to address Barry's depression.

_____
_____
_____
_____
_____
_____

3. Using the concept of multiple transferences from psychoanalytically oriented groups, describe what benefit Barry may expect from therapy in this group.

_____
_____
_____
_____
_____
_____

4. Using the concepts from the _redecision school_ of transactional analysis, describe what processes Barry might experience in this type of psychotherapy group.

_____
_____
_____
_____
_____
_____

**Journal and Reflection**

Space for journaling about your group work experiences is provided below. Use this space to reflect on your reading about group work, your classroom presentations and activities, the group dynamics of your classes themselves, and any simulations or actual group participation opportunities you may have. Comment here thoughtfully. Be sure to carefully honor your ethical commitment to uphold the confidentiality of others in your group. Reflections are yours and are not to reveal anyone else's information. Recording your thoughts and feelings will provide a written history of this phase of your group work education. (Attach additional sheets of paper if desired.)

_Entry date_ _____

# PERSON-CENTERED AND EXISTENTIAL GROUPS

**Outcome Objectives**

1.  I understand and can describe person-centered groups, including:
    a.  the premises upon which person-centered groups are built;
    b.  the application of person-centered theory in a group;
    c.  the role of the person-centered group leader; and
    d.  the desired outcome of personal-centered groups.
2.  I understand and can describe existential groups, including:
    a.  the premises upon which existential groups are built;
    b.  the application of existential theory in a group;
    c.  the role of the existential group leader; and
    d.  the desired outcome of existential groups.

## Chapter Overview

Although person-centered groups (most commonly thought of as encounter groups) are not as prevalent as they were in the 1960s and 1970s, they have an important place in the history and subsequent development of the group movement. Existential groups have increased in popularity in recent years, thanks in part to the writings of Irvin Yalom, Rollo May, and Victor Frankl. These two types of groups focus mainly on relationships. They have had and continue to have considerable impact on much group work done today.

## Chapter Highlights

Person-centered and existential theories of group work are humanistically based ways of working with people. In these two models of group work, an emphasis is placed on here-and-now phenomena, that is, being present in the moment. There is also a focus within these theories on the creation of personal and interpersonal awareness and finding meaning in life (Day & Matthes, 1992; Frankl, 2000).

### PERSON-CENTERED GROUPS

The growth and development of person-centered group work is linked to the theory and personal influence of Carl Rogers (Rogers, 1967, 1970, 1980).

Rogers developed what he termed a *nondirective* counseling approach in reaction to the directive methods used by psychoanalytic therapists and other counselor-practitioners of the 1940s.

In the 1960s, Rogers expanded his focus to the small group as well as to the individual.

Rogers, working with people from the general population, developed the **basic encounter group**, in which "individuals come into much closer and direct contact with one another than is customary in ordinary life" (Rogers, 1967, p. 270).

Rogers became interested in large-group phenomena in the 1970s and initiated a new group format — the **community for learning** — in which about 100 people lived and worked together for 2 weeks at a time.

## Premises of Person-Centered Groups

Basic encounter groups are built on several premises: a trust in the inner resources of persons; a sense of trust in the group to help members develop their potential without being directed in a certain way by a leader; the idea that certain conditions must be created within the group for the group and its members to maximize their full potential (Rogers, 1970); and the understanding that a qualified person with special training and experience will facilitate them.

Members are free to talk about their past and present because encounter groups do not make a distinction between "growth and development goals and psychotherapy goals" (Shaffer & Galinsky, 1989, p. 211).

Both personal deficit and enhancement issues may be dealt with in the group.

Basic encounter groups are established on the premise that individuals who participate in them are relatively healthy.

## Practice of Person-Centered Theory in a Group

Certain procedures (i.e., techniques and processes) are common to all encounter groups. One of the most crucial is the creation of a psychological climate in which group members can risk being themselves.

Feedback and communication are also critical components in encounter group experiences.

The process in which these basic techniques are employed and the **Rogerian-oriented encounter group stages** are well defined, although they do not always occur in a clear-cut sequence and may vary from group to group. Rogers (1970) delineates a 15-stage process.

## Role of the Person-Centered Group Leader

Person-centered group leaders derive their direction from group members. Their leadership style is generally less active than in many other approaches to group work.

Leaders of Rogerian-based groups are paradigms "for interpersonal effectiveness, modeling the therapeutic norms of openness, congruence, warmth, genuineness, and acceptance" and creating a climate within the group that promotes the development of relationships (Ohlsen, Horne, & Lawe, 1988, p. 68).

Person-centered group leaders participate as a member of the group and share their struggles with the group.

Overall, person-centered group leaders carry out five distinct functions: (1) conveying warmth and empathy, (2) attending to others, (3) understanding meaning and content, (4) conveying acceptance, and (5) linking (Boy & Pine, 1999; Posthuma, 1999).

Leaders use themselves as instruments of change (Raskin, 1986a,b) and convey the core conditions of empathy, congruence, and acceptance (Thorne, 1992).

### Desired Outcome of Person-Centered Groups

Person-centered encounter groups are intended for group members to develop self-awareness, awareness of others, and growth.

Another goal is more openness to experience, especially as it relates to intimacy and meaningfulness with others.

### Evaluation of Person-Centered Groups
#### *Strengths and Contributions*

Up to the 1960s, the focus of group psychotherapists was on reduction, rather than expansion, of their group participants' experiences. After encounter groups gained popularity, group psychotherapists were inclined to stress patients' assets as well as try to alleviate their deficiencies (Yalom, 1995).

The heart of the basic encounter group is the group facilitator (Donigian & Hulse-Killacky, 1999; Yalom, 1995). The facilitator's task is to have a genuine interest in others and be able to set up conditions for personal growth.

The basic encounter group model emphasizes improving personal communication skills.

A fourth positive influence of basic encounter groups has been in the area of research technology. Empirical research has become more sophisticated and is rooted in the encounter group tradition of investigation (e.g., Bates & Goodman, 1986; Yamamoto, 1990).

The Rogerian model of conducting groups has led to several other educational models that use it as the basis for their work. For instance, some parent education programs are based on Rogerian group theory.

Person-centered encounter groups have made group work acceptable for "normals."

#### *Limitations*

Encounter groups may be dangerous to participants who need therapy or structure and who try to use these groups as they would more organized psychotherapy groups (Lieberman et al., 1973; Vander Kolk, 1985).

A second limitation of basic encounter groups is the way in which members and leaders are chosen. The ethical issue of not screening members and not requiring rigor in the training of group facilitators is critical.

The emphasis on the personhood of the facilitator and the lack of emphasis on technique may not be productive for some groups (Cain, 1993).

A limitation of basic encounter groups centers on the research methods used to evaluate them and their success.

### EXISTENTIAL GROUPS

The focus of existential therapy is human existence, particularly the thoughts and anxieties that come with being a human, such as the importance of values, freedom, and responsibility in living one's life.

"Existentialism focuses on understanding of the person's subjective view of the world" and, thus, is a phenomenological approach (Corey, 2000, p. 248).

Existentialism is not united as a theory. Rather, what is described as existentialism is built on the diverse work of prominent existential writers.

Because many existential writers are literary figures, atheists, and theologians, and therefore write out of different traditions, a great deal of misunderstanding and misinterpretation arises of what existentialism is in traditional helping situations.

Existential groups in the United States have become popular since the 1960s thanks to at least two factors: the rapid change in lifestyles among Americans, and the writings and media presentations of Irvin Yalom (1995), Rollo May (1953, 1977), and Viktor Frankl (2000).

## Premises of Existential Groups
Existential groups are based on several premises, among them the belief that people form their lives by the choices they make.

From an existentialist's perspective, a person who does not actively seek meaning in life chooses despair or psychopathology.

Humans are constantly challenged to relinquish actions and values that are meaningless to them and to embrace new behaviors and thoughts that give them a sense of meaning.

This demand to discard and obtain so that life can be lived to the fullest creates tension and anxiety.

## Practice of Existential Theory in a Group
Existential groups are usually conducted with an emphasis on psychotherapy, counseling, and occasionally psychoeducation.

In existential groups, one of the first goals is to increase **self-awareness** and **personal responsibility** as it relates to interpersonal modes of behavior.

Group members must face their anxiety by seeing their lives as a journey that will ultimately never stop changing or be secure and will end.

Along with handling anxiety comes a struggle to **search for** personal **meaning** in life.

## Role of the Existential Group Leader
Leadership in existential groups carries with it a responsibility to be active and reflective; leaders are always thinking and taking risks.

Anxiety and other uncomfortable emotions help group members realize that these feelings will lead them toward deeper awareness.

Group leaders work hard to develop close relationships with all members of a group. Meaningful change is believed to occur only when there is personal contact and interaction.

Group leaders use themselves in existential groups as a source of knowledge in regard to human experience and a model of how to be.

### Desired Outcome of Existential Groups

Members will be more aware of themselves and the choices they have in regard to growth and development.

Members of existential groups will also become more self-determining in what they do.

An outcome of an existential group experience may be that members find new meaning in all aspects of their lives.

The paradox of the human experience is that we are both alone and connected; present, here-and-now experiences are highlighted in existential groupwork.

Emphasis is placed on becoming authentic. Like the other qualities people strive to develop in an existential group, the process to be true to oneself and develop one's abilities is a lifelong challenge.

Members of existential groups better understand themselves, interpersonal relationships, and their immediate worlds.

### Evaluation of Existential Groups
#### *Strengths and Contributions*

Existential groups deal with ultimate issues in life and present their members with opportunities to explore their values and lifestyles in depth. Members in an existential group often question both how they are living and the meaning of events in their lives.

After participating in an existential group, participants often let go of past patterns, customs, and beliefs and come to find a different focus for their lives.

Existential groups provide a framework for other forms of group work.

They deal with group members in a holistic way in the present (Lowenstein, 1993). Concerns about specific behaviors or past events are not the focus.

The versatility of existential theory in groups is another of its strengths.

Existential groups are applicable to individuals from a wide range of cultures.

Overall, existential group work has a wide appeal because the theory behind the approach focuses on one's reason for being and the unavoidable exigencies of life in an unpredictable world.

#### *Limitations*

This approach (a drawback to other humanistic approaches as well) is most useful and beneficial for members who are verbal, can communicate effectively, and are not afraid to confront issues that are painful (Lowenstein, 1993).

The existential theory supports these groups has limited applicability outside counseling and psychotherapy settings.

A limitation of existentialism in groups is that it takes maturity, life experience, and close supervision for a leader to practice this approach (Deurzen-Smith, 1990). The nature of existentialism as a theory and practice presents problems in training future existential group leaders.

Group members who need information or immediate answers for specific behaviors are not good candidates for this way of working in groups.

## Key Concepts

active listening
anxiety
authenticity
basic encounter group
community for learning
confront
confrontation
crash-program mentality
facilitators
group therapy for normals
Parent Effectiveness Training (PET)
personal growth
personal responsibility
Rogerian-oriented encounter group 15-stage process
search for meaning
self-actualization
self-awareness
self-report research format
unstructured group

## Key Personalities

*Can you identify and discuss the contributions of the following experts?*

Frankl, Victor
May, Rollo
Rogers, Carl
Yalom, Irvin

**In-Class or Small-Group Discussion Prompts and Activities:**

A. What are your initial reactions to person-centered and existential theoretical approaches to working with groups? What in particular feeds this reaction? Be specific in order to support your position to others in the group.

- After sharing your reaction and hearing what others think and feel, how has your initial reaction changed, if at all? What elements of others' reactions are you drawn to? How did others' positions affect your own?

- Do you notice any subgroups forming within your class or study group arising from your unique positions? Talk about the potential detrimental effect that such a subgroup might have in your discussion group.

_____
_____
_____
_____
_____
_____
_____
_____
_____

B. These theories share some things in common that allow them to be paired even if only for such academic purposes as the organization of chapters in your group work text. What do person-centered and existential group approaches share in a very academic way? What do they share in a more affective/felt way? How are these theories uniquely different?

_____
_____
_____
_____
_____
_____
_____
_____

C. What elements (e.g., terms, concepts, procedures, techniques) from this theoretical approach to group work are you unsure of or confused by? Discuss them; help one another to better understand. Analyze your questions. Do you conclude anything about either theory as a result?

_____
_____
_____
_____
_____
_____
_____
_____

**Activity:** For a moment, imagine yourself to be a group leader practicing from this theory, this approach.

1. Imagine yourself leading this group from either the person-centered or existential theoretical vantage point. What fits you best from this vantage? And what does not fit? Why? Which of your personality features (states or traits) do you become aware of while leading this imaginary group?

_____
_____
_____
_____
_____
_____
_____
_____

2. Who in your small discussion group do you picture most able to lead a group from this theoretical orientation? Why? What do you see in him or her that forms your opinion? What does that individual think and feel about your "nomination" as either a person-centered or existential group leader? Who is the member "least" aligned with this approach, in your opinion? Why? What is her or his reaction?

_____
_____
_____
_____
_____
_____
_____
_____

3. Envision your group members, each carefully screened as appropriate for the group you are leading. What are they like? How does "seeing" them through this theoretical lens affect "who" you see? What about these imaginary group members is distinctive to the theory that you are adhering to for this group?

- How does your understanding of this theory influence your member selection? What do you see as advantages or disadvantages to leadership from either person-centered or existential group approach with underrepresented group members (e.g., an African American member, a gay male, a physically challenged member)?

_____
_____
_____
_____
_____
_____
_____

4. Divide your class or small group into two (or three) "theory teams" and discuss one of the following prompts for a few moments. Then, if you wish, switch "teams" and try again. Following this activity discuss your reactions—remember to include what you felt not just what you thought.

- The way "we" conceptualize and implement our task as group leaders affords "us" the best opportunity to reach our intended goals. Members are best served by this approach to leadership.

- Members in "our" groups are at an advantage over "your" members because "our members" are/have/will/can _____ *(list several advantages)* _____ .

_____
_____
_____
_____
_____
_____
_____
_____
_____

5. Consider the chapters on working with children, adolescents, adults, and the elderly in groups. Identify and share in your small group elements from these two theoretical perspectives that you believe would appeal to members from each of these four developmental groups. Is there anything that you agree would disadvantage one or more of these age groups by adhering to either of these two theories?

_____
_____
_____
_____
_____
_____
_____
_____

**Activity:** Without exception the ten theories covered in the Gladding text and here in this workbook are left wanting for empirical support of their approach. Theorists and practitioners alike would greatly value sound research that would show one theory as superior over others (although, perhaps thankfully, such a claim is unlikely to ever emerge).

For person-centered or existential theories of group leadership and practice covered in this chapter, design one or more research projects to learn more about one of these theories.
1. What are the questions that you would like to investigate through your research? Knowing what you do about research design (and keeping in mind ethical practice) how might you go about testing your hypotheses?
2. What do you see as dependent and independent variables in your research?
3. Are you drawn toward any particular research design? Are either quantitative or qualitative methods more appealing to you for asking and answering questions about these theories?
4. What are the complexities and challenges that you encounter in your design?

5.  Extend this activity if you wish by reviewing the professional literature. Look for actual empirical research that attempts to accomplish what you and your group member colleagues have proposed.

_____
_____
_____
_____
_____
_____
_____
_____
_____

**Activity:** Individually locate one or two texts written by recognized authors who claim allegiance to either person-centered or existential group theory. After skimming (or reading if time permits) these original sources, prepare a short statement (one page) that you will read to your class or to study group members "selling" your theoretical perspective! How do others receive your statement? What reactions do they have? Discuss either as a class or in small groups.

## Self Assessment Questions

### True or False Statements

The following statements check your comprehension of terms and identification of individuals (knowledge and comprehension level); your ability to apply that knowledge to solve more challenging questions (application level), and your ability to evaluate given information (analysis and evaluation level).

Indicate whether each statement is true or false. If you believe a statement is false, identify the error in the space provided. When necessary, refer to your text, *Group Work: A Counseling Specialty* (4th ed.). An answer key appears at the end of this book.

1.  Carl Rogers found that when clients were in charge of their own therapy and were accepted and understood by the therapist they improved faster than when directed by their therapist.

_____
_____
_____

2.  Confronting incongruencies in verbal and nonverbal messages is called *active listening* in person-centered groups.

_____
_____
_____

3.  *Communities for learning* was an interesting large-group phenomenon in the 1940s.

_____
_____
_____

4. "Cracking of facades" is one step in the 15-stage encounter group (Rogers, 1970).

_____

_____

_____

5. Person-centered group facilitators carry out five distinct functions, one being "interpreting meaning."

_____

_____

_____

6. Three means by which people can make their lives meaningful are achieving something, experiencing love, and initiating social reform (Frankl, 2000).

_____

_____

_____

7. *Parent Effectiveness Training* is an outgrowth of the Rogerian person-centered theory and group approach.

_____

_____

_____

8. Existentialists encounter a paradox: as more fully one lives life, the more one becomes aware of death.

_____

_____

_____

9. The existentialist Martin Heidegger is a key philosophical writer whose work influences existential counseling and psychotherapy theory.

_____

_____

_____

10. The scope of "death and non-being" from the existential perspective includes "boredom" (Greenstein & Breitbart, 2000).

_____

_____

_____

11. Tillich's (1952) intent to make the most of discovering and using one's talents and creativity is a desired existential group psychotherapy outcome.

_____

_____

_____

12. A "T" group, first designed by Carl Rogers, is a place where people can come together in a much closer and more direct way than in regular life.

_____

_____

_____

13. Person-centered group leaders see their role as facilitators of the group process.

_____

_____

_____

14. Existential group leaders often find their roles to be an intense and personal experience.

_____

_____

_____

15. Becoming authentic refers to being able to affirm oneself and make the most of discovering one's talents and creativity.

_____

_____

_____

16. One of the primary goals of existential work is to search for meaning in one's life.

_____

_____

_____


**Multiple Choice Questions**

1. Group leaders in person-centered group therapy are known as facilitators. Which of the following statements best illustrates the rationale behind facilitation?
    a. The group leader rebukes techniques and planned procedures.
    b. The group leader attempts to understand each person on a genuine, personal basis.
    c. The group leader participates as a group member and shares his or her struggles with the group.
    d. all of the above are correct.

2. After Jill shared some deeply held emotions with others in the group, it seemed that several other members let down their defenses and opened up in group, sharing and empathizing. Following that session, it seemed that things were substantively different in group. This scenario best illustrates which of the following Rogerian-oriented encounter group processes.
    a. revealing past feelings
    b. communication of immediate interpersonal feelings
    c. development of a healing capacity in the group
    d. expressions of closeness

3. One critical issue worthy of careful exploration regarding person-centered group therapy is
_____.
    a. not requiring rigor in the training of group facilitators
    b. not screening potential group members
    c. (both a and b)
    d. (neither a nor b)

4. Two reasons for the growth in popularity of existential group counseling and therapy since the 1960s are _____ and _____.
    a. changing lifestyles / celebrated writings of experts
    b. political and social unrest / changing lifestyles
    c. celebrated writing of experts / political and social unrest
    d. (none of the above)

5. Which of the following examples, taken from life events of existential group members, illustrates existential group therapy's *search for meaning in life?*
    a. When diagnosed with terminal cancer, Angelina worked fervently to repair her estranged relationship with her mother.
    b. Following a midlife career crisis, Barrett decided he wanted to return to culinary arts school to complete his early goal of becoming a chef.
    c. After the divorce of her parents, Shelia began to work diligently to improve some current challenges in her marriage.
    d. (all of the above)

**Group Work Scenario**

Irene is 27 years old, married, and a mother of two. In her family of origin she is the youngest of three children. Her mother died of breast cancer when Irene was 39 years old, and her father remarried only several years ago after all the children were adult and well established on their own. Irene seeks counseling in either a person-centered group or an existential counseling group (student's choice). She states to others in the opening session of the group, "I just have this nagging fear that I will die the same way as my mother did, or that I won't, and I will live longer than she was able to."

1. What approach have you selected? What is your rationale for your decision?
_____
_____
_____
_____
_____
_____

2. Irene is quite open to talking about her fears. What other hopes do you have for Irene through her participation and membership in this group?
_____
_____
_____
_____
_____
_____

3. Describe the potential benefits membership will provide for Irene. What are the helping mechanisms (therapeutic/curative factors) in person-centered and/or existential group counseling and psychotherapy?

_____

_____

_____

_____

_____

_____

4. What is a possible limitation to these two theoretical approaches in working with Irene? How would you mention any possible limitations in an _informed consent_ for Irene?

_____

_____

_____

_____

_____

_____

## Journal and Reflection

Space for journaling about your group work experiences is provided below. Use this space to reflect on your reading about group work, your classroom presentations and activities, the group dynamics of your classes themselves, and any simulations or actual group participation opportunities you may have. Comment here thoughtfully. Be sure to carefully honor your ethical commitment to uphold the confidentiality of others in your group. Reflections are yours and are not to reveal anyone else's information. Recording your thoughts and feelings will provide a written history of this phase of your group work education. (Attach additional sheets of paper if desired.)

_Entry date_ _____

# ADLERIAN AND REALITY THERAPY GROUPS

## Outcome Objectives

1.  I understand and can describe Adlerian groups, including:
    a.  the premise upon which Adlerian groups are built;
    b.  the application of Adlerian theory in group work;
    c.  the role of the Adlerian group leader; and
    d.  the desired outcome of Adlerian oriented groups.
2.  I understand and can describe reality therapy groups, including:
    a.  the premises upon which reality therapy groups are built;
    b.  the application of reality theory in group work;
    c.  the role of the reality therapy group leader; and
    d.  the desired outcome of reality therapy groups.

## Chapter Overview

Adlerian and reality therapies are considered socially oriented therapies. Adler believed that social forces motivate people. Adlerian groups emphasize change in the present while analyzing past beliefs and behaviors that have resulted from family and peer groups. Reality therapy is based on Glasser's theory that people have social needs that they try to meet in multiple ways. Both of these approaches are especially popular in educational settings.

## Chapter Highlights

Adlerian therapy and reality therapy (RT) are both socially oriented approaches to working with groups.

Despite similarities, these two theories originated more than forty years apart.

Both ways of working with groups have continued to evolve and are especially popular in educational settings.

## ADLERIAN THERAPY GROUPS

Adlerian theory has always had a group focus. It concentrates on the inherent social interest of persons and emphasizes social development, cooperation, and education.

Rudolf Dreikurs became the major impetus behind the establishment of group procedures based on Adlerian theory.

Christensen, Sonstegard, and Corsini applied Adlerian principles to family counseling groups (Christensen & Marchant, 1983; Dreikurs, Corsini, Lowe, & Sonstegard, 1959).

Dinkmeyer and his colleagues (Dinkmeyer, & Sperry, 2000) are most noted for packaging Adlerian group models.

### Premises of Adlerian Groups

Chief among the major tenets of Adlerian theory is that people are primarily motivated by social interest (Corsini, 1988; Donigian & Hulse-Killacky, 1999).

Other major beliefs that undergird Adlerian theory include:

The purposefulness of all behavior;

The subjective nature of perception;

The holistic nature of people;

The importance of developing a healthy style of life; and

The self-determinism of the individual to chart a future based on expected consequences of behavior.

### Practice of Adlerian Theory in a Group

Adlerian groups are primarily psychoeducational in nature although the emphasis in some of these groups is therapeutically oriented and they are often conducted in a counseling context.

The idea in all Adlerian groups is that people can learn from each other.

In **Adlerian parent education groups**, for example, developmental and preventive aspects of parenting are stressed; the focus is on empowering parents to consider the dynamics and purposes of their children's behaviors.

One variation of an Adlerian psychoeducational group is the **C group**: collaboration, consultation, clarification, confrontation, concern, confidentiality, and commitment.

Three unifying factors that link Adlerian groups together are the emphasis on an **interpretation of a person's early history**; the practice of stressing individual, interpersonal, and group process goals during the duration of the group; and the four phases of Adlerian group counseling.

### Role of the Adlerian Group Leader

The ideal leader is a well-balanced person who possesses certain characteristics: adaptability, courage, humor, sincerity, an acceptance of others, and an openness that promotes honest interchange with group members.

Group leaders must have good knowledge of their clients and be active in attacking in a timely manner the **faulty logic** (i.e., irrational ideas) their clients hold.

The group leader is a participant in the group process in a collaborative manner.

Adlerian leaders strive to stay true to the theory behind the process yet also be inventive.

### Desired Outcome of Adlerian Groups

The outcomes of Adlerian group practice focus primarily on the growth and actions of the individual within the group rather than the group itself.

On a global level, members of an Adlerian group experience should be more socially oriented, personally integrated, and goal directed when the group ends.

Children in Adlerian groups should recognize more clearly the logical consequences of their actions and who they can be.

Adolescents in Adlerian groups are specifically helped to deal better with their own and others' perceptions of themselves and to realize they do not have to engage in competitive behaviors to be accepted.

With families and adults, Adlerian groups are directed toward social adjustment.

In Adlerian task/work groups, the outcome from these groups should also be one that emphasizes social cooperation and teamwork (Larson & LaFasto, 1989).

## Evaluation of Adlerian Groups
### *Strengths and Contributions*
Adlerian groups are generally helpful to participants because of their educational emphasis. Many Adlerian groups are based on a healthy rather than a sick model of operating (Moask, 2000).

The methods associated with the Adlerian approach are logical and based on "common sense" (Corsini, 1988; Sweeney, 1999). Most group participants do not feel put off by the terms or procedures used.

Adlerian groups are holistic.

Adlerians are not tied to rigid procedures and methods.

Another strong point of the Adlerian approach is its flexibility in working with varied populations.

### *Limitations*
A drawback of Adlerian group work is the leader's style in regard to procedure. If the group leader deviates somewhat from Adlerian principles, the group may have difficulty.

One limitation of the groups derived from Adlerian theory is the narrowness of their scope, in assuming that all problems are socially based.

Adlerian groups lack a uniformity of method and lack concreteness of techniques in group work.

## REALITY THERAPY GROUPS

**Reality therapy** has a dynamic history. Since its original development in the 1950s and 1960s, reality therapy has evolved.

Reality therapy was initially employed more in groups than with individuals.

The success of reality therapy in education has been so successful that there is even a Quality School Consortium composed of over 200 schools using reality therapy principles.

Reality therapy has been applied to many populations of those seeking mental health services (Glasser, 1969, 1976, 1986b; Glasser & Breggin, 2001) and in task/work environments.

## Premises of Reality Therapy Groups
Unlike most other helping theories, Glasser claims that human behavior is not a reaction to outside events but rather to internal needs.

**Reality therapy's four human psychological needs** are belonging, power, freedom, and fun, whose origin is the "new" human brain. There is also one physiological need, survival, which originated in the "old" human brain (Glasser, 1985).

Glasser believes that third-force psychology with its humanistic emphasis, as represented by the writings of Abraham Maslow, is closely aligned to reality therapy.

A main emphasis of reality therapy is also cognitive and behavioral in nature, as illustrated in Wubbolding's (1991, 1992, 2001) acronym WDEP, where $W$ = wants, $D$ = direction and doing, $E$ = evaluation, and $P$ = planning.

## Practice of Reality Therapy in a Group

The practice of reality therapy in a group setting is basically a rational and pragmatic process. It emphasizes observable behavior in a here-and-now setting (Glasser, 1992, 2000).

Wubbolding (2001) stressed that there are two main components involved in using reality therapy in groups—setting up the environment and applying proper procedures using the WDEP framework.

In addition to Glasser's current eight-step procedure, Wubbolding (1988, 1991) suggests four special techniques that are applicable to setting up the environment of a reality therapy group: (a) skillful use of questioning, (b) self-help procedures, (c) use of humor, and (d) use of paradox.

## Role of the Reality Therapy Group Leader

Reality therapy group leaders are active and involved with group members.

Glasser (1965) lists four criteria for effective reality therapy leaders.

Corey (2000) states reality therapy practitioners must serve as a personal model of responsible behavior (i.e., being a success identity).

## Desired Outcome of Reality Therapy Groups

Among the most important is the change members will experience in moving past self-defeating patterns of behavior.

Group members come away from the reality therapy experience with a greater awareness of their values.

Outside events and past histories lose much of their power if individuals learn one of the basic premises of the reality therapy approach — they are responsible and can choose to change.

Reality therapy has been used in a number of different kinds of groups and is among the most versatile of the theories used in groups.

## Evaluation of Reality Therapy Groups
### *Strengths and Contributions*

Reality therapy emphasizes accountability (Wubbolding, 2001).

A strength of this approach is its stress on action and thinking, as opposed to feeling and physiology (Glasser, 1986a, 2000).

A valuable dimension of a reality therapy group is its viability with people in the society on which others have given up (Glasser & Breggin, 2001).

A strength of this approach is its emphasis on definable procedures for working with individuals in groups (Glasser, 1986b; Wubbolding, 1987, 1999).

Using reality therapy in groups allows that the treatment continues only until participants are able to resolve difficulties. As a way of promoting positive change, reality therapy is a relatively brief approach (Wubbolding, 1988, 1999).

### *Limitations*
Individuals who cannot or will not communicate, either verbally or in writing (Glasser, 1984) do not benefit very much from this approach.

Another limitation is its apparent simplicity. Glasser's eight-step method of conducting a group or Wubbolding's WDEP model may be misapplied by "mechanical" group leaders who do not understand or appreciate the complexity of human nature and change.

A drawback of reality therapy is its extreme position on some issues (e.g., that people choose to behave in mentally ill ways).

A limitation of this theory in group work is its lack of proven effectiveness.

A final limitation of reality therapy is its emphasis on conformity and utility.

## Key Concepts

acting "as if"
Adlerian parent education
"C" group
control theory
eight basic steps of reality therapy
encouragement
group process goals
individual goals
insight
insight and reorientation phases of the group
interpretation of a person's early history
integrity therapy
interpersonal goals
natural consequences
paradox
push button
reality therapy
reality therapy's four human psychological needs
reality therapy's original eight basic steps
reorientation
setting up the environment
social interest
style of life
Systematic Training for Effective Parenting (S.T.E.P.)

task setting
total quality movement (TQM)

## Key Personalities

*Can you identify and discuss the contributions of the following experts?*

Adler, Alfred
Christensen, Oscar
Corsini, Raymond
Dinkmeyer, Donald
Dreikurs, Rudolf
Glasser, William
Sonstegard, Manford
Wubbolding, Robert

## In-Class or Small-Group Discussion Prompts and Activities:

A. What are your initial reactions to Adlerian and reality therapy approaches to working with groups? What in particular feeds this reaction? Be specific in order to support your position to others in the group.

- After sharing your reaction and hearing what others think and feel, how has your initial reaction changed, if at all? What elements of others' reactions are you drawn to? How did others' positions affect your own?

- Do you notice any subgroups forming within your class or study group arising from your unique positions? Talk about the potential detrimental effect that such a subgroup might have in your discussion group.

B. These theories share some things in common that allow them to be paired even if only for such academic purposes as the organization of chapters in your group work text. What do Adlerian and reality therapy share? Consider answering this question in two ways: What do they share in a very academic way? What do they share in a more affective/felt way? How are these theories uniquely different?

_____
_____
_____
_____
_____
_____
_____
_____

C. What elements (e.g., terms, concepts, procedures, techniques) from this theoretical approach to group work are you unsure of or confused by? Discuss them; help one another to better understand. Analyze your questions. Do you conclude anything about either theory as a result?

_____
_____
_____
_____
_____
_____
_____
_____
_____

**Activity:** For a moment, imagine yourself to be a group leader practicing from this theory, this approach.

1. Imagine yourself leading this group from either an Adlerian or reality therapy theoretical vantage point. What fits you best from this vantage? And what does not fit? Why? Which of your personality features (states or traits) do you become aware of while leading this imaginary group?

_____
_____
_____
_____
_____
_____
_____

2. Who, in your small discussion group, do you picture most able to lead a group from this theoretical orientation? Why? What do you see in him or her that forms your opinion? What does that individual think and feel about your "nomination" as an Adlerian or reality therapy group leader? Who is the member "least" aligned with this approach, in your opinion? Why? What is her or his reaction?

_____
_____
_____
_____
_____
_____
_____
_____

3. Envision your group members, each carefully screened as appropriate for the group you are leading. What are they like? How does "seeing" them through this theoretical lens affect "who" you see? What about these imaginary group members is distinctive to the theory that you are adhering to for this group?

- How does your understanding of this theory influence your member selection? What do you see as advantages or disadvantages to leadership from Adlerian or reality therapy with underrepresented group members (e.g., an African American member, a bisexual client, a deaf member)?

_____
_____
_____
_____
_____
_____
_____
_____
_____

4. Divide your class or small group into two (or three) "theory teams" and discuss one of the following prompts for a few moments. Then, if you wish, switch "teams" and try again. Following this activity discuss your reactions—remember to include what you felt not just what you thought.

- The way "we" conceptualize and implement our task as group leaders affords "us" the best opportunity to reach our intended goals. Members are best served by this approach to leadership.

- Members in "our" groups are at an advantage over "your" members because "our" members" are/have/will/can _____ *(list several advantages)* _____.

_____
_____
_____
_____
_____
_____
_____
_____

**206**

5. Consider the chapters on working with children, adolescents, adults, and the elderly in groups. Identify and share in your small group elements from both Adlerian and Reality therapy's theoretical perspectives that you believe would appeal to members from each of these four developmental groups. Is there anything that you agree would disadvantage one or more of these age groups by adhering to either of these two theories?

_____
_____
_____
_____
_____
_____
_____
_____
_____

**Activity:** Without exception the ten theories covered in the Gladding text and here in this workbook are left wanting for empirical support of their approach. Theorists and practitioners alike would greatly value sound research that would show one theory as superior over others (although, perhaps thankfully, such a claim is unlikely to ever emerge).

For Adlerian or reality therapy theories of group leadership and practice covered in this chapter, design one or more research projects to learn more about one of these theories.

1. What are the questions about Adlerian or reality therapy that you would like to investigate through your research? Knowing what you do about research design (and keeping in mind ethical practice) how might you go about testing your hypotheses?
2. What do you see as dependent and independent variables in your research?
3. Are you drawn toward any particular research design? Are either quantitative or qualitative methods more appealing to you for asking and answering questions about these theories?
4. What are the complexities and challenges that you encounter in your design?
5. Extend this activity if you wish by reviewing the professional literature. Look for actual empirical research that attempts to accomplish what you and your group member colleagues have proposed.

_____
_____
_____
_____
_____
_____
_____
_____
_____

**Activity:** Individually locate one or two texts written by recognized authors who claim allegiance to either Adlerian or reality therapy theory. After skimming (or reading if time permits) these original sources, prepare a short statement (one page) that you will read to your class or to study group members "selling" your theoretical perspective. How do others receive your statement? What reactions do they have? Discuss either as a class or in small groups.

## Self Assessment Questions

### True or False Statements

The following statements check your comprehension of terms and identification of individuals (knowledge and comprehension level); your ability to apply that knowledge to solve more challenging questions (application level), and your ability to evaluate given information (analysis and evaluation level).

Indicate whether each statement is true or false. If you believe a statement is false, identify the error in the space provided. When necessary, refer to your text, *Group Work: A Counseling Specialty* (4th ed.). An answer key appears at the end of this book.

1. Adler's concept of *social interest* has to do with feelings of concern for others and a positive attitude toward people.

_____
_____
_____

2. Adlerian group leaders believe that members can learn from one another, which represents a critical theoretical underpinning.

_____
_____
_____

3. Adlerian "C group" components have contributed to widely popular psychoeducational parent education programs, including STEP and Active Parenting.

_____
_____
_____

4. Group members are encouraged to act differently and take more control of their lives as a result of Adlerian group counseling. This outcome is called acting "as if."

_____
_____
_____

5. Adlerian group work upholds that all problems are socially based.

_____
_____
_____

6. Adlerian group leaders rely on members as leaders.

_____
_____
_____

7. Glasser's control theory is the current theoretical underpinning of reality therapy.

_____
_____
_____

8. The four human psychological needs addressed in reality therapy are freedom, relationships, power, and love.

_____

_____

_____

9. The main emphases of reality therapy are cognitive and behavioral in nature.

_____

_____

_____

10. Reality therapy's original eight basic steps includes "never give up."

_____

_____

_____

11. Wubbolding's (1999) acronym SAMIC stands for "simple, attainable, measurable, immediate, and courageous."

_____

_____

_____

12. Reality therapy's perspective that ALL behavior is chosen is a notable drawback for all community mental health practitioners.

_____

_____

_____

13. Group leaders of reality therapy groups are completely accepting.

_____

_____

_____

14. William Glasser, who founded reality therapy, rejects the idea that there are genetically based mental illnesses.

_____

_____

_____

15. A common belief, shared by adherents of both reality and Adlerian therapies is the power and influence of society on people.

_____

_____

_____

## Multiple Choice Questions

1. Jonathan has been in and out of residential treatment facilities for most of his 16 years. He continually appears to sabotage any progress he makes, rendering his treatment goals unattainable. According to _____, Jonathan would be a strong candidate for *this* therapy.

        a. control theory                      c. TQM
        b. choice theory                    d. integrity theory

2. Wubbolding's WDEP model and Glasser's eight-step model of conducting reality therapy in groups risk misapplication resulting in _____.

        a. mechanical leadership          c. self-help groups
        b. devaluing group process      d. inability to work through impasses

3. The theoretical underpinnings of Reality therapy contend that human behavior is a reaction to _____ NOT _____.

        a. outside events / internal needs
        b. outside events / environmental needs
        c. internal needs / outside events
        d. environmental events / internal needs

4. Adlerian group leaders use all of the following techniques with when working with children EXCEPT _____.

        a. encouragement                  c. natural consequences
        b. task setting                    d. acting "as if"

5. The Adlerian concept of *social interest* is best illustrated by which of the following examples?

        a    Selena is studying much harder this semester because both she and her parents were quite disappointed with her last grades.
        b    Mark will volunteer at an urban soup kitchen next month because he believes it will look great on his application.
        c    Juan received a monetary award to honor his "care for the environment."
        d    Lu Wei will specialize in public health following the completion of her residency in epidemiology next spring.

## Group Work Scenario

Jeremy is an 11-year-old African American who lives with his mother and two younger siblings in rural, predominantly White, lower-middle class community in central Indiana. Jeremy is a "B-C" student who, for the first time, has encountered some "behavioral difficulties" in his 6th grade classroom. Prior to now, he has been quite quiet and "level-headed." His current behavior is described by his classroom teacher as "argumentative, impulsive, and rude." Jeremy willingly sees his school counselor who decides to invite Jeremy to join a counseling group she is beginning. The group will include 5 to 7 students, all from the sixth grade. Sessions will meet for approximately 40 minutes, once a week for 9 weeks. The membership is rather "issue homogeneous" but Jeremy is the only student of color in the group.

1. Considering only Adlerian and reality therapy theory, which would you use for this group and why?

_____
_____
_____
_____
_____
_____

2. What would you like to know more about before you begin counseling Jeremy? How might you go about accessing any additional information that you desire?

_____
_____
_____
_____
_____
_____

3. What are the most outstanding issues standing before this school counselor? What qualities do you hope she exhibits as she undertakes this counseling group?

_____
_____
_____
_____
_____
_____

4. How will Adlerian theory benefit Jeremy? What will the Adlerian-oriented school counselor likely emphasize, and how will those be apparent to Jeremy?

_____
_____
_____
_____
_____
_____

5. Describe the process of this group if the approach is based on reality therapy. What would Jeremy likely encounter in terms of interpersonal interactions if the school counselor led the group in this way?

_____
_____
_____
_____
_____
_____

## Journal and Reflection

Space for journaling about your group work experiences is provided below. Use this space to reflect on your reading about group work, your classroom presentations and activities, the group dynamics of your classes themselves, and any simulations or actual group participation opportunities you may have. Comment here thoughtfully. Be sure to carefully honor your ethical commitment to uphold the confidentiality of others in your group. Reflections are yours and are not to reveal anyone else's information. Recording your thoughts and feelings will provide a written history of this phase of your group work education. (Attach additional sheets of paper if desired.)

_Entry date_ _____

# GESTALT AND PSYCHODRAMA GROUPS

## Outcome Objectives

1. I understand and can describe Gestalt groups, including:
   a. the premises upon which Gestalt groups are built;
   b. the application of Gestalt theory in group work;
   c. the role of the Gestalt group leader; and
   d. the desired outcome of Gestalt groups.
2. I understand and can describe psychodrama groups, including:
   a. the premises upon which psychodrama groups are built;
   b. the application of psychodrama in group work;
   c. the role of the psychodrama group leader; and
   d. the desired outcome of psychodrama groups.

## Chapter Overview

Gestalt and psychodrama are experiential in nature. Gestalt group work focuses primarily on client awareness and interpersonal interactions. Psychodrama is one of the most active and powerful group approaches to be found. The psychodrama requires a highly experienced director/group leader, and within psychodrama, individuals can release old feelings and try out new behaviors in the safety of the group.

## Chapter Highlights

Gestalt and psychodrama groups are experiential in nature and generally stress interpersonal interactions and learning through awareness and enactment.

## GESTALT GROUPS

Gestalt therapy is an experiential and humanistic approach to change, which focuses on working with client awareness.

Gestalt group therapy complements individual and couples work, but does not replace them as treatment modalities.

In his original workshops, "Perls and his immediate disciples preferred to focus on the group solely as a backdrop for individual work"; they would concentrate on one individual at a time (Shaffer & Galinsky, 1989, p. 121).

It was the ideas and processes generated by Perls, however, combined with those of Kepner (1980) and Zinker (1977) that have evolved into what is now known as the Gestalt group process.

## Premises of Gestalt Groups

Four basic assumptions (principles) underlie Gestalt groups: holism, awareness, figure/ground, and polarities (Latner (1973).

Gestalt group process is based on the assumption that groups are multidimensional systems that operate on several levels at once.

Gestalt therapy is premised on the idea that individuals will experience a certain amount of "elasticity" between their more pressing needs (figure) and their less pressing needs (background).

Gestalt group process stresses increasing awareness, choice, meaningfulness, integrative wholeness, and closure (Mullan & Rosenbaum, 1978; Vander Kolk, 1985).

### Practice of Gestalt Theory in a Group
Gestalt group process is often misperceived as individual "hot seat" psychotherapy in a group setting (Shaffer & Galinsky, 1989; Yalom, 1995).

A Gestalt leader focuses on one person in the presence of other group members and works with him or her.

Gestalt group practitioners share many common beliefs and practices: the here and now (i.e., present experiences), work on a specific problem to help foster greater awareness, emphasis on behavioral, rather than cognitive, processes (Zinker, 1977), and the use of experiments and exercises to help their members achieve greater awareness and growth (Resnikoff, 1988).

Experiments and exercises revolve around five main themes: (a) enactment, (b) directed behavior, (c) fantasy, (d) dreams, and (e) homework (Polster & Polster, 1973).

### Role of the Gestalt Group Leader
The group leader is central to the functioning of the Gestalt group.

One of the leader's jobs is to help group members locate their **impasses** (the places in which they get stuck) and work through them so awareness and growth will take place (Corey, 2000).

The leader balances challenging group members with supporting them.

Gestalt group leaders play several roles over the group's life span: (a) expert-helper; (b) seer, communications expert; (c) frustrator; (d) creator; and (e) teacher (Levin & Shepherd, 1974).

### Desired Outcome of Gestalt Groups
As a result of a Gestalt group, members should be more aware of themselves in the here and now.

Members will be more congruent in themselves (mind and body) and with others. They will not be mired down in worrying about the past and will become more self-regulating. The experiential quality of Gestalt groups is especially beneficial for persons who are predominantly cognitive, for it forces them to use other ways of relating.

The key to whether a Gestalt group is beneficial is whether the leader is well trained.

### Evaluation of Gestalt Groups
#### Strengths and Contributions

Gestalt group work lends itself well to leaders who are creative and who strive to bring out the creativity in others.

Gestalt groups focus within the groups on working through impasses and becoming more integrated.

A strong point of Gestalt groups is the variety of exercises and experiences they foster. Gestalt group work is usually intense and active (Day & Matthes, 1992).

Gestalt groups are also quite powerful in working with a variety of client difficulties.

Another strength of the Gestalt groups is the abundance of training institutes available to professionals who wish to learn this approach.

### *Limitations*
The Gestalt approach tends to eschew the cognitive side of human nature.

Gestalt group leaders are sometimes not able to help the group help itself — that is, to work through impasses.

A limitation of the Gestalt approach is the potential danger of abusing techniques and people.

Gestalt groups are extremely difficult to research (Fagan & Shepherd, 1970); therefore very little empirical research has been conducted on them.

## PSYCHODRAMA GROUPS

**Psychodrama**, a way of exploring the human psyche through dramatic action, was created and developed by Moreno in the 1920s and 1930s (D'Amato & Dean, 1988; Goldman & Morrison, 1984).

Psychodrama (Moreno, 1923, 1984) as a formal system was conceptualized with Moreno stressing the uniqueness of the approach by having clients relive, instead of retell or analyze, their conflicts.

## Premises of Group Psychodrama
Psychodrama is similar to psychoanalysis in that it emphasizes a freeing of individuals from the irrational forces that bind them into dysfunctional patterns of behaving.

In psychodrama, the client is removed from the usual one-to-one relationship with the psychotherapist or counselor and given an opportunity to act out and experience various aspects of his or her problem(s) within a group setting.

A focused emphasis of psychodrama is on the holistic interaction of the protagonist in his or her drama. The group leader is the producer of the drama.

Enactments are based on a client's memories and shown in dramatic form rather than discussed.

At the heart of psychodrama is the **encounter**, an existentialist concept that involves total physical and psychological contact between persons on an intense, concrete, and complete basis in the here and now.

The main concepts emphasizing Moreno's premise of experiencing one's situation fully in the here and now are spontaneity and creativity, situation, tele, catharsis, insight (Greenberg, 1974b).

## Practice of Psychodrama in a Group

Physical and personal factors must be considered in psychodrama, such as a stage, a protagonist, actors, a director, and an audience (Blatner, 1996, 1989; Haskell, 1973), and techniques must be employed in a methodological manner (Holmes & Karp, 1991; Moreno, 1959).

The techniques employed in psychodrama are dependent on many variables. Among the most important factors that influence which techniques will be used are the situation of the protagonist, the skill of the director, the availability of actors, the size of the audience, the goals of the session, and the phase in which the psychodrama is operating.

The psychodrama process generally goes through three phases: warm-up (pre-action), action, and integration.

There are literally hundreds of psychodrama techniques with many variations, including: creative imagery, magic shop, sculpting, soliloquy, monodrama, double and multiple double, role reversal, and mirror.

## Role of the Psychodrama Group Leader

The director is the leader of a psychodrama and as such wears many hats. Moreno (1953, 1964) suggests that the **director** serves as a producer, a facilitator, an observer, and an analyzer.

Overall, Corsini (1966) concludes that effective group directors possess three qualities: creativity, courage, and charisma.

## Desired Psychodrama Group Outcome

The desired outcome of psychodrama can be described as the creation of catharsis, insight, and emotional resolution (Moreno, 1964).

Through psychodrama, individuals should be able to experience and work through past, present, or anticipated events that have caused them distress.

Participants in psychodramas must be willing to take risks and be open to constructive feedback from the audience and director.

## Evaluation of Psychodrama Groups
### *Strengths and Contributions*

A major strength of psychodrama is its diversity (Greenberg, 1974a). Psychodrama is appropriately used in psychotherapeutic environments, as well as in psychoeducational and business settings.

Psychodrama can be employed with individuals of all age, educational, and socioeconomic levels.

Another positive aspect of psychodrama is its teaching potential.

One strength of a psychodrama group is its fostering of creativity and spontaneity within leaders and members (Coven, Ellington, & Van Hull, 1997).

Psychodrama has an integrative and vicarious effect. Psychodrama emphasizes action coupled with emotional release. A by-product of this process is the change in thoughts that accompanies changes in behavior and emotion (Coven et al., 1997).

Another strength of psychodrama is the input and feedback the audience and actors give the protagonist and each other (Moreno, 1964).

### *Limitations*
A major limitation of psychodrama is the danger of overexposing the protagonist to him- or herself, as well as to the audience (Greenberg, 1974a).

An area of considerable concern to many professional group workers is the quantity and quality of the research underlying psychodrama (D'Amato & Dean, 1988; Kellermann, 1987); the central tenets of the theory have not been empirically verified.

Another limitation of psychodrama is connected with the availability of training (Greenberg, 1974a). At present, there are few training centers for directors.

Psychodrama is may focus too much on expression of feelings rather than change in behavior.

## Key Concepts
        action exercises
        action phase
        actors
        amplify
        audience
        awareness
        body language
        catharsis
        changing questions to statements
        condemning questions
        creative imagery
        dialogue
        director
        double and multiple double
        dream work
        dual-focused Gestalt group work
        elasticity
        emotional debris
        empty chair technique
        encounter
        energy field
        exercises
        experiments
        fantasy exercises
        floating hot seat
        "Greek chorus"
        here and now
        homework
        "hot seat"
        impasses
        insight
        integration phase
        intrinsically neutral

"Living Newspaper"
layers of nuerosis
magic shop
making the rounds
mirror
monodrama
multiple double
principle of awareness
principle of figure/ground
principle of holism
principle of polarities
protagonist
psychodrama
rehearsal
role reversal
sculpting
situation
soliloquy
spillover effect
spontaneity
stage
surplus reality
tele
"Theater of Spontaneity"
top dog/ underdog dialogue
trilevel model of Gestalt group work
unfinished business
warm-up phase


## Key Personalities

*Can you identify and discuss the contributions of the following experts?*

Blatner, A.
Goodman, P.
Kepner, E
Lewin, Kurt
Moreno, Jacob
Moreno, Zerka
Perls, Fritz

**In-Class or Small-Group Discussion Prompts and Activities:**

A. What are your initial reactions to Gestalt and psychodrama theoretical approaches to working with groups? What in particular feeds this reaction? Be specific in order to support your position to others in the group.

- After sharing your reaction and hearing what others think and feel, how has your initial reaction changed if at all? What elements of others' reactions are you drawn to? How did others' positions affect your own?

- Do you notice any subgroups forming within your class or study group arising from your unique positions? Talk about the potential detrimental effect that such a subgroup might have in your discussion group.

_____
_____
_____
_____
_____
_____
_____
_____

B. These theories share some things in common that allow them to be paired even if only for such academic purposes as the organization of chapters in your group work text. What do Gestalt and psychodrama share? Consider answering this question in two ways: What do they share in a very academic way? What do they share in a more affective/felt way? How are these theories uniquely different?

_____
_____
_____
_____
_____
_____
_____
_____

C. What elements (e.g., terms, concepts, procedures, techniques) from these theoretical approachs to group work are you unsure of or confused by? Discuss them; help one another to better understand. Analyze your questions. Do you conclude anything about the theory as a result?

_____
_____
_____
_____
_____
_____
_____

**Activity:** For a moment, imagine yourself to be a group leader practicing from this theory, this approach.

1. Imagine yourself leading this group from either the Gestalt or psychodrama theoretical vantage point. What fits you best from this vantage? And what does not fit? Why? Which of your personality features (states or traits) do you become aware of while leading this imaginary group?

_____
_____
_____
_____
_____
_____
_____
_____
_____

2. Who in your small discussion group do you picture most able to lead a group from this theoretical orientation? Why? What do you see in him or her that forms your opinion? What does that individual think and feel about your "nomination" as either a Gestalt or psychodrama group leader? Who is the member "least" aligned with this approach, in your opinion? Why? What is her or his reaction?

_____
_____
_____
_____
_____
_____
_____
_____
_____

3. Envision your group members, each carefully screened as appropriate for the group you are leading. What are they like? How does "seeing" them through either a Gestalt or a psychodrama lens affect "who" you see? What about these imaginary group members is distinctive to the theory that you are adhering to for this group?

- How does your understanding of this theory influence your member selection? What do you see as advantages or disadvantages to leadership from Gestalt or psychodrama with underrepresented group members (e.g., a Hispanic member, a lesbian client, a physically challenged member)?

_____
_____
_____
_____
_____
_____
_____
_____
_____

4. Divide your class or small group into two (or three) "theory teams" and discuss one of the following prompts for a few moments. Then, if you wish, switch "teams" and try again. Following this activity discuss your reactions—remember to include what you felt not just what you thought.

- The way "we" conceptualize and implement our task as group leaders affords "us" the best opportunity to reach our intended goals. Members are best served by this approach to leadership.

- Members in "our" groups are at an advantage over "your" members because "our" members" are/have/will/can _____ *(list several advantages)* .

_____
_____
_____
_____
_____
_____
_____
_____

5. Consider the chapters on working with children, adolescents, adults, and the elderly in groups. Identify and share in your small group elements from Gestalt and psychodrama perspectives that you believe would appeal to members from each of these four developmental groups. Is there anything that you agree would disadvantage one or more of these age groups by adhering to either of these two theories?

_____
_____
_____
_____
_____
_____
_____
_____

**Activity:** Without exception the ten theories covered in the Gladding text and here in this workbook are left wanting for empirical support of their approach. Theorists and practitioners alike would greatly value sound research that would show one theory as superior over others (although, perhaps thankfully, such a claim is unlikely to ever emerge).

For Gestalt or psychodrama theories of group leadership and practice covered in this chapter, design one or more research projects to learn more about one of these theories.
1. What are the questions that you would like to investigate through your research? Knowing what you do about research design (and keeping in mind ethical practice) how might you go about testing your hypotheses?
2. What do you find to be important variables in your research of either Gestalt or psychodrama?
3. Are you drawn toward any particular research design? Are either quantitative or qualitative methods more appealing to you for asking and answering questions about these theories?

4. What are the complexities and challenges that you encounter in your research design for these two theories?

5. Extend this activity by reviewing the professional literature. Look for actual empirical research that attempts to accomplish what you and your group member colleagues have proposed.

_____
_____
_____
_____
_____
_____
_____
_____
_____

**Activity:** Individually locate one or two texts written by recognized authors who claim allegiance to either Gestalt or psychodrama theory. After skimming (or reading if time permits) these original sources, prepare a short statement (one page) that you will read to your class or to study group members "selling" your theoretical perspective. How do others receive your statement? What reactions do they have? Discuss either as a class or in small groups.

## Self Assessment Questions

### True or False Statements

The following statements check your comprehension of terms and identification of individuals (knowledge and comprehension level); your ability to apply that knowledge to solve more challenging questions (application level), and your ability to evaluate given information (analysis and evaluation level).

Indicate whether each statement is true or false. If you believe a statement is false, identify the error in the space provided. When necessary, refer to your text, *Group Work: A Counseling Specialty* (4th ed.). An answer key appears at the end of this book.

1. Gestalt therapy focuses on working toward change through increasing client awareness.

_____
_____
_____

2. Many Gestalt therapists disagree with Perl's belief that clients can be treated by group Gestalt therapy.

_____
_____
_____

3. The empty chair is seen by Perls as "the royal road to integration" and can be done either individually or with the help of the group.

_____
_____
_____

4. A likely goal of a Gestalt therapist is to bring about a client's integration with an unresolved loss of a love object.

_____

_____

_____

5. Elasticity describes how individuals experience great difficulties moving from one set of needs (i.e., foreground) to another (i.e., background) and back again.

_____

_____

_____

6. An exercise early in a Gestalt group called the "floating hot seat" is where members might be asked to share something that they rarely share with others.

_____

_____

_____

7. Gestalt group therapy fantasy exercises can help client/members express feelings of guilt and shame and become more involved in group.

_____

_____

_____

8. A result of Gestalt group therapy would be that the client deals effectively with learning to "be authentic", "see themselves as they really are", and "get past where his or her maturity is stuck."

_____

_____

_____

9. Psychodrama is a way of exploring the psyche through dramatic action.

_____

_____

_____

10. One result of psychodrama that Moreno noticed in all members was for the clients to observe the lives of others.

_____

_____

_____

11. Insight involves often intense physical and psychological contact and is the heart of psychodrama.

_____

_____

_____

12. In a psychodrama, *tele* involves the experience of dialogue that transcends physical reality.

_____

_____

_____

13. Group members form the "audience," a role that includes giving feedback and acting as auxiliary cast members.

_____

_____

_____

14. During "warm-up," members are led by the psychodrama director through exercises, which aid members focusing on individual concerns.

_____

_____

_____

15. Psychodrama directors observe and instigate group member conflict.

_____

_____

_____

16. Soliloquy is used when the protagonist plays all the parts of the psychodrama rather than employing other actors.

_____

_____

_____

17. The emotional experience that results in a release of pent up feelings is known as catharsis.

_____

_____

_____

**Multiple Choice Questions**

1. The *purpose* of the "floating hot seat" is for members in Gestalt group therapy to work on exploring their own personal issues when _____.
    a. it is their turn        c. members' issues trigger their own
    b. the leader calls on them    d. another finishes

2. Alison continues to hold on rather frantically to her guilt and suffering related to the tragic death of her younger sibling nearly 20 years earlier. It seems all she talks about in group. This "holding on" is referred to by Gestalt therapists as _____.
    a. cathexis        c. garbage thinking
    b. emotional debris    d. dialogue

3. Which of the following does NOT represents a *layer of neurosis* that successful Gestalt group members shed in therapy.
    a. the phony        c. the impasse
    b. the phobic        d. the protagonist

4. The task of conducting multiple roles that the leader takes on in psychodrama (e.g., facilitator, observer, and analyzer) is often called the _____.
   a. director  c. sculptor
   b. orchestra  d. (all of the above)

5. One potential drawback for the promulgation of psychodrama is, at the present, psychodrama's _____.
   a. lack of training opportunities
   b. inconclusive empirical support
   c. failure to work effectively with culturally diverse members
   d. dwindling public interest in light of managed care

**Group Work Scenario**

Elaine comes to counseling reluctantly. She is "coming only because I'm losing my patience with my kids, my partner, and my business contacts, and I am seriously stressed-out about my whole life!" She is very bright and very successful in academic and professional accomplishments. Elaine is "psychologically-minded" but admittedly has not been handling herself well for months. Beyond "stress" she reports not sleeping well, having little interest in her life-partner of 17 years, and says, "I would sort of like to climb under a big rock and hide for the next century or so!"

1. Envision yourself as either (or at least one at a time) a Gestalt group therapist or a psychodrama director. What are key elements, principles, beliefs that you hold?

_____
_____
_____
_____
_____
_____

2. As a Gestalt group therapist, what do you think Elaine's group counseling experience will look like? What kinds of interventions would she be introduced to?

_____
_____
_____
_____
_____
_____

3. Select two or three *experiments* or *exercises* that you would utilize while working with Elaine. What is it about her presenting difficulties that drew you toward these interventions?

_____
_____
_____
_____
_____
_____
_____

4. Describe Elaine's experience joining a psychodrama group. What are several things that Elaine is likely to do there?

_____
_____
_____
_____
_____
_____
_____

5. What are the roles of other members in the psychodrama group that Elaine joins? What functions will Elaine play for others as the group moves from warm-up through integration?

_____
_____
_____
_____
_____
_____
_____

6. As either a Gestalt leader or a psychodrama director, what do you believe will be the most challenging aspect of working with Elaine?

_____
_____
_____
_____
_____
_____
_____

## Journal and Reflection

Space for journaling about your group work experiences is provided below. Use this space to reflect on your reading about group work, your classroom presentations and activities, the group dynamics of your classes themselves, and any simulations or actual group participation opportunities you may have. Comment here thoughtfully. Be sure to carefully honor your ethical commitment to uphold the confidentiality of others in your group. Reflections are yours and are not to reveal anyone else's information. Recording your thoughts and feelings will provide a written history of this phase of your group work education. (Attach additional sheets of paper if desired.)

_Entry date_ _____

# RATIONAL-EMOTIVE BEHAVIORAL THERAPY (REBT) AND BEHAVIORAL THERAPY GROUPS

## Outcome Objectives

1. I understand and can describe rational emotive behavior therapy groups, including:
    a. the premises upon which rational emotive behavior therapy groups are built;
    b. the application of rational emotive behavior theory in group work;
    c. the role of the rational emotive behavior therapy group leader; and
    d. the desired outcome of rational emotive behavior therapy groups.

2. I understand and can describe behavioral therapy groups, including:
    a. the premises upon which behavioral therapy groups are built;
    b. the application of behavioral therapy in group work;
    c. the role of the behavioral therapy group leader; and
    d. the desired outcome of behavioral therapy groups.

## Chapter Overview

Rational-emotive behavioral therapy groups and behavioral groups are popular approaches to working with groups. REBT utilizes many affective, behavioral, and cognitive methods with group members to bring about change. The belief that feelings emanate from thoughts, not events, is key to this approach. Behavioral therapy groups build upon a long tradition of behaviorism. Within groups, members in addition to the leader offer support toward attaining clearly specified goals. Behavioral group therapy has impressive empirical support for its methods.

## Chapter Highlights

Cognitive and behavioral theories of group work focus primarily on how thought processes and actions affect the overall functioning of group members.

Cognitive and behavioral approaches to human relations are based on a theory of personality which maintains that how one thinks and/or behaves largely determines how one feels and functions (Beck & Weishaar, 2000; Wilson, 2000) and what one does indicates who one is.

These approaches have a history of being used extensively in psychoeducational, counseling, and psychotherapeutic groups and occasionally in task/work groups.

### RATIONAL-EMOTIVE BEHAVIORAL THERAPY GROUPS

**Rational-emotive behavioral therapy (REBT)** was originally known as rational-emotive therapy (RET) but changed its name when its founder, Albert Ellis (2000), decided his approach needed to be more reflective of what the theory actually did: focus on behavior as well as cognitions.

From the beginning, REBT groups have been quite varied (Ellis, 1997).

Groups with as many as 100 meet for the purpose of demonstrating REBT principles, a psychoeducational, skills-learning approach.

Groups conducted by REBT practitioners include open-ended and closed-ended psychotherapy and counseling sessions that may include group marathons (Ellis & Dryden, 1997).

Numbers in REBT counseling and psychotherapy groups are usually limited to a dozen.

## Premises of Rational-Emotive Behavioral Therapy Groups

Rational-emotive behavioral therapy is based on the idea that one's thinking about events, not external circumstances, produces feelings and behaviors.

To behave rationally, individuals need first to control their thoughts and behaviors (Ellis, 1962, 1995, 2000).

The process of change is built on an **A-B-C model of human interaction**, in which "A" is the event, "B" is the thought process, and "C" is the feeling state resulting from one's thoughts.

Rational-emotive behavioral therapy stresses the **dual nature of human beings**. Individuals have both rational and irrational beliefs that can be modified through disputation (Ellis, 1976).

## Practice of Rational-Emotive Behavioral Therapy Groups

REBT groups tend to be didactic, philosophical, and skills oriented (Corey, 2000; Hansen, Warner, & Smith, 1980).

The leader introduces REBT theory to the group, and then group members are asked to share troublesome problems or concerns that are usually of a personal nature.

Group members, as well as the leader, give feedback and suggestions to the person who initially presented (Ellis, 2000). The feedback is in the form of disputation, which takes three main forms: cognitive, imaginal, and behavioral (Gladding, 2000).

Very little attention is paid to past events in the group.

In many ways, REBT groups can be conceptualized as psychoeducational in both theory and practice. Members learn a new way of life and, through sharing with each other, reinforce appropriate ideas and behaviors.

Participants in REBT groups are exposed to a wide variety of cognitive and behavioral methods. Techniques include actively disputing clients' thoughts, persuading them to work from a REBT viewpoint, teaching clients the ABCs of REBT, and giving clients feedback on the rational outcomes of their thoughts.

## Role of the Rational-Emotive Behavioral Therapy Group Leader

"The Rational-Emotive group is leader-centered. It is the leader's task to make sure that the group is philosophically and cognitively based" (Hansen et al., 1980, p. 246).

The leader encourages rational thinking in a number of ways (Ellis, 1974).

In psychotherapeutic and counseling groups, the group leader encourages members to work as **auxiliary counselors** once someone has presented a problem.

## Desired Outcome of Rational-Emotive Behavioral Therapy Groups

A primary desired outcome of a REBT group is for group members to learn how to think rationally.

Knowing how to implement the REBT theory is not enough; it must be practiced, both inside and outside of the group context

REBT group members should have a better knowledge of how REBT can be employed in situations with which they have no firsthand experience

Members gain the experience of personally understanding the process of change.

## Evaluation of Rational-Emotive Behavioral Therapy Groups
### *Strengths and Contributions*

Rational-emotive behavioral therapy is one of the few integrative theories used in a group that places primary importance on cognitions as they are related to behaviors and affect.

It is relatively easy for everyone involved in the group process to learn how to take charge of themselves and help others in the group (Ellis, 1997).

REBT groups may be the perfect environments for clients who are phasing out of individual therapeutic counseling (Wessler & Hankin, 1988).

REBT theory applied to group work is versatile.

REBT groups emphasize action as well as talk (Rieckert & Moller, 2000).

### *Limitations*

Rational-emotive behavioral therapy is individually oriented.

REBT is confrontive and directive. Group leaders and members may push a member to get rid of faulty beliefs and adopt new thought patterns before he or she is ready.

A limitation of REBT groups is the lack of rigorous research specifically on them.

## BEHAVIORAL THERAPY GROUPS

Behavioral theories have a long and diversified history stretching back to the beginning of the 20th century (Wilson, 2000).

Behaviorists emphasize learning and modification of behaviors as opposed to the treatment of underlying symptoms.

## Premises of Behavioral Therapy Groups

In general, **behaviorists** inside and outside group settings emphasize overt processes, here-and-now experiences, learning, changing of maladaptive actions, definition of specific goals, and scientific support for techniques (Spiegler & Guevremont, 1993).

As a group, behaviorists offer a wide variety of concrete and pragmatic procedures that are tailored to the needs of particular individuals and are empirically verified.

**Behavioral groups** are either interpersonal or transactional depending on the purposes of the leader and members.

## Practice of Behavioral Therapy in a Group

Behavioral groups may form for a variety of purposes; there are specific stages and principles that universally apply to behavioral groups (Rose 1977, 1983; Hollander & Kazaoka, 1988).

Seven stages include: (1) forming the group; (2) establishing the initial group attraction and identity; (3) establishment of openness and sharing in the group; (4) establishing a behavioral framework for all participants; (5) establishing and implementing a model for change; (6) generalization and transference of treatment to the natural environment; and (7) maintaining behavior change and fading out of the need for the group's support.

Some of the most frequently used techniques are reinforcement, extinction, contingency contracts, shaping, modeling, behavioral rehearsal, coaching, cognitive restructuring, and the buddy system (Posthuma, 1999).

## Role of the Behavioral Therapy Group Leader

The behavioral group leader is a participant-observer (Hansen et al., 1980; Rose, 1983).

Behavioral group leaders may come from any of the major mental health professions or from the business and management domains.

## Desired Outcome of Behavioral Therapy Groups

Members will be more aware of what specific behaviors they and others have that need changing and how to accomplish that.

Participants will be able to assess how well they have altered their behaviors as well as what they still need to do to generalize them to their daily living environments.

Group members may realize more fully the power of group reinforcement.

As a result of this psychological and social support, they may structure their life within groups differently and become more behaviorally oriented in resolving their own difficulties outside a group setting.

## Evaluation of Behavioral Therapy Groups

Because behaviorism has a long history and strong research methods, groups based on this theory are probably among the easiest to evaluate.

### *Strengths and Contributions*

A major strength of behavioral groups is their focus on helping their members learn new ways of functioning (Spiegler & Guevremont, 1993).

A notable strength of the behavioral approach is the impressive research it has generated (Rose, 1983).

Behavioral groups are relatively short term and here and now focused (Gazda, et al., 2001; Hollander & Kazaoka, 1988).

There are very few problems behaviorists do not address. Each group is tailored to the needs of its members (Rose, 1983).

The behavioral approach emphasizes promoting self-control among its members once the group ends.

Behavioral theories can be combined with other approaches (e.g., cognitive theories) to create a multimodal way of working with groups and their members.

### *Limitations*

Group members may become overdependent on the group for support and encouragement.

A limitation of behavioral group work is that some of its methods can be too rigidly applied.

The behavioral approach has a tendency to ignore the past and the unconscious (Rose, 1977).

Behavioral groups are much more likely to concentrate on particular events or skills in their members' lives than on members' lives as a whole.

The behavioral approach is also limited in its concentration on just behavior, whether overt or covert.

Behavioral groups are not unified theoretically and work best with well-motivated members (Hollander & Kazaoka, 1988).

## Key Concepts

*Can you define and describe each of the following terms? Be able to offer a brief example or relevant context for these concepts.*

> A-B-C model of human interaction
> antecedent-response-consequence model of behaviorism
> A-R-C model
> Association for Advancement of Behavioral Therapy (AABT)
> auxiliary counselors
> behavioral disputation
> behavioral groups
> behavioral rehearsal
> behaviorist
> behavior therapy
> buddy system
> chaining
> coaching
> cognitive behaviorists
> cognitive and behavioral approaches to human relations
> cognitive disputation
> cognitive restructuring

contingency contracts
dual nature of human beings
extinction
feedback
four types of thoughts (negative, positive, neutral, and mixed)
generalization
imaginal disputation
maintenance
making wishes into demands
modeling
operant conditioning
positive expectations
radical behaviorists
Rational-Emotive Behavioral therapy (REBT)
REBT viewpoint
reinforcement
respondent conditioning
self-instructional training
self-monitoring
self-talk
shame attack
shaping
social modeling

## Key Personalities

*Can you identify and discuss the contributions of the following experts?*

Bandura, Albert
Beck, Aaron
Ellis, Albert
Krumboltz, J.
Lazarus, Arnold
Maultsby, Maxie
Meichenbaum, Donald
Pavlov, Ivan
Skinner, B. F.
Watson, J. B.
Wolpe, J.

**In-Class or Small Group Discussion Prompts nd Activities:**

A. What are your initial reactions to rational emotive behavior therapy and behavioral group therapy approaches to working with groups? What in particular feeds this reaction? Be specific in order to support your position to others in the group.

- After sharing your reaction and hearing what others think and feel, how has your initial reaction changed if at all? What elements of others' reactions are you drawn to? How did others' positions affect your own?

- Do you notice any subgroups forming within your class or study group arising from your unique positions? Talk about the potential detrimental effect that such a subgroup might have in your discussion group.

_____
_____
_____
_____
_____
_____
_____
_____
_____

B. These theories share some things in common that allow them to be paired even if only for such academic purposes as the organization of chapters in your group work text. What do rational emotive behavior therapy and behavioral therapy groups share? Consider answering this question in two ways: What do they share in a very academic way? What do they share in a more affective/felt way? How are these theories uniquely different?

_____
_____
_____
_____
_____
_____
_____
_____

C. What elements (e.g., terms, concepts, procedures, techniques) from REBT or behavioral group therapy approaches to group work are you unsure of or confused by? Discuss them; help one another to better understand. Analyze your questions. Do you conclude anything about either theory as a result?

_____
_____
_____
_____
_____
_____
_____
_____

**Activity:** For a moment, imagine yourself to be a group leader practicing from this theory, this approach.

1. Imagine yourself leading this group from either the rational emotive behavior therapy or a behavioral therapy group theoretical vantage point. What fits you best from this vantage? And what does not fit? Why? Which of your personality features (states or traits) do you become aware of while leading this imaginary group?

_____
_____
_____
_____
_____
_____
_____
_____
_____

2. Who in your small discussion group do you picture most able to lead a group from this theoretical orientation? Why? What do you see in him or her that forms your opinion? What does that individual think and feel about your "nomination" as rational emotive behavior therapy or behavioral therapy group leader? Who is the member "least" aligned with this approach, in your opinion? Why? What is her or his reaction?

_____
_____
_____
_____
_____
_____
_____
_____
_____

3. Envision your group members, each carefully screened as appropriate for the group you are leading. What are they like? How does "seeing" them through this theoretical lens affect "who" you see? What about these imaginary group members is distinctive to the theory that you are adhering to for this group?

- How does your understanding of this theory influence your member selection? What do you see as advantages or disadvantages to leadership from rational emotive behavior therapy or behavioral therapy group with underrepresented group members (e.g., a Hispanic member, a lesbian client, a physically challenged member)?

_____
_____
_____
_____
_____
_____
_____
_____

4. Divide your class or small group into two (or three) "theory teams" and discuss one of the following prompts for a few moments. Then, if you wish, switch "teams" and try again. Following this activity discuss your reactions—remember to include what you felt, not just what you thought.

- The way "we" conceptualize and implement our task as group leaders affords "us" the best opportunity to reach our intended goals. Members are best served by this approach to leadership.

- Members in "our" group are at an advantage over "your" members because "our members" are/have/will/can _____ *(list several advantages)* _____.

_____
_____
_____
_____
_____
_____
_____
_____
_____
_____

5. Consider the chapters on working with children, adolescents, adults, and the elderly in groups. Identify and share in your small group elements from rational emotive behavior therapy or behavioral therapy's theoretical perspectives that you believe would appeal to members from each of these four developmental groups. Is there anything that you agree would disadvantage one or more of these age groups by adhering to either of these two theories?

_____
_____
_____
_____
_____
_____
_____
_____
_____
_____

**Activity:** Without exception the ten theories covered in the Gladding text and here in this workbook are left wanting for empirical support of their approach. Theorists and practitioners alike would greatly value sound research that would show one theory as superior over others (although, perhaps thankfully, such a claim is unlikely to ever emerge).

For the two theories of group leadership and practice covered in this chapter, design one or more research projects to learn more about one of these theories.

1. What are the questions that you would like to investigate through your research? Knowing what you do about research design (and keeping in mind ethical practice) how might you go about testing your hypotheses?
2. What do you see as dependent and independent variables in your research?
3. Are you drawn toward any particular research design? Are either quantitative or qualitative methods more appealing to you for asking and answering questions about these theories?

4. What are the complexities and challenges that you encounter in your design?
5. Extend this activity if you wish by reviewing the professional literature. Look for actual empirical research that attempts to accomplish what you and your group member colleagues have proposed.

_____
_____
_____
_____
_____
_____
_____
_____

**Activity:** Individually locate one or two texts written by recognized authors (primary authors) who claim allegiance to one of these two theories. After skimming (or reading if time permits) these original sources, prepare a short statement (one page) that you will read to your class or to study group members "selling" your theoretical perspective. How do others receive your statement? What reactions do they have? Discuss either as a class or in small groups.

## <u>Self Assessment Questions</u>

### True or False Statements

The following statements check your comprehension of terms and identification of individuals (knowledge and comprehension level); your ability to apply that knowledge to solve more challenging questions (application level), and your ability to evaluate given information (analysis and evaluation level).

Indicate whether each statement is true or false. If you believe a statement is false, identify the error in the space provided. When necessary, refer to your text, _Group Work: A Counseling Specialty_ (4th ed.). An answer key appears at the end of this book.

1. REBT group leaders spend considerable time during the orientation phase on the REBT viewpoint in order to validate this theory and approach.

_____
_____
_____

2. Cognitive and behavioral theories of group work focus on observable behaviors in a social learning format.

_____
_____
_____

3. REBT groups tend to be didactic, philosophical, and skills oriented (Corey, 2000).

_____
_____
_____

4. Faulty beliefs may not really be discarded by some clients, and that is a potential limitation regarding the use of REBT.

_____
_____
_____

5. Donald Meichenbaum and Aaron Beck are cognitive behaviorists.

_____
_____
_____

6. Behaviorists are often viewed as esoterically oriented practitioners who emphasize overt processes, defining specific goals, and scientific support for techniques.

_____
_____
_____

7. Negative reinforcement is a behavioral process geared toward lessening unwanted behaviors.

_____
_____
_____

8. By vocalizing their self-talk aloud in the group and learning to change it when necessary, behavior therapy group members are practicing cognitive restructuring.

_____
_____
_____

9. REBT is based on the premise that messages people give themselves internally are a negative influence on their behavior and mental health.

_____
_____
_____

10. Imaginal disputation, employed in the REBT group, asks members to imagine themselves as if one day their problem or difficulty had miraculously disappeared.

_____
_____
_____

11. In REBT groups, leaders often encourage group members to serve as "helping members" following someone's disclosure to the group.

_____
_____
_____

12. A primary goal for REBT group members is to learn to think rationally.

_____
_____
_____

13. Teaching new behaviors through observation of someone else is called "coaching."

_____
_____
_____

14. Generalization, which is displaying desired behaviors outside of the learning environment, is an outcome goal for behavioral group counseling.

_____
_____
_____

15. Behavioral group leaders consider a member's unconscious processes.

_____
_____
_____

16. REBT group leaders focus on the client's past.

_____
_____
_____

**Multiple Choice Questions**

1. Based upon the confrontive and directive stance of REBT, and that the client-counselor relationship is not highly emphasized, which of the following populations might actually get worse?
    a. a depressed group member      c. a highly anxious group member
    b. a borderline group member      d. a rigid group member

2. In REBT, questions such as *"Where is holding this belief getting me?"* or *"Is my belief logical?"* are examples of _____ .
    a. disputing yourself      c. identifying irrational beliefs
    b. motivating yourself      d. (all of the above)

3. Behavioral groups that are essentially psychoeducational are usually referred to as _____ groups.
    a. interpersonal      c. radical
    b. transactional      d. social modeling

4. The process of gradually shaping a behavior by practice and feedback is known as _____.
    a. extinction      c. rehearsal
    b. chaining      d. coaching

5. REBT and behavioral group therapy share all of the following concepts EXCEPT _____.
    a. irrational beliefs      c. cognitive restructuring
    b. involuntary thoughts      d. life scripts

**Group Work Scenario**

Rachel is a fourth-year school counselor. She is responsible for the school counseling services for children grades 5, 6, and 7 in a suburban, culturally diverse community. Early in October, Sandra, a fifth-grade teacher, asks Rachel for her help. She says, "In all of my years of teaching (11), I have never had a more challenging group of students. I am having no luck controlling their unruly behavior and I fear two boys and three girls initiate it. I have spoken with them individually and they are willing to come in to see you to talk about their behavior, which, by the way, they all seem to know is obnoxious!" The two girls are Latina, from upper-middle class, rather socially precocious, and "very able to behave when they want." The three boys on the other hand often seem out of control. One, Hector, is an 11-year old who has learning difficulties and is on medication for ADHD. The other two are "very nice boys" who seem to feed off of picking relentlessly on Hector. The "oddest thing" is that Hector doesn't seem to care!

1. Rachel has been very interested in both behavioral groups and REBT for several years. She has had excellent training in both and had a good group work education in graduate school. Using the scenario (and embellishing as you wish), what would Rachel's first steps be if she in fact decides to see these five children in either a behavioral or an REBT group?

_____
_____
_____
_____
_____
_____

2. Hector says, "I am not doing some stupid 'reward chart'; I've done that at home with my last counselor! It was lame. No way!" What other interventions might Rachel rely on—using the group context—as a tool to help him manage his behavior?

_____
_____
_____
_____
_____
_____

3. Describe several steps you might recommend Rachel take to enhance member cohesion, goal setting, and norming.

_____
_____
_____
_____
_____
_____

4. Although lots of excellent work seems to be accomplished in the 40-minute weekly group, the teacher, Sandra, reports VERY little progress seems to be noticeable after 6 weeks. What might you do to enhance the generalization from in-group to in-class interventions?

_____
_____
_____
_____
_____
_____

5. What are your general reactions to this scenario? What additional information do you feel would really benefit you in this case?

_____
_____
_____
_____
_____
_____

## Journal and Reflection

Space for journaling about your group work experiences is provided below. Use this space to reflect on your reading about group work, your classroom presentations and activities, the group dynamics of your classes themselves, and any simulations or actual group participation opportunities you may have. Comment here thoughtfully. Be sure to carefully honor your ethical commitment to uphold the confidentiality of others in your group. Reflections are yours and are not to reveal anyone else's information. Recording your thoughts and feelings will provide a written history of this phase of your group work education. (Attach additional sheets of paper if desired.)

_____
_____
_____
_____
_____
_____
_____
_____
_____
_____
_____
_____
_____
_____
_____
_____
_____
_____
_____
_____
_____
_____
_____
_____
_____
_____
_____
_____
_____
_____
_____
_____
_____
_____

_Entry date_ _____

# ASSOCIATION FOR SPECIALISTS IN GROUP WORK: BEST PRACTICE GUIDELINES

**Discussion Questions:**

What does the "conceptual framework" for *Best Practice Guidelines* offer beginning group workers? In other words, how do group work specialists benefit by having such a conceptual framework articulated?

Describe the relationship between the American Counseling Association *Code of Ethics and Standards of Practice* (1995 Revision) and this document, ASGW's *Best Practice Guidelines* (1998).

From *Section A: Best Practice in Planning,* A.7. "Group and Member Preparation," discuss what implications related to this section you currently face in your practicum, internship, or employment settings.

From Section A.9. discuss some of the technological changes that you have experienced recently. How have you handled these changes; what, if anything, do you continue to struggle with?

Consider *Section B: Best Practice in Performing,* B.8. "Diversity," and describe and discuss areas of personal growth that present some challenges for you regarding this standard. What are you doing to continue your work on these issues?

In *Section C: Best Practice in Group Procession*, C.2 "Reflective Practice," what theories that guide group practice are appealing to you? Why? What do you find yourself thinking about as you prepare for your current group experiences?

# ASSOCIATION FOR SPECIALISTS IN GROUP WORK: PRINCIPLES FOR DIVERSITY-COMPETENT GROUP WORKERS

**Discussion Questions:**

From the *Preamble,* describe and discuss your experiences with the "isms" listed (e.g., heterosexism, able-ism, racism). "It is ourpersonal responsibility to address these issues through awareness, knowledge, and skills." What are you doing toward this personal responsibility? What do you see others doing that you actively support?

Under *I. Awareness of Self* "Attitudes and Beliefs," what "movement" have you shown toward being increasingly aware? What beliefs do you hold that impede your personal movement? How do others with whom you study or practice encourage your personal growth in these areas?

In your immediate circle of colleagues, your family of origin, or your current friendships, what process covertly and overtly perpetuate oppression? Asking this question perhaps will open dialogue toward change. Do you sense or feel any resistance as you consider personal change?

*Section II. Group Worker's Awareness of Group Member's Worldview*, Section B, "Knowledge," asks that you become an active scholar in the vast arena of diversity. Where are you in terms of such knowledge? Do you have strengths that you can identify, where you are knowledgeable regarding specific populations and persons? What are they? What about arenas where you are lacking? Are their marginalized or oppressed peoples that you know very little about? Who might they be, and what might you do to gain knowledge about them?

In *Section III. Diversity-Appropriate Intervention Strategies*, Section C, "Skills," you are asked to consider your current skills, strengths, and weaknesses in working with peoples perhaps different from yourself. Who do you see as different? What makes them so? What do you see as YOUR needs for strengthening your existing skills in working with any particular self-identified status of various group members?

At the conclusion to this document, *ASGW* reminds readers that this document is a "starting point." Discuss with your colleagues what that might mean on a personal level and a professional level. Where are you beginning from, do you sense a long road, a long rough road ahead? Identify through your discussion a path, a map that you can refer to as you embark on this journey toward diversity-competency in life as in group work.

# ASSOCIATION FOR SPECIALISTS IN GROUP WORK: PROFESSIONAL STANDARDS FOR THE TRAINING OF GROUP WORKERS

**Discussion Questions:**

Describe the group work training opportunities that you are undergoing currently (as student, as instructor, as curious bystander). As you read these standards both for content and clinical instruction, how does your program of study compare? Are there areas where you feel your program is fully compliant, perhaps even exceed the recommendations? Are there areas of weakness that arise? Carefully articulate these strengths and weakness. Generate and discuss your list of confidences and concerns.

Core training in group work acts as a foundation upon which additional skills toward specialization are extended. Assess your "core skills." What does the term "mastery" mean to you? What feedback have you received about your core group work skills mastery? Discuss ways that you continue to improve, and what you will do to ensure such professional growth.

Rarely do group work specializations emerge at the end of formal education or coursework; specializations, as you read in this document, require additional course work, and supervised experience. What aspirations do you have toward such specialization? Do you envision your career path to include an expertise in leading task/work groups, or perhaps psychotherapy groups? Identify sources where continuing education, training, and supervision are available.

**Journal and Reflection**

Space for journaling about your group work experiences is provided below. Use this space to reflect on your reading about group work, your classroom presentations and activities, the group dynamics of your classes themselves, and any simulations or actual group participation opportunities you may have. Comment here thoughtfully. Be sure to carefully honor your ethical commitment to uphold the confidentiality of others in your group. Reflections are yours and are not to reveal anyone else's information. Recording your thoughts and feelings will provide a written history of this phase of your group work education. (Attach additional sheets of paper if desired.)

_____
_____
_____
_____
_____
_____
_____
_____
_____
_____
_____
_____
_____
_____
_____
_____
_____
_____
_____
_____
_____
_____
_____
_____
_____
_____
_____
_____
_____
_____
_____

*Entry date* _____

# GLOSSARY

**A-B-C model of human interaction** "A" is the event, "B" is the thought process, and "C" is the feeling state resulting from one's thoughts. To change negative or nonproductive feelings, individuals need to think differently (i.e., positive or neutral).

**A-B-C-D-E worksheet** an approach to ethical decision making that uses a mnemonic device to remind group leaders and members of what they should do. The letters of this worksheet stand for Assessment, Benefit, Consequences and Consultation, Duty, and Education.

**accommodating** a behavior in which individuals neglect their own concerns to satisfy the concerns of others

**action-centered view of groups** the view that groups for children under 12 years of age should involve play and action

**action exercises** sensory awareness methods or guided imagery used in the psychodrama warm-up phase to help members discover common themes within the group as well as focus more on individual concerns

**action-oriented group techniques** techniques that require group members to behave in an active manner (e.g., role-playing, using "I" statements)

**action phase** the second part of the psychodrama process that involves the enactment of protagonists' concerns

**active listening** to hear the tone and meanings behind verbal communication and to pick up on messages in nonverbal behaviors

**activity group guidance (AGG)** group guidance involving activities that are developmental in nature; typically includes coordinated guidance topics

**actors** those who play the parts of other important people or objects in a psychodrama play. They are called *auxiliaries,* and with prompting from the protagonist, they can play the protagonist's double, an antagonist, or even a piece of furniture. In the same psychodrama, an auxiliary could play more than one part, such as being the protagonist's best friend and worst enemy.

**Adlerian parent education** stresses the cooperation among family members as a goal and emphasizes the use of logical and natural consequences to avoid power struggles. There is a democratic emphasis to this orientation, and regular family council meetings are held in order for all members to voice concerns and needs. The Adlerian approach stresses parent discussion groups with a trained leader and a set curriculum.

**adolescence** the age span from 13 to 19 but extended to include some individuals up to age 25; a time of unevenness and paradoxes marked by extensive personal changes

**adult children of alcoholics (ACoAs)** adults who grew up in families in which one or both parents abused alcohol. These individuals developed coping mechanisms for dealing with their alcoholic family system, such as denial or overcompensation, that are usually not functional for a mature lifestyle. Dealing with feelings about the past as well as learning behaviors for coping and life skills are therapeutic foci for these persons.

**Adult ego state (TA)** the realistic, logical part of a person; functions like a computer in that it receives and processes information from the Parent, the Child, and the environment

**adulthood** a somewhat nebulous term implying that a person has reached physical, mental, social, and emotional maturity

**advice/evaluation** telling people how to behave or judging them

**advice giving** instructing someone what to do in a particular situation. It is seldom appropriate or needed in most groups. It prevents members from struggling with their own feelings and keeps advice givers from having to recognize shortcomings in their own lives.

**ageism** discrimination against older people based on their age

**aging process** a biological phenomenon composed of physiological changes as well as a mental process of considering oneself older

**airtime** the amount of time available for participation in the group

**Alcoholics Anonymous (AA)** an organization that helps alcoholics gain and maintain control of their lives by remaining sober; established in the late 1930s

**altruism** sharing experiences and thoughts with others; helping them by giving of one's self; working for the common good

**American Association of Retired Persons (AARP)** a leading group for those age 55 and above to learn what social and political events impact them most

**American Group Psychotherapy Association (AGPA)** a psychoanalytically oriented organization established by Samuel R. Slavson in 1943

**American Society of Group Psychotherapy and Psychodrama (ASGPP)** a professional group association established by Jacob L. Moreno between 1941 and 1942

**amplify** to emphasize statements made by the protagonist in psychodrama. Examples include verbalizing nonverbal communications, questioning one's self, interpreting statements for what is being said and not said, contradicting feelings, self-observing, and engaging in denial.

**analyzing/interpreting** explaining the reasons behind behavior without giving the person an opportunity for self-discovery

**antecedent-response-consequence model of behaviorism** a model that basically states that behavior is functionally related to its antecedents and consequent events

**anxiety** tension; an uneasy feeling that accompanies decision making or performance

**apprehension** anxiety; a moderate amount helps group members key in on what they are experiencing and what they want to do

**A-R-C model** (see *antecedent-response-consequence model of behaviorism*)

**assessing members' growth and change** a technique similar to personal reviews, but in assessment, the emphasis is on individuals' memories of themselves at the beginning of the group and now. The idea of such an exercise is to have members see and share significant gains with themselves and others.

**Association for Advancement of Behavioral Therapy (AABT)** the major professional organization for behavioral therapists

**Association for Specialists in Group Work (ASGW)** formed in 1973; a division within the American Counseling Association

**attack on the leader** when members of the group become hostile or rebellious in regard to a leader's authority or conduct of the group. Underlying reasons for such attacks are subgrouping, fear of intimacy, and extragroup socializing.

**attractiveness** a multidimensional concept that basically refers to members positively identifying with others in the group

**audience** a term used to describe others who may be present during the psychodrama. Some may become auxiliaries.

**authenticity** the ability to affirm oneself and to make the most of discovering and using one's talents and creativity

**authoritarian** group leaders leaders who envision themselves as experts. They interpret, give advice, and generally direct the movement of the group much like a parent controls the actions of a child. They are often charismatic and manipulative. They feed off of obedience, expect conformity, and operate out of the wheel model.

**authoritative power** power predicated on social position or responsibility in an organization

**autonomy** the promotion of self-determination or the power to choose one's own direction in life. In groups, it is important that group members feel they have a right to make their own decisions.

**auxiliary counselors** when a rational-emotive therapy group leader encourages members of the group to act as types of cocounselors once someone has presented a problem. When they do, participants benefit from multiple input.

**avoiding** when individuals do not immediately pursue their concerns or those of other persons

**avoiding conflict** when the group ignores areas of tension or silences or discounts members who expose the group's disagreements

**awareness** Gestalt term for a total organismic response to the environment so that a person gains insight and control over situations and becomes responsible in achieving a healthy response to life events

**"BA" (basic assumption) activity** a classification devised by Wilfred Bion for the emotional pattern of an antiwork group (as opposed to a "W" [work group]). BA groups can be broken down further into three subpatterns: *BA Dependency* (where members are overdependent on the group leader), *BA Pairing* (where members are more interested in being with each other than in working on a goal), and *BA Fight-Flight* (where members become preoccupied with either engaging in or avoiding hostile conflict).

**band-aiding** the misuse of support; process of preventing others from fully expressing their emotional pain

**basic encounter group** also known as *encounter group;* first established by Carl Rogers to describe his approach to group work; focuses on individuals' awareness of their own emotional experiences and the behaviors of others; emphasis is placed on the awareness and exploration of intrapsychic and interpersonal issues. Encounter groups are often known as *personal growth groups* because the emphasis in these groups is on personal development.

**BASIC ID** A. Lazarus's multimodal model for helping; includes the components of behavior, affect, sensation, imagery, cognition, interpersonal relations, and drugs

**basic skills training (BST)** approach to groups developed at the National Training Laboratories in the 1940s; predecessor of the *T-group* movement

**behavior therapy** the collective behaviorist point of view, a combination of opinions and procedures about behavior and how to influence it

**behavioral disputation** rational-emotive behavioral therapy treatment that involves many forms from reading (bibliotherapy) to role-playing in the group. Often enactment of the problem within the group setting and possible ways of handling it are used. Homework may then be assigned in the form of *shame attacks* (in which the person actually does what he or she dreaded and finds the world does not fall apart regardless of the outcome).

**behavioral groups** either interpersonal or transactional groups depending on the purposes of the leader and members. (a) *Interpersonal groups* are highly didactic and involve specified goals that usually center on self-improvement. (b) *Transactional groups* are more heterogeneous and focus on broader, yet specific, goals.

**behavioral parent education** an approach associated with direct change and manipulation. Parents are trained to be change agents and to record and reinforce certain behaviors in their children.

**behavioral rehearsal** consists of practicing a desired behavior until it is performed the way one wishes. The process consists of gradually shaping a behavior and getting corrective feedback.

**behaviorists** inside and outside group settings, leaders who emphasize overt processes, here-and-now experiences, learning, changing of maladaptive actions, defining specific goals, and scientific support for techniques

**beneficence** promoting the good of others. It is assumed in groups that leaders and members will work hard for the betterment of the group as a whole.

**blind quadrant** information originally unknown to oneself but known to others when the group began

**blocking** related to protecting, in which the leader intervenes in the group activity to stop counterproductive behavior. This intervention can be done on a verbal or nonverbal level.

**blocking role** an anti–group member role. Individuals who take this role act as aggressors, blockers, dominators, recognition seekers, and self-righteous moralists.

**body language** a Gestalt concept in which emphasis is placed on what a person's body is doing, such as a hand tapping

**boundaries** physical and psychological parameters under which a group operates, such as starting and ending on time

**brainstorming** a way to stimulate divergent thinking, requires an initial generating of ideas in a nonjudgmental manner. The premise of this approach is that creativity and member participation are often held back because of the critical evaluation of ideas and actions by other group members.

**burnout** becoming physically and emotionally exhausted

**C group** a type of Adlerian parent education group; each component of the group—collaboration, consultation, clarification, confrontation, concern, confidentiality, and commitment—begins with a *c*. The group is primarily psychoeducational. It emphasizes developmental and preventive aspects of parenting.

**capping** the process of easing out of emotional interaction and into cognitive reflection; especially useful during termination

**career awareness and self-exploration (CASE) groups** groups that combine brief lectures on particular subjects, such as types of careers, self-disclosure, trust, self-esteem, and communications, with small-group interaction

**career change groups** groups for adults in midlife that are both psychoeducational and psychotherapeutic in nature

**career support groups** groups geared to life-span issues of work

**caring** a genuine concern for others

**catharsis** a release of pent-up feelings such as anger or joy; a psychoanalytic concept

**cathexis school of TA** a branch of TA that emphasizes reparenting

**chain** in this group arrangement, people are positioned or seated along a line, often according to their rank. Communication is passed from a person at one end of the configuration to a person at the other end through others. The chain is a popular way to run some group organizations, such as the military. Disadvantages of the chain include the indirectness of communication, the lack of direct contact with others, and the frustration of relaying messages through others.

**chaining** specific behavioral response sequences linked or chained to each other and used in shaping behavior

**changing questions to statements** Gestalt procedure that requires a group member who has raised a question to rephrase it as a statement

**Child ego state (TA)** divided into two parts (a) *Adapted Child* conforms to the rules and wishes of Parent ego states within the self and others; (b) *Free Child* (or natural child) reacts more spontaneously, has fun, and is curious and playful. It takes care of its needs without regard for others while using its intuition to read nonverbal cues.

**circle** in this group configuration, all members have direct access to each other and there is implied equality in status and power. The disadvantage of this arrangement is the lack of a perceived leader in the structure unless the identified leader is active and direct. Overall, the circle is probably the best structured way to ensure group members have an opportunity for equal airtime.

**clarify the purpose** when group leaders remind members and the group as a whole what the appropriate behavioral interactions or foci in the group are and why

**clarity of purpose** the first step in the preplanning process; determining what the group is set up to accomplish

**classic school of TA** a branch of TA that emphasizes present interactions

**closed-ended groups** groups that do not admit new members after the first session

**coaching** a process of providing a group member with general principles for performing desired behaviors. It works best when the coach sits behind the group member who is rehearsing.

**code of ethics** a set of standards and principles that organizations create to provide guidelines for their members to follow in working with the public and each other

**cognitive and behavioral** approaches to human relations based on a theory of personality that maintains that how one thinks largely determines how one feels and behaves

**cognitive behaviorists** behaviorists who believe thoughts play a major part in determining action and that thoughts are behaviors

**cognitive disputation** a process in REBT that involves direct questioning, reasoning, and persuasion

**cognitive restructuring** to think and perceive of oneself differently; a process in which group members are taught to identify, evaluate, and change self-defeating or irrational thoughts that negatively influence their behavior

**cohesion** the togetherness of a group; "we-ness"

**cohesiveness** (see *cohesion*)

**coleader** a professional or a professional-in-training who undertakes the responsibility of sharing the leadership of a group with another leader in a mutually determined manner. The use of coleaders in groups occurs often when membership is 12 or more.

**collaborating** the process in which individuals work with others to find some solution that fully satisfies the concerns of everyone

**collaboration** sharing facts and feelings with other members in a group; helping a member obtain a personal goal when there is no observable reward for the other members of a group

**collective counseling** Alfred Adler's form of group counseling

**commitment** when participants begin to evaluate their performances and the performances of others in terms of accomplishment of the group's goals

**communication facilitator** when the group leader reflects the content and feeling of members and teaches them how to do likewise. This process focuses on both the expression of words and the emotion behind these communications. In addition, the leader stresses the importance of speaking congruently—that is, using "I" messages to state what one wants or thinks.

**community for learning** a large-group phenomenon in the 1970s initiated by Carl Rogers in which about 100 people live and work together for 2 weeks at a time

**competing** when individuals pursue their own concerns at other people's expense

**compromising** when individuals attempt to find some expedient, mutually acceptable solution that partially satisfies both parties

**conceptual skills** thinking skills that enable group leaders to delineate dominant themes and concerns of clients while simultaneously choosing a particular helpful response

**condemning questions** questions that put people down and prevent them from seeing situations more honestly and openly (e.g., "Don't you think you should feel differently?")

**conductors** the term used to refer to psychoanalytically oriented group leaders who do not wish to be the main attention of the groups they facilitate

**confidentiality** the explicit agreement that what is said within a group will stay in the group; the right of group members to reveal personal thoughts, feelings, and information to the leader and other members of the group and expect that in no way will nonmembers of the group learn of this. Not keeping confidences is like gossiping and destructive to the group process.

**conflict** involves matters in which people struggle in resolving significant issues in their lives such as authority, intimacy, growth, change, autonomy, power, and loss

**conflict management** an approach premised on the basis that conflict can be positive. Thus, the focus in conflict management is on directing conflict toward a constructive dialogue.

**conflict management orientations** ways of handling conflict in a group (e.g., competing, accommodating, collaborating, sharing, avoiding)

**conflict resolution** based on the underlying notion that conflict is essentially negative and destructive, with the primary focus on ending a specific conflict

**confront** to challenge incongruencies in thoughts and actions

**confrontation** challenging group members to look at the discrepancies and incongruencies between their words and actions

**consciousness-raising (C-R) group** a group set up to help its participants become more aware of the issues they face and choices they have within their environment

**consensual validation** involves checking out one's behaviors with a group of other people

**contact-focused group theory** a conceptualization of groups in which the purpose of groups is highlighted; three primary contact groups described in this model are group guidance, group counseling, and group psychotherapy

**contagion** the process in which member behavior elicits group interaction on either an emotional or behavioral level

**content functions** the actual words and ideas exchanged between leaders and members

**contingency contracts** contracts that spell out the behaviors to be performed, changed, or discontinued; the rewards associated with the achievement of these goals; and the conditions under which rewards are to be received

**continuing education units (CEUs)** credits for participating in professional educational programs

**contract** an agreement, verbal or written, of what group members or the group as a whole will do and when

**control theory** a complete system for explaining how the brain works; added to base of reality therapy in the 1980s to make it more complete

**cooperation** when group members work together for a common purpose or good

**cooperative learning groups** study groups established so that assigned tasks can be divided and accomplished; members are responsible for meeting regularly and teaching each other what they have learned

**core mechanisms of group leadership** core skills of group leadership (i.e., emotional stimulation, caring, meaning attribution, and executive function)

**corrective recapitulation of the primary family group** reliving early familial conflicts correctly and resolving them

**counseling/interpersonal** problem-solving groups that focus on each person's behavior and growth or change within the group in regard to a particular problem or concern

**countertransference** a leader's emotional responses to members that are a result of the leader's own needs or unresolved issues with significant others

**couples group therapy** proponents of couples group therapy list many advantages for it including (a) identification by group members of appropriate and inappropriate behaviors and expectations by others, (b) development of insight and skills through observing other couples, (c) group feedback and support for the ventilation of feelings and changed behavior, and (d) lower cost

**crash-program mentality** when group experiences are carried out to excess

**creative imagery** a warm-up technique consisting of inviting psychodrama participants to imagine neutral or pleasant objects and scenes. The idea is to help participants become more spontaneous.

**crisis-centered groups** groups formed because of some emergency, such as conflict between rival groups

**critical incident in the life of the group** an event that has the power to shape or influence the group positively or negatively

**critical-incident model** a model focusing on a number of critical incidents in the life of a group of any type. The trainee, after studying group dynamics, watches a videotape of his or her instructor handling a number of different situations in a group. Then the trainee coleads a group under the instructor's supervision and makes strategic interventions geared to the incidents in the particular group. Trainees are taught self-management skills, as well as ways to deal with specific group situations.

**critical incident stress debriefing (CISD) groups** groups that help victims of violence deal with its repercussions, such as feelings of helplessness, anxiety, depression, and disorganization, lasting one 1- to 3-hour session

**crystallized intelligence** the ability to do something as a result of experience and education

**culturally encapsulated** individuals who hold stereotyped views of others who differ from themselves and act accordingly

**curative (therapeutic) factors within groups** eleven group factors (instillation of hope, universality, imparting of information, altruism, corrective recapitulation of the primary family group, development of socialization techniques, imitative behavior, interpersonal learning, group cohesiveness, catharsis, and existential factors) that contribute to the betterment of individuals in the group; first researched by Irvin Yalom

**cutting off** another term for blocking; defined two ways: (a) making sure that new material is not introduced into the group too late in the session for the group to adequately deal with it; (b) preventing group members from rambling

**cyclotherapy process** the idea that after the group meets, it continues to evolve and can be conceptualized as forever forming, with certain issues returning from time to time to be explored in greater depth

**defense mechanisms** ways of protecting a person from being overwhelmed by anxiety, such as repression or denial; overused when a person is not coping adequately

**delegating** when the group leader assigns a task to the group or one or more of its members

**democratic group leaders** group-centered leaders who trust group participants to develop their own potential and that of other group members; serve as facilitators of the group process and not as directors of it. They cooperate and collaborate with the group and share responsibilities with group members.

**denial** acting as if an experience does not exist or will never end

**density of time** the fullness of time and eventfulness; both seem to lessen with age

**dependency** group members who present themselves as helpless and incapable but refuse to listen to feedback. They are help-rejecting complainers and encourage the behavior of advice givers and band-aiders in a group.

**Developing Understanding of Self and Others—Revised (DUSO-R)** a commercial classroom guidance program based on Adlerian theory

**development of socializing techniques** learning basic social skills

**developmental factors** variables such as the age, gender, and maturity level of those involved in a group

**developmental group counseling** psychoeducational groups often used for teaching basic life skills

**developmental psychoeducational/guidance groups** groups that focus on common concerns of adolescents such as identity, sexuality, parents, peer relationships, career goals, and educational/institutional problems. Individuals who join these groups do so out of a sense of need.

**devil's advocate procedure** a procedure in which one or more members in the group are asked to question group decisions with a firm skepticism before the group reaches a conclusion

**diagnosing** an activity in which the leader identifies certain behaviors and categories into which a person or group fits. Diagnosing in groups does not usually include psychological instruments but is based more on leader observations.

**dialogue** talk between others and oneself or between different aspects of oneself; one of the two primary therapeutic tools in Gestalt therapy (along with *awareness*)

**director** the person who guides the protagonist in the use of the psychodramatic method to help that person explore his or her problem. The director is roughly equivalent to the group leader in other theoretical approaches but serves as a producer, a facilitator, an observer, and an analyzer.

**discussion teams** small groups used to promote involvement in guidance activities. In this arrangement, a large group is divided into four or five teams that are then seated in semicircles around the room. This formation has the advantage of getting members involved with one another and raising the level of excitement among them. The disadvantages are that interaction is mainly limited to a small number of individuals and other group members do not get the advantage of participating in all the groups, just one.

**displaced homemakers** women who have lost their source of economic support and are now forced back into the workforce after spending a number of years at home caring for their families

**double and multiple double** important techniques in psychodrama. The *double* consists of an actor taking on the role of the protagonist's alter ego and helping the protagonist express true inner feelings more clearly. In cases in which the protagonist has ambivalent feelings, the *multiple double* technique is used. In these situations, two or more actors represent different aspects of the protagonist's personality. The doubles may speak at once or take turns, but through their input, the protagonist should gain a better idea of what his or her thoughts and feelings are.

**drawing out** the opposite of cutting off or blocking; the process whereby group leaders purposefully ask more silent members to speak to anyone in the group, or to the group as a whole, about anything on their minds

**dream analysis** a psychotherapeutic technique. In group psychotherapy individuals must first be prepared to share. This preparation can occur through the group leader asking members in an early session to describe a recent dream, a recurring dream, or even a daydream. Through sharing, group members get to know each other better and at the same time are able to be more concrete in handling their feelings associated with the dream, and in managing themselves in general. *Dream content* is either *manifest* (conscious) or *latent* (hidden). Manifest content consists of the obvious and recallable features of the dream, such as who was in it. Latent content is the symbolic features of the dream that escape first analysis.

**dream work** seen by Fritz Perls as "the royal road to integration." It is used by having those who dream re-create and relive the dream in the present. By doing so, these individuals become all parts of the dream. They may do this through working alone in the group setting or having others in the group act out different parts of the dream (i.e., *dream work as theater*).

**dual-focused Gestalt group work** a Gestalt approach in which attention is concentrated on group process with the power of individual work within the group

**dual nature of human beings** a REBT concept that states individuals are both rational and irrational

**dual relationships** when group leaders find themselves in two potentially conflicting roles with their group members

**eating disorders groups** professionally led psychotherapeutic and support groups for individuals who have obsessive and distorted ideas in regard to thinness and body image

**eclectic** a composite of theoretical approaches

**educational and developmental procedure** a group training model consisting of four components: (a) content, (b) decision making, (c) eventual leadership style, and (d) dual process

**educational growth group (EGG)** a group composed of 8 to 15 students who meet for a total of five sessions and cover specific topics chosen by the students. The aim of the group is to help members assimilate and personalize this information.

**ego (psychoanalysis)** the "executive of the mind"; works according to the reality principle and tries to reduce the tension of the id

**egogram (TA)** a bar graph showing how people structure their time in six major ways: (a) withdrawal, (b) ritual, (c) pastimes, (d) work, (e) games, and (f) intimacy

**ego state (TA)** a system of feelings accompanied by a related set of behavior patterns; three basic TA ego states: Parent, Adult, and Child

**eight basic steps of reality therapy** (see *reality therapy's eight basic steps*)

**elasticity** a Gestalt term describing the ability to move from one set of needs to another and back

**elder hostel** a place where older individuals live and study together for a select period of time

**emotional ambivalence** feelings of loss, sadness, and separation mixed with those of hope, joy, and accomplishment

**emotional debris** unfinished business

**emotional impact of separation** includes dealing with loss, putting the separation in perspective, becoming aware of the limited value of searching for causes of separation, becoming more cognizant of systems interactions (family, work, social network), using the past as a guide to the future, and moving from a dyadic to a monadic identity

**emotional response of separation** focuses on continuing relationships with an ex-spouse; recognizing the influence of the separation on family, friends, and children; working and dating; and making sexual adjustments

**emotional stimulation** sharing on an affective level as well as intellectual level

**empathizing** to put oneself in another's place in regard to subjective perception and emotion and yet keep one's objectivity. It demands a suspension of judgment and a response to another person that conveys sensitivity and understanding.

**empty chair technique** a Gestalt technique designed to help group members deal with different aspects of their personalities (e.g., a person is given an opportunity to role-play and speak to a missing person with whom he or she has unfinished business)

**encounter** an existentialist concept that involves total physical and psychological contact between persons on an intense, concrete, and complete basis in the here and now; a psychodrama concept

**encounter group** (see *basic encounter group*)

**encouragement** an Adlerian technique of having group members examine their lifestyles in regard to mistaken perceptions and to take note of their assets, strengths, and talents. Encouragement is one of the most distinct Adlerian procedures.

**ethics** suggested standards of conduct based on a set of professional values

**evaluation questionnaire** serves the purpose of helping group members be concrete in assessing the group in which they have participated. This questionnaire can take many forms but is best if kept brief. An evaluation questionnaire should cover at least three aspects of the group: the leadership of the group, the facilities in which the group was held, and the group's effectiveness in achieving its objectives.

**excursions** a part of synectics in which members actually take a break, a vacation, from problem solving and engage in exercises involving fantasy, metaphor, and analogy. The idea is that the material generated in these processes can be reintegrated back into the group later.

**executive function** the role of the leader to manage the group as a social system that allows the group and its members to achieve specific goals

**exercises** planned activities that have been used previously to help group members become more aware; structured activities that the group does for a specific purpose

**existential factors** accepting responsibility for one's life in basic isolation from others, recognition of one's own mortality, and the capriciousness of existence

**existential variables** immediate feelings and interactions, such as conflict, withdrawal, support, dominance, and change

**experiments** nonplanned experiences that occur spontaneously in the group session

**extinction** the process of lowering the rate at which a behavior occurs by withdrawing the reinforcers that have been maintaining it so the targeted behavior will stop altogether

**facilitating** as done by group leaders, helping open up communication between group members

**facilitative feedback** telling another person the effect they have on you as a compliment or confrontation

**facilitative/building role** a role that adds to the functioning of a group in a positive and constructive way. Members who take on such a role may serve as initiators of actions and ideas, information seekers, opinion seekers, coordinators, orienters, evaluators, or recorders

**facilitators** term for Rogerian group leaders

**families in high-risk environments** families living in neighborhoods prone to violence

**family councils** a form of family group meetings originated by Alfred Adler

**family reenactment** a situation in which family of origin issues continue to be an influence on people throughout their lives, such as in groups that resemble families in many ways

**fantasy exercises** a method used in Gestalt group work to help group members (a) be more concrete in assessing their feelings, (b) deal with catastrophic experiences, (c) explore and express feelings of guilt and shame, and (d) become more involved in the group. It is not necessary that group members live out their fantasies.

**farewell-party syndrome** a dynamic in which group members emphasize only the positive aspects of what has occurred in the group, instead of what they have learned. This type of focus tends to avoid the pain of closure.

**faulty logic** irrational ideas that clients hold

**feedback** involves one person giving another his or her perception of a behavior, sharing relevant information with other people, such as how they appear to others, so they can make decisions about whether they would like to change. Feedback information should be given in a clear, concrete, succinct, and appropriate manner.

**fidelity** refers to loyalty and duty. It is keeping one's promise and honoring one's commitment. In group work, fidelity involves stating up front what the group will focus on and then keeping that pledge.

**field theory** Kurt Lewin's approach to groups that emphasizes the interaction between individuals and their environments. It is based on the ideas of Gestalt psychology, in which there is an interdependence of part-whole relationships.

**fishbowl** the use of in and out circles in conducting a group

**fishbowl procedure** (see *group observing group*)

**fixation** a tendency to cope with the outside world in a manner similar to that employed in an earlier stage of development in which one is stuck. To overcome fixation requires that people regress to that time and come to terms with themselves and significant others who were involved in the fixation process.

**floating hot seat** Gestalt technique in which interaction is promoted by encouraging group members to work on exploring their own personal issues when someone else in the group touches on an issue that has personal relevance for them

**focus groups** temporary groups composed of representative samples of individuals concerned with issues, products, and/or outcomes, increasingly used by businesses and politicians

**focusers on others** those who become self-appointed group "assistant leaders" by questioning others, offering advice, and acting as if they did not have any problems

**follow-up** reconnecting with group members after they have had enough time to process what they experienced in the group and work on their goals/objectives

**formal feedback** structured; may be set up through use of a *time-limited round*

**forming or orientation stage of the group** a stage characterized by initial caution associated with any new experience. During this time, group members try to avoid being rejected by others, the leader, or even themselves.

**four stages of psychosexual development** oral, anal, phallic, and genital

**four-step process of termination** orientation, summarization, discussion of goals, follow-up

**four types of thoughts**: negative, positive, neutral, and mixed; REBT concept; (a) negative thoughts concentrate on painful or disappointing aspects of an event, (b) positive thoughts focus on just the opposite, (c) neutral cognitions are those that are neither positive nor negative, and (d) mixed thoughts contain elements of the other three thought processes

**free association** in group psychoanalysis, used to promote spontaneity, interaction, and feelings of unity in the group. In a group, free association works as a type of "free-floating discussion" in which group members report their feelings or impressions immediately.

**game analysis (TA)** an examination of destructive and repetitive behavioral patterns and an analysis of the ego states and types of transactions involved

**games (TA)** an ongoing series of complementary ulterior transactions progressing to a well-defined, predictable outcome. Games are played on three levels, and almost all of them are destructive and result in negative payoffs (i.e., *rackets*). *First-degree* games are the least

harmful; minor faults are highlighted. *Second-degree* games are more serious; interactive process in second-degree games leaves the people involved feeling negative. *Third-degree* games are deadly and often played for keeps; there is nothing socially redeemable about third-degree games. People who play games operate from three distinct positions: (a) the *victim* (who appears to be innocent), (b) the *persecutor* (who appears to cause problems), and (c) the *rescuer* (who is seen as a problem-solver or hero to the victim). Individuals who play games often switch between these roles.

**general systems theory** a theory that emphasizes circular causality as opposed to linear causality

**generalization** the display of behaviors in environments other than where they were originally learned

**generativity** a goal of midlife, according to Erik Erikson, in which people seek to be creative in their lives and work for the benefit of others and the next generation

**genogram** a type of family tree

**goals** specific objectives that individuals in the group or the group as a whole wish to accomplish

**go-rounds** also known as rounds is a procedure in which every group member of a group comments briefly (usually a sentence or two) as his or her turn comes up around the circle

**Greek chorus** (see *hot seat*)

**group** a collection of two or more individuals who meet in face-to-face interaction, interdependently, with the awareness that each belongs to the group and for the purpose of achieving mutually agreed-on goals

**group analysis** a term first applied to the treatment of individuals in psychoanalytically oriented groups by Trigant Burrow. He emphasized that social forces affect individuals' behaviors.

**group-based training** in this model, specific skills used in groups are first identified and defined by trainers. Examples are given in which this skill might be used. The flexibility of using various skills is stressed in this presentation. Next, both videotapes and role plays are used to show trainees how a particular skill is employed. The third step in this procedure is structured practice in which each trainee demonstrates how he or she would use the skill that has been previously demonstrated. This enactment is then critiqued. Finally, group leader trainees, after learning all the group skills, are asked to demonstrate their group facilitation skills in 20-minute unstructured practice sessions. They are observed leading a group and given feedback on the use of skills they implemented during this time, as well as those that they did not use.

**group-centered perspective** focuses on members and interpersonal processes

**group cohesion** a sense of "we-ness"

**group cohesiveness** the proper therapeutic relationship between group members, group members and the group leader, and the group as a whole so that a sense of we-ness is fostered

**group collusion** involves cooperating with others unconsciously or consciously to reinforce prevailing attitudes, values, behaviors, or norms. The purpose of such behavior is self-protection, and its effect is to maintain the status quo in the group.

**group content** information discussed within a group

**group dynamics** a term originally used by Kurt Lewin to describe the interrelations of individuals in groups

**group exercises** (see *exercises*)

**group generalist model** a model entailing five steps: (a) the trainer models leader behavior for the total group; (b) the group is broken down into subgroups of five or six, and each subgroup member practices leading a small group discussion; (c) after each discussion, some aspect of the subgroup's behavior is processed (e.g., anxiety); (d) the subgroup critiques the leader's behavior; and (e) following practice by each trainee, the total group shares observations and conclusions about the activity.

**group interaction** the way members relate to each other with nonverbal and verbal behaviors and the attitudes that go with them. Group interaction exists on a continuum, from extremely nondirective to highly directive.

**group norming** (see *norming*)

**group observing group** when a group breaks up into two smaller groups and each observes the other function (as outsiders) for a set amount of time; sometimes called a *fishbowl procedure*

**group process** the interactions of group members as the group develops

**group process goals** in Adlerian groups, goals center around promoting and experiencing a cooperative climate within the group

**group processing** when a neutral third party observes and offers feedback to the group about what is occurring between members and in the group itself

**group psychoanalysis** a model that emphasizes the whole group is the client and that group dynamics are an essential feature to analyze

**group psychotherapy** a group that addresses personal and interpersonal problems of living among people who may be experiencing severe and/or chronic maladjustment; specializes personality reconstruction. It is meant to help people who have serious, long-term psychological problems. As such, this type of group is found most often in mental health facilities, such as clinics or hospitals.

**group setting** the group's physical environment

**group structure** the way a group is set up physically as well as how the group members interact or structure themselves in relationship to others

**group for survivors of suicide** group for adults that helps them break out of isolation and resolve grief issues specific to suicide; can also be conducted on a self-help and support group basis

**group techniques** exercises that are structured so that group members interact with one another

**group therapy for normals** premise of basic encounter groups that states individuals who participate in them are relatively healthy

**group work** "a broad professional practice involving the application of knowledge and skill in group facilitation to assist an interdependent collection of people to reach their mutual goals, which may be intrapersonal, interpersonal, or work related. The goals of the group may include the accomplishment of tasks related to work, education, personal development, personal and interpersonal problem solving, or remediation of mental and emotional disorders" (p. 330).

**groupthink** a group situation in which there is a deterioration of mental efficiency, reality testing, and moral judgment that results from in-group pressures

**groupware** the collective name of computer support for something a group does

**groups for victims of abuse** groups set up to help victims of abuse break the cycle of isolation so common to this population and interrelate in a healthy, dynamic way

**growing times** when fresh learning occurs on an individual and interpersonal level

**growth-centered groups** groups that focus on the personal and social development of people and are set up to explore feelings, concerns, and behaviors about a number of everyday subjects

**"guidance hour"** also called *"guidance room"*; the term used for a homeroom at school in the

1930s; responsibilities of the teacher in the room were to establish friendly relationships with students, discover their abilities and needs, and develop right attitudes with them toward school, home, and the community.

**guidance/psychoeducational group** originally developed for use in educational settings, specifically public schools. Primary function of the group is the prevention of personal or societal disorders through the conveying of information and/or the examining of values. Guidance/psychoeducational groups stress growth through knowledge. Content includes, but is not limited to, personal, social, vocational, and educational information.

**Hawthorne effect** changes in behavior as a result of observation/manipulation conditions under which a person or group works

**HELPING** D. B. Keat's multimodal framework for helping: Health, Emotions, Learning, Personal Interactions, Imagery, Need to Know, and Guidance

**here and now** the present

**heterogeneous groups** groups composed of dissimilar persons. Such groups can broaden members' horizons and enliven interpersonal interactions.

**heuristic dimension** research component

**hidden quadrant** in the Johari window, contains undisclosed information known only to oneself

**highly structured groups** groups with a predetermined goal and a plan designed to enable each group member to reach an identified goal with minimum frustration. Such groups are usually used in teaching skills that may be transferred to a wide range of life events.

**high-risk families** families prone to violence

**holding the focus** helping members concentrate on a specific topic or person for a set length of time

**homework** working outside the group itself, members implement behaviors they have addressed or practiced within the group. These real-life situations help them realize more fully what they need to work on in the group.

**homogeneous groups** groups composed of similar persons

**hope** both a cognitive and emotional experience in groups. Cognitively, the belief that what is desired is also possible and that events will turn out for the best. Emotionally, the feeling that what one believes will occur. The importance of hope is that it energizes group members and the group as a whole.

**hot seat** the place in Gestalt group therapy where the person who wants to work sits with his or her chair facing that of the therapist or leader; the rest of the group serves as a kind of "Greek chorus" in the background of the encounter where they resonate and empathize with the one who is working and gain insights into themselves and others through the process of identification.

**humor** the ability to laugh at oneself and the group in a therapeutic and nondefensive manner; an especially important quality during the working stage of the group

**hybrids** groups that defy fitting any category. They encompass multiple ways of working with their members and may change their emphasis frequently. For example, some groups that are instructive are also simultaneously or consequentially therapeutic. The prototype for a hybrid group is a *self-help* group.

**hypokinesis** physical inactivity

**I/We/It** a conceptualization of the group process in which attention is given to personal, interpersonal, and product outcomes

**icebreaker** an activity designed to promote communication between two or more people in a group

**ice-breaking exercises** introductory activities that link people together. Such exercises increase the group's awareness of each other and/or remind members of what they did in previous sessions.

**id (psychoanalysis)** the first system within the personality to develop; primarily where human instincts reside. It is amoral, functions according to the pleasure principle, and contains the psychic energy *(libido)* of the person.

**identification** a "normal" developmental process in which individuals see themselves as being similar to one another

**imaginal disputation** a technique that has participants see themselves in stressful situations and examine their self-talk

**imago (i.e., image) relationship therapy** image therapy; an eclectic approach to working with couples that includes elements of psychoanalysis, transactional analysis, Gestalt psychology, cognitive therapy, and systems theory

**imitative behavior** modeling actions of other group members

**imparting of information** instruction on how to deal with life problems, usually through group discussion

**impasses** in Gestalt theory, the places where group members get stuck

**in and out circles** often referred to as the *fishbowl*. The inner circle promotes a sense of closeness, but those in the outer circle may feel left out and become bored. To help promote participation by everyone, group leaders can assign tasks for the outside group members to do while they observe the inside group.

**incorporation** a personal awareness and appreciation of what the group has accomplished both on an individual and collective level

**individual goals** in Adlerian groups, involves developing insight into the creation of a mistaken lifestyle and taking corrective measures

**individually conducted** pregroup screening procedure intake interview used to determine who will join a particular group

**influential power** based on the idea of persuasion and manipulation of others through convincing them that a certain course of action is correct

**informal feedback** when the group leader asks members to give their reactions to a group session in an unstructured way at any time they wish. Such an invitation is likely to increase spontaneity and sensitivity.

**information statement** a written description of what a group is about and what is expected of its members

**informational** power premised on the idea that those who know more are able to exert control over situations, including those involving people

**informed consent statement** a document a group member signs acknowledging that the individual is aware of the group activity in which he or she is about to participate and is doing so voluntarily

**injunctions (TA)** parent commands recorded internally by a child that call for the individual to adopt certain roles

**insight** consists of immediate new perceptions and understandings about one's problems; often occurs during or after the experience of catharsis

**insight and reorientation phases of the group** in Adlerian groups, involves helping individuals understand why they made the choices they did in the past, often accompanied by the use of interpretation on the group leader's part that is offered as a tentative hypothesis

**instillation of hope** a process in which group members come to realize that their issues are resolvable

**integrating conflicting ideas to form new solutions** the idea behind integration is consensus. In using this strategy, group leaders try to get all parties to reexamine a situation and identify points of agreement.

**integration phase** last phase of psychodrama; involves discussion and closure

**integrity** one of Erikson's virtues; the total integration of life experiences into a meaningful whole

**integrity therapy** stresses helping people live up to their own moral convictions; has some commonality with reality therapy

**intellectualization** behavior that is characterized by an emphasis on abstraction with a minimal amount of affect; the use of thoughts and a sophisticated vocabulary to avoid dealing with personal feelings

**intentional civil liability** cases include situations such as (a) *battery* (the unconsented touching of a person); (b) *defamation* (injury to a person's character or reputation either through verbal *[slander]* or written *[libel]* means); (c) *invasion of privacy* (violation of the right to be left alone); (d) *infliction of mental distress* (outrageous behavior on the part of the therapist or group leader)

**interactional catalyst** when group leaders promote interaction between group members without calling attention to themselves. It is a functional process that continues throughout the group and can take various forms such as questioning whether two or more group members have something to say to one another and then being silent to see what happens.

**interpersonal goals** in Adlerian groups, involves becoming more socially oriented and involved with other individuals experiencing life difficulties

**interpersonal learning** gaining insight and correctively working through past experiences

**interpersonal style of group leadership** leadership that focuses on transactions between individuals in the group

**interpretation** a psychoanalytic technique that focuses on helping group members gain insights into their past or present behavior; generally made by group leaders in the earliest stages of the group, because group members seldom possess the sophistication to do so adequately and appropriately at this time. There are three levels of interpretation: *thematical*—broad based, covering the whole pattern of a person's existence such as self-defeating behavior; *constructional*—focusing on thought patterns and the way group members express themselves; and *situational*—context centered, emphasizing the immediate interactions within the group.

**interpretation of a person's early history** in Adlerian groups, when group members recognize and understand the ways they created their own lifestyles

**intervention cube** concept model for training group leaders (see *critical-incident model*)

**intrapersonal style of group leadership** leadership that concentrates on the inward reactions of individual members of the group

**intrinsically neutral** as an approach, Gestalt theory views individuals as neither positive nor negative (i.e., without a predetermined set of responses)

**involvement** when group members actively participate with each other and invest themselves in the group

**job support group** a group for people who have lost their jobs and need emotional support, who want to learn how to achieve career goals and are willing to spend a good deal of time in doing so, and who are unemployed and are emotionally struggling with the stigma, shame, and isolation of their situations

**jogging group** approach built on the premise that physical exercise is an important element that contributes to people's abilities to perform better in all areas of life. The jogging group itself combines an hour of exercise in the form of walking, jogging, or running, with another hour of group process.

**Johari Awareness Model** also known as *Johari Window;* a representative square with four quadrants that is often used to show what happens in group interactions when the group and its members are working or not working

**joining** the process by which leaders and group members connect with one another psychologically and/or physically

**journals** also known as *logs;* in this experience, group members are required to write their reactions to the events of each session. This process enables them to spot inconsistencies in their reactions more quickly than if they simply talked about them.

**justice** fairness; refers to the equal treatment of all people. This virtue implies that everyone's welfare is promoted and that visible differences in people, such as gender or race, do not interfere with the way they are treated.

**laissez-faire leaders** leaders in name only. They do not provide any structure or direction for their groups. Members are left with the responsibility of leading and directing.

**law** a body of rules recognized by a state or community as binding on its members

**Law of Triviality** the time a group spends discussing any issue is in inverse proportion to the consequences of the issue

**layers of neurosis** in Gestalt theory, those aspects of people that keep them from being healthy: the *phony*—being unauthentic; the *phobic*—being afraid to really see themselves as they are; and the *impasse*—where their maturity is stuck

**leader-centered group** autocratic; the leader instructs the followers in the "right" way. The leader-centered group is based on obedience from followers.

**leaderless groups** groups that rotate the leadership role among their members (e.g., self-help groups)

**leveling** a process in which group members are encouraged to interact freely and evenly with each other. In leveling, group members who are underparticipatory are drawn out and those who are excessively active are helped to modify their behavior.

**life script analyses (TA)** an examination of people's basic life plans involving transactions and games

**life-skill development group** a type of guidance/psychoeducational group, especially designed for those who have a deficit of behavior. Emphasis is on a "how-to" approach to learning new behaviors; may include the use of films, plays, demonstrations, role-plays, and guest speakers (see *developmental group counseling*).

**life-skills training** focuses on helping persons identify and correct deficits in their life-coping skills and learn new appropriate behaviors

**limits** the outer boundaries of a group in regard to behaviors that will be accepted within the group

**linear** a cause-and-effect explanation

**linking** the process of connecting persons with one another by pointing out to them what they share in common. Linking strengthens the bonds between individuals and the group as a whole.

**living newspaper** a dramatic technique devised by Jacob Moreno in psychodrama in which recent happenings—sometimes local incidents, sometimes developments in world politics—were spontaneously dramatized

**logs** (*see journals*)

**low facilitative responses** (a) *advice/evaluation* (telling people how to behave or judging them); (b) *analyzing/interpreting* (explaining the reasons behind behavior without giving the person an opportunity for self-discovery); (c) *reassuring/supportive* (trying to encourage someone, yet dismissing the person's real feelings)

**magic shop** a warm-up technique in psychodrama that is especially useful for protagonists who are undecided or ambivalent about their values and goals. It involves a storekeeper (the director or an auxiliary ego) who runs a magic shop filled with special qualities. The qualities are not for sale but may be bartered.

**maintenance** in this stage, an emphasis is placed on increasing group members' self-control and self-management (e.g., when a behavioral group member is consistent in doing the actions desired without depending on the group or its leader for support)

**maintenance role** a person who contributes to the social–emotional bonding of members and the group's overall well-being. When interpersonal communication in the group is strained, there is a need to focus on relationships. Persons who take on such roles are social and emotionally oriented. They express themselves by being encouragers, harmonizers, compromisers, commentators, and followers.

**major transactions** a TA term that describes when the major focus of the group is on group leader–member interactions

**making the rounds** a warm-up technique in which each member is given a chance to speak about a particular topic. In Gestalt groups, confrontation is heightened as group members are asked to say something they usually do not verbalize.

**making wishes into demands** using *should, ought,* and *must* in regard to a desired action

**malpractice** bad practice; implies the group leader has failed to render proper service because of either negligence or ignorance

**malpractice suit** a claim against a professional made by a "plaintiff" who seeks a monetary award based on a specific amount of damages—physical, financial, and/or emotional

**manipulators** group members who use feelings and behaviors to get their way regardless of what others want or need. Often they are angry.

**marathon groups** originated by George Bach and Fred Stoller in 1964 as a way of helping people become more authentic with themselves; usually held for extended periods of time, such as 24 or 48 hours; group members are required to stay together. As time passes, members become tired and experience a breakdown in

their defenses and an increase in their truthfulness.

**marriage enrichment** a psychoeducational and growth group for marrieds aimed at helping them have healthier relationships

**masculine mystique** the belief that men are superior to women and therefore have the right to devalue and restrict women's values, roles, and lifestyles

**meaning attribution** refers to the leader's ability to explain to group members in a cognitive way what is occurring in the group

**mediation** having a third party hear arguments about a situation and then render a decision

**member-specific groups** related to topic-specific groups; focus on particular transitional concerns of individual members, such as grief, hospitalization, or institutionalized day care. Basically, member-specific groups may be conducted for older adults or for members of their families.

**middle adulthood** approximately ages 40 to 65; begins somewhere between the late 30s and the early 40s. Individuals at this time realize that life is half over and death is a reality.

**midlife** ages 40 to 65 years

**midlife transition** a time for evaluating, deciding, and making adjustments at midlife. It is a difficult time for many individuals as they give up the dreams of adolescence and come to terms with their own mortality.

**minor transactions** a TA term to describe when the group is functioning properly, when group members interact with one another

**mirror** in this psychodrama activity, the protagonist watches from offstage while an auxiliary ego mirrors the protagonist's posture, gesture, and words. This technique is often used in the action phase of psychodrama to help the protagonist see him- or herself more accurately.

**mixed-gender groups** groups composed of both males and females

**modeler of appropriate behavior** when group leaders consciously pick and choose actions they think group members need to learn through passive and active demonstrations; can include deliberate use of self-disclosure, role-plays, speech patterns, and acts of creativity

**modeling a social behavioral** method used to teach group members complex behaviors in a relatively short period of time by copying/imitating

**modification** a technique in which the group leader must use a logical sequence by first "acknowledging the emotional reaction of a member" receiving negative feedback and then affirming the "potentially constructive intent" of the sender

**monodrama** also known as *autodrama;* in this technique, the protagonist plays all the parts of the enactment; no auxiliary egos are used. The person may switch chairs or talk to different parts of the self.

**monopolizers** group members who, because of their own anxiety, dominate conversation by not giving other persons a chance to participate verbally

**monopolizing** when a person or persons within the group dominate the group's time through talking

**multimodal method** using verbal and nonverbal means for conveying information

**multiple-family group therapy** involves treating several families together at the same time. It requires the use of coleaders and has many of the same advantages that couple group therapy has, including the fact that families can often serve as cotherapists for each other.

**multiple transferences** in psychoanalytic groups when group members can experience transference feelings with others in the group as well as with the group leader

**mutual help groups** when members mutually assist one another; another term for self-help groups

**mythopoetic** refers to a process of ceremony, drumming, storytelling/poetry reading, physical movement, and imagery exercises designed to create a "ritual process"; a process often used in men's groups

**narcissistic groups** groups that develop cohesiveness by encouraging hatred of an out-group or by creating an enemy. As a result, regressive group members are able to overlook their own deficiencies by focusing on the deficiencies of the out-group.

**National Training Laboratories (NTL)** a group training facility in Bethel, Maine, established by Kurt Lewin and associates in the late 1940s

**natural consequences** living with the results of a particular behavior, such as not following instructions (an Adlerian concept)

**negative group variables** group action that includes, but is not limited to, avoiding conflict, abdicating group responsibilities, anesthetizing to contradictions within the group, and becoming narcissistic

**nominal-group technique (NGT)** a six-step process involving the generation both verbally and in writing of a number of ideas/solutions connected with a problem statement. This exercise does not require the open exposure of members as much as brainstorming and ends with a vote, discussion, and revote on priorities for resolving a situation. The time period for the group takes 45 to 90 minutes, after which the group, composed of people from diverse settings, is disbanded and the members thanked for their participation.

**nondevelopmental counseling and psychotherapy groups** adolescent groups that tend to focus mainly on concerns of adults and society, such as drug use, school problems (e.g., poor grades, truancy), or deviant behavior. Usually, these groups are set up by a school, agency, or court, and troubled adolescents are forced to attend.

**nondevelopmental factors** encompass unpredictable qualities such as the nature of a problem, the suddenness of its appearance, the intensity of its severity, and the present coping skills

**nonmaleficence** avoiding doing harm. To act ethically, leaders and members of groups must be sure the changes they make in themselves and help others to make are not going to be damaging.

**nonverbal behaviors** behaviors that make up more than 50% of the messages communicated in social relationships such as in groups and are usually perceived as more honest and less subject to manipulation than verbal behaviors. Four categories of nonverbal behavior are body behaviors, interaction with the environment, speech, and physical appearance.

**nonverbal cues** such behaviors as body posture or facial expression

**norming** where members form an identity as a group and a sense of "we-ness" prevails; there is enthusiasm, cooperation, and cohesiveness at this time. In many ways, the norming stage parallels the forming stage in regard to its emphasis on positive feelings. Norming, like storming, lasts only for a few sessions; it sets the pattern for the next stage: performing (i.e., working).

**norms** rules and standards of behavior. Groups typically accept both *prescriptive* norms, which describe the kinds of behaviors that should be performed, and *proscriptive* norms, which describe the kinds of behaviors that are to be avoided.

**old-old** individuals over the age of 76; they are likely to experience declines in health and overall functioning

**old-timers** more experienced members of self-help groups (see *pros*)

**open quadrant** in the Johari window, one that contains information that is generally known to self and others

**open-ended groups** groups that admit new members at any time

**open-ended questions** questions that invite more than a one- or two-word response

**operant conditioning** emphasizes that behavior is a function of its consequences

**operations** specific techniques employed by TA group leaders, such as interrogation, specification, confrontation, explanation, illustration, confirmation, interpretation, and crystallization

**paradox** asking members to do the opposite of what you want in the hope they will disobey

**parent education groups** primarily psychoeducational groups focusing on the raising of children. Rudolph Dreikurs began setting up these groups in the 1950s using Alfred Adler's theory and ideas.

**Parent Effectiveness Training (PET)** a Rogerian-based parent education program. In PET, there is an emphasis on communication skills, and parents are encouraged to recognize their positive and negative feelings toward their children and come to terms with their own humanness. A major hypothesis of this approach is that *active listening* (i.e., hearing what is implied as well as what is actually said) and *acceptance* (acknowledging what is happening as opposed to evaluating it) will decrease family conflicts and promote individual growth.

**Parent ego state (TA)** dualistic in being both nurturing and critical (or controlling). The function of the *Critical Parent* is to store and dispense the rules and protection for living. The function of the *Nurturing Parent* is to care for, to nurture.

**Parents Without Partners (PWP)** a popular national organization whose groups for the divorced and widowed tend to be psychoeducational or self-help

**pat on the back** a closing exercise in which members draw the outline of their hand on a piece of white paper that is then taped on their back. Other group members then write closing comments that are positive and constructive about the person on the hand outline or on the paper itself.

**peer power** people helping people in a group setting

**peer supervision** when practitioners meet on a regular basis to consult with each other about particularly difficult group situations

**permission (TA)** centers on giving group members directives to behave against the injunctions of their parents

**personal growth** Rogerian term; a global emphasis that stresses development as a result of experiences such as travel or encounter; the opposite of *personal growth issues*—an individual emphasis that springs from a perceived deficit or need

**personal power** a strategy often used in mature relationships. Personal power's source is from the individual and his or her ability to persuade others to follow a select course of action.

**personal responsibility** an existentialist concept, being responsible for making meaning out of what one does or what occurs

**personalization skills** using one's own personal attributes, such as openness or humor, to full advantage in a group setting

**phyloanalysis** the biological principles of group behavior

physical structure the arrangement of group members in relationship to one another

**planning for continued problem resolution** this activity may be completed in a group before or after individual good-byes are said. It involves making a specific plan of what group members will do to continue their progress after the group ends. It should include when and how certain activities will be carried out, but others' expectations should not be part of the plan.

**polarities** two interrelated, interdependent, opposite poles such as career and family

**polarization** when a group becomes divided into different and opposing subgroups or camps

**position power** a strategy often used when there are immature relationships between individuals. Position power is derived from the status of people's titles, such as "group leader" or "group facilitator."

**positive expectations** behavioral theory that individuals who expect to be successful are much more likely to achieve their goals

**positive group variables** a collection of favorable group factors such as member commitment; readiness of members for the group experience; the attractiveness of the group for its members; a feeling of belonging, acceptance, and security; and clear communication

**potency** the use of appropriate counseling techniques in certain situations to bring about change

**power** the capacity to bring about certain intended consequences in others' behavior

**preadolescents** children in the latency period with an age range from 9 to 13 years

**premature termination** when individuals quit a group abruptly or when the group experience ends suddenly because of actions by the leader. There are three types of premature termination: the termination of the group as a whole, the termination of a successful group member, and the termination of an unsuccessful group member.

**preschool and early school-aged children** ages 5 through 9

**pretraining** orienting members of a group on what to expect of the group before it meets

**primal horde** Freud's conceptualization of a group; he thought leaders within the group function as *parental figures*

**primary affiliation groups** those groups with which people most identify as belonging, such as a family or peers

**primary tension** awkwardness about being in a strange situation

**principle ethics** ethics based on obligations. They focus on finding socially and historically acceptable answers to the question "What shall I do?" Codes of ethics are based on principle ethics (i.e., actions stemming from obligations).

**principle of awareness** Gestalt assumption that people are free to choose only when they are *self-aware*—that is, in touch with their existence and what it means to be alive; awareness includes all sensations, thoughts, and behaviors of the individual

**principle of figure/ground** Gestalt principle. The *figure* in one's personal life is composed of experiences that are most important; the *background* is composed of experiences that are less pressing.

**principle of holism** Gestalt term for integration

**principle of polarities** Gestalt belief that if people are to meet their needs, they must first differentiate their perceptual field into opposites/poles, for example, active/passive, good/bad. People fail to resolve conflicts because they are not in contact with the opposite sides of the situation.

**problem-centered groups** small groups set up to focus on one particular concern (e.g., coping with stress)

**process functions** identifiable sequences of events over time that influence a group's development

**process observer** a professional human services person who is neutral in regard to the group agenda and personalities; as part of the procedure of group processing, observes and gives feedback to the group on what and how they are doing

**process skills** observable behaviors used to run groups such as summarization, immediacy, and confrontation. By improving these skills group leaders become more versatile in their interactions with group members and the group as a whole.

**professional liability insurance** insurance designed specifically to protect a group worker from financial loss in case of a civil suit

**professional skills** actions such as behaving appropriately in a crisis, safeguarding confidentiality, and turning in reports connected with the group in a timely manner

**projecting the future** when group members are asked to imagine what changes they would like to make in the short term and long term

**projective identification**, sometimes just referred to as *identification,* is a one of the most complex and potentially disruptive behaviors that can occur in a group. The manifestation of projective identification involves multiple members and occurs, for example, when an individual who experiences marked self-contempt projects these feelings onto another person in the group.

**promoting a positive interchange among group members** a condition that, when created, can help members become more honest with themselves and others and promote cohesion in the group

**promoting hope** one of the basic "therapeutic" factors described by Irving Yalom. If members believe that their situations can be different and better, they are likely to work harder within the group.

**pros** self-help group leaders who gain their position from experience and longevity (see *old-timers*)

**protagonist** the person who is the subject of the psychodrama enactment; may play many parts

**protecting** involves the leader safeguarding members from unnecessary attacks by others in the group

**protection** involves a group leader keeping members safe from psychological or physical harm

**pseudo-acceptance** false acceptance; harmony is stressed over everything; prevents anxiety but also progress in a group

**psychic numbing** members anesthetizing themselves to contradictions in the group

**psychoanalysis** in groups, focus is on the individual; the major tools of the psychoanalytic method are transference, dreams interpretation, historical development analysis, interpretation of resistance, and free association

**psychodrama** an interpersonal group approach in which participants act out their emotions and attempt to clarify conflicts; a way of exploring the human psyche through dramatic action; created and developed by J. L. Moreno; psychodrama process generally goes through three phases: (a) warm-up (preaction), (b) action, and (c) integration

**psychotherapy and counseling groups for the elderly** geared toward the remediation of specific problems faced by the aging, such as role changes, social isolation, physical decline, and fear of the future

**publicizing a group** the way a group is announced; an appropriate activity in the planning substage of forming

**quality circles** groups established in businesses on the idea of participative management; composed of workers in the same work area who meet on a weekly basis to discuss and try to resolve work-related problems

**quality groups** task/work groups first set up and used by the Japanese under the direction of W. Edwards Deming to assure work was done correctly the first time and efficiently; today these groups are a major part of many American businesses/industries

**questioning** a query that is sometimes a disguise for a statement. If group members are constantly questioning each other, they are safe from exposing their true selves. Questions keep the group focused on why something occurred and prevent members from concentrating on what is happening now.

**radical behaviorists** behaviorists who avoid any mentalistic concepts and concentrate exclusively on observable actions

**rape survivors' group** a group for victims of rape aimed at helping them decrease their sense of isolation and stigma while learning to model effective coping strategies

**rating sheet** an evaluation form members fill out and return before they terminate a group or a group session. Members can rate themselves, other members, and the leader on a number of dimensions including involvement, risk taking, goals, emotional involvement, feedback, and productivity

**rational-emotive behavioral therapy** based on the idea that it is one's thinking about events that produces feelings, not situations themselves. Individuals who have negative, faulty, or irrational thoughts become emotionally disturbed or upset and act in nonproductive ways, whereas those with more

neutral or positive thoughts feel calmer and behave constructively.

**reality-oriented groups** set up for older individuals who have become disoriented to their surroundings. These groups, while educationally focused, are therapeutically based in that their emphasis is on helping group members become more attuned to where they are with respect to time, place, and people.

**reality testing** a skill used when a group member makes an important decision, (e.g., changing jobs or taking a risk). At such moments, the leader will have other group members give feedback to the one who is contemplating a change on how realistic they see the decision. Through this process, the person is able to evaluate more thoroughly his or her decision.

**reality therapy** founded by William Glasser. It emphasizes that all behavior is generated within ourselves for the purpose of satisfying one or more basic needs.

**reality therapy's eight basic steps** (a) Make friends; establish a meaningful relationship. (b) Emphasize present behaviors; ask, "What are you doing now?" (c) Stress whether clients' actions are getting them what they want. (d) Make a positive plan to do better. (e) Get a commitment to follow the positive plan. (f) No excuses. (g) No punishment. (h) Never give up.

**reality therapy's four human psychological needs** belonging, power, freedom, and fun; one physiological need: survival

**reassuring/supportive** trying to encourage someone, yet dismissing the person's real feelings

**REBT viewpoint** involves getting group to believe the premises on which REBT is based are valid and applicable to their situations

**recycling** when individuals who have not benefited from a group experience go through a similar group to learn lessons missed the first time

**redecision school of TA** emphasis is on intrapsychic processes; groups provide a living experience in which members are able to examine themselves and their histories in a precise way. Individuals can then change their life scripts.

**redecision theory** a special form of TA; helps clients make redecisions while they are in their Child ego state. This task is accomplished by having these individuals reexperience a past event as if it were now present.

**referrals** transfers of members to another group; made when group leaders realize they cannot help certain members achieve designated goals or when there is a conflict between leaders and members that is unresolvable. The group leader should make appropriate referrals since he or she cannot be all things to all people. The referral process itself involves four steps: (a) identifying the need to refer, (b) evaluating potential referral sources, (c) preparing the client for the referral, and (d) coordinating the transfer.

**reframing** conceptualizing potentially negative actions in a positive way

**regressive-reconstructive model of group psychoanalysis** emphasizes that participants will become responsible for themselves and for society. It stresses the importance of being a creator of society as well as a transmitter of patterns. It pushes participants to continue to change after the group has ended.

**rehearsal** (a) when members show others in the group how they plan to act in particular situations; (b) in Gestalt groups when members are invited to say out loud what they are thinking

**reinforcement** any behavior, positive or negative, that increases the probability of a response

**relationship groups** groups that focus on helping women break out of the dependency and caretaking roles they often find themselves in and connecting with oneself and others in a healthy, growth-producing way. In such groups the emphasis is on being-in-relation where one's needs as well as others' needs are met. The groups are short term (6 weeks) and goal oriented.

**reminiscing groups** originated in the 1960s; based on the importance of "life review." They help individuals who are not yet at the older life stage to comprehend and appreciate more fully who they are and where they have been. Persons in these groups share memories, increase personal integration, and become more aware of their lives and the lives of those their age. Insight gained from this process helps these persons realize more deeply their finiteness and thus prepare for death.

**remotivation therapy groups** groups aimed at helping older clients become more invested in the present and future. Their membership is composed of individuals who have "lost interest" in any time frame of life except the past.

**reorientation** in Adlerian groups, when members are encouraged to act differently and take more control of their lives. Such a procedure means taking risks, acting "as if" they were the person they wished to be, and "catching themselves" in old, ineffective patterns and correcting them.

**repressive-constructive model of group psychoanalysis** focuses on adaptation and adjustment of participants without stressing the creation of newness within culture

**resistance** any behavior that moves the group away from areas of discomfort or conflict and prevents it from developing; works in overt and covert ways (e.g., rebellion by group members against the leader; getting bogged down in details; becoming preoccupied with the unimportant)

**resisters** group members who do not actively participate in the group and/or act as barriers to helping the group develop

**respondent conditioning** also known as *classical conditioning;* behavioral view that human responses are learned through association

**reviewing and summarizing the group experience** a procedure during termination in which group members recall and share special moments they remember from the group

**Rogerian-oriented encounter group 15-stage process**

1. *Milling around*—In the initial stage of the group, members are often confused about who is responsible for conducting the group and what they are supposed to be doing. This confusion results in frustration, silence, and a tendency to keep conversations on a superficial level.

2. *Resistance*—Group members tend to avoid exposing their private selves until they have built trust in other members. Members try to protect themselves and others from revealing too much too fast.

3. *Revealing past feelings*—As trust begins to develop, group members start to talk about their feelings, but only those that are safe to expose (e.g., the past). The talk at this point is on there-and-then experiences (i.e., those that are historical) that are nonthreatening to expose.

4. *Expression of negative feelings*—As the group develops, initial here-and-now feelings are expressed, but generally in a negative manner. Most of these feelings are directed toward the leader, and they are in the form of blame for not providing enough structure.

5. *Expression of personally meaningful material*—Real trust in the group is established at this stage. Group members feel free to explore and talk about important meaningful events in their lives.

6. *Communication of immediate interpersonal feelings*—At this point in the life of the group, members begin to be affected by and

respond to other group members. They indicate to others how their comments and actions are perceived.

7. *Development of a healing capacity in the group*—After members have expressed personal feelings about themselves and others, they begin reaching out to one another. This is accomplished by offering warmth, compassion, understanding, and caring to group members who have shared their concerns.

8. *Self-acceptance and the beginning of change*—As members are accepted more, they become increasingly aware of their own behaviors and feelings and are consequently less rigid. In the process, they open themselves to changes.

9. *Cracking of facades*—The tendency in encounter groups for members to drop the masks they have been wearing and become more genuine.

10. *Feedback*

11. *Confrontation*

12. *Helping relationships outside the group*—This stage is a parallel to stage 7, but group members experience healing and helping relationships with each other outside the formal group experience.

13. *The basic encounter*—Genuine person-to-person contact is the overriding characteristic at this point in the group.

14. *Expressions of closeness*—As the group nears completion, group members express positive feelings about their experience and about one another. A sense of group spirit develops.

15. *Behavior changes*—Behavior changes, the result of increased congruence, are more pronounced; members tend to act in a more open, honest, caring manner; and their behaviors are carried with them into everyday life experiences after the group terminates.

**role** a dynamic structure within an individual (based on needs, cognitions, and values) that usually comes to life under the influence of social stimuli or defined positions. The manifestation of a role is based on the individual's expectation of self and others and the interactions one has in particular groups and situations.

**role collision** when there is a conflict between the role an individual plays in the outside world (such as being a passive observer) and the role expected within the group (such as being an active participant)

**role confusion** occurs when a group member (or members) simply does not know what role to

perform. This often happens in leaderless groups where members do not know if they are to be assertive in helping establish an agenda or to be passive and just let the leadership emerge.

**role incompatibility** when a person is given a role within the group (such as being the leader) that he or she neither wants nor is comfortable exercising

**role-playing** assuming an identity that differs from one's present behavior. Role-playing is a tool for bringing a specific skill and its consequences into focus. It is vital for experiential learning within the group.

**role reversal** a psychodrama technique in which the protagonist literally switches roles with another person on stage and plays that person's part; group members act the opposite of what they feel

**role transition** when a person is expected to assume a different role as the group progresses but does not feel comfortable doing so

**rounds** also known as *go-rounds;* the process of giving members of a group an equal chance to participate in the group by going around the circle in which they are sitting and asking each person to make a comment on a subject that is presently before the group

**row formation** a group in which attention is focused toward the front. This arrangement is good for making a presentation, but it limits, and even inhibits, group interaction.

**rules** the guidelines by which groups are run

**sarcasm** masked feelings disguised through the use of clever language such as biting humor

**saying good-bye** the final words members exchange with others at the end of a group that wraps it up, at least on an affective/cognitive level. Members are encouraged to own their feelings and express their thoughts at this time, especially in regard to what others in the group have meant to them.

**scapegoat** to blame others for one's own problems

**screened** when potential group members are interviewed prior to the group in regard to their suitability for the group

**screening** a three-part process that begins when group leaders formulate the type of group they would like to lead. Next is the process of *recruitment,* in which the leader must make sure not to misrepresent the type of group that is to be conducted and to publicize it properly. Finally, there is the task of interviewing applicants by the leader to determine whether they will benefit from and contribute to the group.

**scripts (TA)** patterns of behavior that influence how people spend their time. Most people initially script their lives as a Child in the *I'm Not OK—You're OK* stance (powerless) but change to an Adult stance in later life as they affirm an *I'm OK—You're OK* position (characterized by trust and openness). Other options open to them are *I'm OK—You're Not OK* (projection of blame onto others) and *I'm Not OK—You're Not OK* (hopeless and self-destructive).

**sculpting** an exercise in which group members use nonverbal methods to arrange others in the group into a configuration like that of significant persons with whom they regularly deal, such as family members, office personnel, or social peers. The positioning involves body posturing and assists group members in seeing and experiencing their perceptions of significant others in a more dynamic way.

**searching for meaning** the search to find significance in one's life, even in the mundane events

**secondary affiliation groups** those groups with which people least identify

**secondary tension** intragroup conflict

**self-actualization** realistically living up to one's potential; being the best one can be

**self-awareness** a state of being in touch with one's existence and what it means to be alive; includes all sensations, thoughts, and behaviors of an individual

**self-disclosure** revealing to the group personal information of which the group was previously unaware. It involves listening and receiving feedback as well as speaking. One of the strongest signs of trust in a group is self-disclosure.

**self-help groups** groups that usually do not include professional leaders but are led by paraprofessionals or group members. Examples of such groups are Alcoholics Anonymous (AA) and Compassionate Friends (see *mutual help group*).

**self-instructional training** in this procedure, the group member is trained to become aware of his or her maladaptive thoughts (self-statements). Next, the group leader models appropriate behaviors while verbalizing the reasons behind these strategies. Finally, the group member performs the designated behaviors while verbally repeating the reasons behind the actions and then conducts these behaviors giving himself or herself covert messages.

**self-monitoring** behavioral group members keeping detailed, daily records of particular events or psychological reactions

**self-report research format** research method used by Rogers and nonbehaviorists in which participants write out or check off how they have changed as a result of the group experience

**self-talk** the messages people give themselves internally

**semicircle arrangement** a half-circle group structure in which members can see each other; discussion is likely to involve almost everyone. However, if the group is too large (e.g., above 20), persons may not feel that they are a group.

**sensitivity group** (see *basic encounter group*)

**settling-down period** a time when members test one another and the group collectively, before the group unifies

**shame attack** a REBT technique in which a person actually does what he or she dreaded and finds the world does not fall apart regardless of the outcome

**shaping** teaching behaviors through successive approximation and chaining. This gradual step process allows group members to learn a new behavior over time.

**shifting the focus** moving group members to a different topic area or person

**silent members** group members who are reticent to speak in the group owing to anger, nonassertiveness, reflection, shyness, or slowness in the assessment of their thoughts and feelings

**single-subject research design** a procedure in which leaders follow one of two methods in evaluating their groups. In the first method, they follow an ABAB design to evaluate the relationship of an intervention on changes that may occur in the group. In the other method, leaders employ a multiple-baseline design that more randomly measures change across subject, variables, or situations.

**SIPA (structure, involvement, process, and awareness)** a model for achieving group goals in group guidance

**situation** a psychodrama technique in which an emphasis is placed on the present; natural barriers of time, space, and states of existence are obliterated

**situational therapy** activity groups for children ages 8 to 15 based on psychoanalytic principles first created by Samuel Slavson

**social ecology** context of a group

**social group work** organizing individuals into purposeful and enriching groups; first begun by

Jane Addams at Hull House in Chicago for immigrants and the poor

**social influence** how interaction in groups exert an influence on actions, attitudes, and feelings of people

**social interest** an Adlerian term defined as not only an interest in others but also an interest in the interests of others

**social modeling** learning as a result of imitation of other's behaviors

**sociogram** a tool of sociometry that plots out group interactions

**sociometry** a phenomenological methodology for investigating interpersonal relationships.

**soliloquy** a psychodrama technique that involves the protagonist (i.e., the client) giving a monologue about his or her situation, as he or she is acting it out. A variation on this activity is the therapeutic soliloquy technique, in which private reactions to events in the protagonist's life are verbalized and acted out, usually by other actors (i.e., auxiliary egos).

**solution-focused debriefing (SFD) groups** groups that help victims of violence deal with its repercussions, such as feelings of helplessness, anxiety, depression, and disorganization, spanning seven stages in 3 weeks for enhanced recovery. These group emphasize a specific distressing incident, focus on the here and now, and include only persons who have witnessed the same violent episode.

**sophistry** a cognitive, psychotherapeutic group technique for assessing offenders' (and involuntary clients') "private logic" (i.e., way of thinking) and helping them change. This method helps counselors get beyond offenders' resistance. It employs paradox (i.e., telling resistant clients not to change), use of hidden reasons in a group debate, and a reorientation phase to get offenders to examine their thinking.

**specialty/standards model** an approach to conceptualizing groups in which they are defined according to their purpose, focus, and needed competencies. ASGW has defined standards for four types of groups: guidance/psychoeducational, counseling/interpersonal problem solving, psychotherapy/personality reconstruction, and task/work.

**spillover effect** the impact for others who are helping or watching a main character in psychodrama reach resolution on important issues; they see themselves as interacting in a new and better way.

**spontaneity** in psychodrama, the response people make that contains some degree of adequacy to a new situation or a degree of novelty to an old situation. The purpose of spontaneity is to liberate one's self from scripts and stereotypes and gain new perspectives on life.

**stage** in psychodrama, the area in which the action takes place

**stages of psychoanalytically oriented groups**

1. *Preliminary individual analysis*—Individuals in the psychoanalytically oriented group are interviewed individually by the group leader for their suitability for the group experience.
2. *Establishment of rapport through dreams and fantasies*—Group members are asked to discuss a recent dream, recurring dream, or a fantasy they have. The idea is to encourage group participation by having all members report on themselves and help others interpret or free associate on their experience.
3. *Analysis of resistance*—When group members become reluctant to share themselves with others and individual defenses are examined and dealt with.
4. *Analysis of transference*—When transference interactions are examined as close to the time of their occurrence as possible. Individual members are also asked to examine their feelings and involvement with other members of the group.
5. *Working through*—When individuals are required to accompany insight with action.
6. *Reorientation and social integration*—When clients demonstrate they are able to deal with the realities and pressures of life in an appropriate fashion without becoming overanxious or overcompliant when requests are made of them.

**storming** a time of conflict and anxiety in a group when it moves from primary tension (awkwardness about being in a strange situation) to secondary tension (intragroup conflict). It is a period when group members and leaders struggle with issues related to structure, direction, control, catharsis, and interpersonal relationships.

**strokes (TA)** verbal, psychological, or nonverbal recognition

**structured activities** (see *exercises*)

**structuring the group** running the group according to a preset prescribed plan or agenda

**study groups** types of task groups, typically involving three to four students who meet at least weekly to share information, knowledge, and expertise about a course in which they are all enrolled. The idea is that each group member will support and encourage the others and will obtain insight and knowledge through the group effort.

**style of life** Adlerian term; the way one prefers to live and relate to others. Adlerians stress that a faulty lifestyle is based on competitiveness and a striving to be superior to others.

**subgroups** cliques of group members who band together, often to the detriment of the group as a whole

**Succeeding in School lessons** a series of 10 lessons created by Gerler and Anderson (in 1986) that deal with modeling after successful people in school while learning to feel comfortable and responsible. Succeeding focuses on promoting cooperative efforts, enhancing student self-concept, and learning appropriate school skills such as listening and asking for help.

**summarizing** reflections by group members that recall significant events or learning experiences in the group

**superego** a psychoanalytic term that represents the values of parents and parental figures within the individual. It operates on the moral principle by punishing the person when he or she disobeys parental messages through the *conscience* and by rewarding the person through the *ego ideal* when parental teachings are followed. The superego strives for perfection.

**support groups** types of self-help groups in which members share a common concern and have a professional group leader

**supporting** the act of encouraging and reinforcing others. Its aim is to convey to persons that they are perceived as adequate, capable, and trustworthy. Through the act of supporting, group members feel affirmed and are able to risk new behaviors because they sense a backing from the group.

**suppression of the conflict** a strategy that consists of playing down conflict. It is often used when issues are minor. It keeps emotions under control and helps group leaders build a supportive climate.

**surplus reality** psychological experience that transcends the boundaries of physical reality. These experiences, which include relationships with those who have died or were never born, or with God, are often as important to people as their actual experiences with physical entities; a psychodrama concept.

**SYMLOG** System for the Multiple Level Observation of Groups

**synectics** from the Greek, means the joining together of different and apparently irrelevant elements. Synectics theory applies to the integration of diverse individuals into a problem-stating, problem-solving group.

**system** a set of elements standing in interaction

**systematic group leadership** training involves the teaching of basic skills to beginning group leaders. It is a six-step method that includes the videotaping of trainees leading a group before being introduced to the skill they are to learn (steps 1 and 2). Then the trainees read about and see a new skill demonstrated (steps 3 and 4). Finally, trainees critique their original videos and then make new videotapes demonstrating the skill they have just been taught (steps 5 and 6).

**Systematic Training for Effective Parenting (S.T.E.P.)** an Adlerian-based parent education program

**systemically** in a circular manner

**systems theory** a theory that focuses on the interconnectedness of elements. From this perspective, a group as an organism is composed of other organisms, commonly called members and a leader, who over time relate to each other face-to-face, processing matter, energy and information (see *general systems theory*).

**task processing** ways of accomplishing specific goals in a group

**task/work groups** groups whose emphasis is on accomplishment and efficiency in completing identified work goals. They are united in their emphasis on achieving a successful performance or a finished product through collaborative efforts. Task/work groups take the form of task forces, committees, planning groups, community organizations, discussion groups, and learning groups.

**Tavistock Institute of Human Relations** a group research facility in Great Britain

**teachable moment** a time when people are ready and able to learn

**team** a number of persons associated together in work or activity such as in athletic or artistic competition in which members of a group act and perform in a coordinated way to achieve a goal. Teams differ from basic groups in four main ways: (a) They have shared goals, as opposed to individual goals in most groups. (b) They stress an interdependency in working more than do groups. (c) They require more of a commitment by members to a team effort. (d) They are by design accountable to a higher level within the organization than are groups.

**team building** effective development of a team through managing conflict, promoting interpersonal relationships, and achieving consensus

**teamwork** all members of a group working together cooperatively

**tele** the total communication of feelings between people; involves complete interpersonal and reciprocal empathy; a psychodrama concept

**termination** a transition event that ends one set of conditions so that other experiences can begin. Termination provides group members an opportunity to clarify the meaning of their experiences, to consolidate the gains they have made, and to make decisions about the new behaviors they want to carry away from the group and apply to their everyday lives.

**Theater of Spontaneity** a forerunner of psychodrama formulated by J. L. Moreno in 1921

**theater style** a type of group structure in which members are seated in lines and rows

**theme group** a group that focuses on a particular problem or theme

**themes** specific topics or subjects related to the genuine interests of the participants, thereby holding their interest and inviting their participation. Many adolescent groups work best when they are structured around themes.

**theory** a way of organizing what is known about some phenomenon in order to generate a set of interrelated, plausible, and, above all, refutable propositions about what is unknown. A theory guides empirical inquiry and is useful in testing hypotheses.

**Theory X leader** an autocratic and coercive leader who basically believes people are unambitious and somewhat lazy

**Theory Y leader** a nondirective and democratic leader who thinks that people are self-starters and will work hard if given freedom

**Theory Z leader** a facilitative leader who helps encourage group members to participate in the group and trust that individual and collective goals will be accomplished through the process of interaction

**therapeutic contracts** in TA groups, specific, measurable, concrete statements of what participants intend to accomplish during the group. They place responsibility on members for clearly defining what, how, and when they want to change. TA contracts have the four major components of a legal contract: (a) *mutual assent*—clearly defining a goal from an adult perspective and joining with the therapist's Adult as an ally; (b) *competency*—

agreeing to what can realistically be expected; (c) *legal object*—an objective; and (d) *consideration*—a fee or price for services.

**therapeutic factors** (see *curative factors*)

**therapeutic fairy tale** a projective group activity meant to help persons focus on the future and renew their effort in the group. In this process, individuals are asked to write a fairy tale in a 6- to 10-minute time frame. They are to begin their story with "Once upon a time," and in it they are to include (a) a problem or predicament, (b) a solution, even if it appears outlandish, and (c) a positive, pleasing ending. The tale is then discussed in regard to personal and group goals.

**time limit for the group** the number of meeting times that the group will meet, usually announced in advance

**time-limited round** a technique in which each individual has the same amount of time, usually 1 or 2 minutes each, to say whatever he or she wishes

**timely teaching** when a particular event stimulates thinking and discussion among students

**top dog/underdog** dialogue in this Gestalt method, group members are asked to examine the *top-dog introjections* they have taken in from parents (usually represented by *should*s and *you*) and their own real feelings about situations (usually represented by "I" statements). They then are asked to carry on a dialogue between these two aspects of themselves before the group or with another group member and try to become more aware of their true self-identity and ways to act that would be appropriate.

**topic-specific groups** centered around a particular topic, such as widowhood, bibliotherapy, sexuality, health, or the arts. They are designed ultimately to improve the quality of daily living for older people. They also assist the aged to find more meaning in their lives and to establish a support group of like-minded people.

**total quality groups** implemented by the Japanese under the direction of task/work group master W. Edwards Deming. These types of groups focus on problem solving related to consumer satisfaction and quality issues in business.

**total quality movement (TQM)** in task/work environments, an emphasis on working cooperatively and productively in small groups

**TRAC model of groups** a model of groups known by the acronym TRAC (tasking, relating, acquiring, and contacting). Each letter represents an area in the total picture of group work. *Tasking* groups are focused on task achievement. *Relating* groups achieve objectives to increase the options for movement within the life of each person. *Acquiring* groups are directed toward learning outcomes that members can apply to others. In contrast, *contacting* groups are focused on the individual growth of members.

**traditional leader** a person who is controlling and exercises power from the top down as an expert; may be appropriate in running a hierarchical group that is diverse and whose members are physically separated

**traffic director** when the group leader helps members become aware of behaviors that open communication channels and those that inhibit communication

**training group** a group for beginning leaders designed to help them recognize and work out major personal and professional issues that affect their ability to conduct groups (e.g., criticism, anxiety, jealousy, need for control)

**training group (T-group)** approach to groups developed at the National Training Laboratories in the 1940s; primary attention to theory, group dynamics, and social material involving groups

**trait approach** the idea that some persons emerge as leaders because of their personal qualities

**transactional analysis (TA)** involves the diagnosing of interactions among group members to determine if they are *complementary* (from appropriate and expected ego states), *crossed* (from inappropriate and unexpected ego states), or *ulterior* (from a disguised ego state)

**transactional skills** qualities that help group members interact

**transactions (TA)** social actions between two or more people, manifested in social (overt) and psychological (covert) levels

**transference** the displacement of affect from one person to another; the projection of inappropriate emotions onto the leader or group members

**transformational leader** a person who empowers group members and shares power with them in working toward the renewal of a group; may be needed when a group is floundering

**transformational skills** helping members and the group achieve new behaviors

**transient children** children who have moved to a new community and a new school

**transition period** the time after the forming process and prior to the working stage; it includes the storming and norming stages

**trilevel model of Gestalt group work** attention is systematically focused on (a) the individual at the intrapersonal level, (b) two or more people at the interpersonal level, and (c) the group as a systematic unit

**tying things together** linking; connecting members with one another in regard to their similarities

**unfinished business** emotional debris from a person's past

**unintentional civil liability** a lack of intent to cause injury

**universality** a sense of commonness that group members feel in regard to their experiences when compared with others

**universalization** one's realization that others may have the same concerns

**unknown quadrant** of the Johari window, contains material hidden from self and others because of a lack of opportunity

**unstructured group** used in experientially based situations and employed where process rather than product is emphasized

**users of sarcasm** persons who mask their feelings through the use of clever language that has a biting humor

**using eyes** to scan the group and notice nonverbal reactions

**using power to resolve the conflict** a strategy involving the imposition of someone's will on someone else. The source of power may either be derived from one's status (position) or personality. *Position* power is most often used when there are immature relationships between individuals. Position power is derived from the status of people's titles, such as "group leader" or "group facilitator." *Personal* power is employed more frequently in mature relationship situations. The source of power in such a situation is from the individual and his or her ability to persuade others to follow a select course of action. By using power, a leader is able to quickly resolve a crisis, but the use of power often creates *win-lose atmospheres.*

**veracity** truthfulness. In group work, veracity is important in almost all phases of the group's development. Group members and leaders who are not truthful with themselves or others set up situations in which a good working relationship is impossible to achieve.

**verbal behavior** when group members speak to each other. The content of speech between people along with its tone and emphases.

**virtue ethics** focus on the character traits of the counselor [or group worker] and nonobligatory ideals to which professionals aspire rather than on solving specific ethical dilemmas

**"W" work group** (see *task/work groups*)

**warm-up phase** in psychodrama, characterized by the director making sure he or she is ready to lead the group and that group members are ready to be led

**we/they mentality** when practitioners of other points of view are seen as "uninformed," "naive," or "heretical"

**we/they tendency** when there is an overemphasis on identifying with a particular group, group members may tend to develop an antagonism toward other groups

**wheel** in this group arrangement, there is a center spoke, a leader, through which all messages go. Members have the advantage of face-to-face interaction with the leader, but they may become frustrated by the inability to communicate with another group member directly.

**wisdom** one of Erikson's virtues; the ability to make effective choices among alternatives

**withdrawal from the conflict** a strategy that involves group leaders distancing themselves from conflict and postponing interventions

**working out a compromise** when each party involved gives up a little to obtain a part of what they wanted and to avoid conflict. The result is a win-win situation in which cooperative behavior and collaborative efforts are encouraged. This approach is effective in groups when resources are limited.

**working stage** most unified and productive group stage that focuses on the achievement of individual and group goals and the movement of the group itself as a system

**wounded healers** fellow sufferers who have overcome their hurt; it is assumed in self-help groups that these individuals are able to deal most effectively with each other by coming together and sharing through disclosing, listening, and learning

**written projections** a process whereby members are asked to see themselves or their groups in the future as having been successful and to describe what the experience is like. They are able to play with their fantasies at times as well as be realistic.

**Y** this group arrangement combines the structural elements of the wheel and chain—there is a perceived leader. The efficiency of the unit is second only to that of the wheel in performance. Like a chain, the Y may frustrate group members who wish to have direct contact and communication with each other. Information is not equally shared or distributed.

**yearbook feedback** saying nice but insignificant things about a person, as high school students do when they write in annuals

**young adulthood** ages 20 to 40 years, in which identity and intimacy are two intense primary issues

**young-old** individuals between ages 65 and 75

# ANSWER KEY TO SELF-ASSESSMENT QUESTIONS

PART I <u>History and Trends of Group Work</u>

## CHAPTER 1

### History and Trends of Group Work

True or False Statements
1. t
2. f
3. f
4. t
5. t
6. f
7. f
8. t
9. t
10. f

Multiple Choice Questions
1. a (p. 4)
2. b (p. 11)
3. d (p. 13)

## CHAPTER 2

### Types of Group Work

True or False Statements
1. f
2. f
3. f
4. f
5. t
6. t
7. t
8. f
9. t
10. f
11. f
12. t
13. t

Multiple Choice Questions
1. a (p. 25)
2. c (p. 26)
3. c (p. 38)

## CHAPTER 3

### Group Dynamics

True or False Statements
1. f
2. t
3. t
4. t
5. t
6. f
7. f
8. f
9. f
10. f
11. t

Multiple Choice Questions
1. a (p. 54)
2. b (p. 51)
3. b (p. 54)

## CHAPTER 4

### Effective Group Leadership

True or False Statements
1. f
2. t
3. f
4. t
5. t
6. f
7. f
8. t
9. t
10. t
11. f
12. t
13. t
14. t
15. t
16. f
17. t
18. t

Multiple Choice Questions
1. d (p. 82)
2. c (p. 82)
3. a (p. 92)
4. c (p. 96)
5. d (p. 101)

## CHAPTER 5

### Beginning a Group

True or False Statements
1. f
2. f
3. t
4. f
5. t
6. t
7. t
8. f
9. t
10. t
11. f
12. t
13. t
14. t
15. f
16. t

Multiple Choice Questions
1. b  (p. 116)
2. b  (p. 112)
3. c  (p. 117)
4. b  (p. 123)

## CHAPTER 6

### The Transition Period in a Group: Norming and Storming

True or False Statements
1. f
2. f
3. t
4. f
5. t
6. t
7. f
8. t
9. f
10. t
11. t
12. f
13. t
14. f

Multiple Choice Questions
1. b  (p. 134)
2. b  (p. 135)
3. d  (p. 136)
4. b  (p. 145)

## CHAPTER 7

### The Working Stage in a Group: Performing

True or False Statements
1. f
2. t
3. t
4. f
5. t
6. f
7. t
8. f
9. t
10. f
11. t
12. t
13. t
14. t

Multiple Choice Questions
1. b  (p. 161)
2. b  (p. 168)
3. d  (p. 171, 172)

## CHAPTER 8

### Termination of a Group

True or False Statements
1. t
2. f
3. t
4. t
5. t
6. f
7. f
8. t
9. f
10. f
11. t
12. f
13. f
14. t
15. t
16. t

Multiple Choice Questions
1. d  (p. 178)
2. c  (p. 186)
3. b  (p. 189)
4. a  (p. 194)

**Group Work with Culturally Diverse
Populations**

True or False Statements

1. f
2. t
3. f
4. f
5. t
6. t
7. t
8. f
9. f
10. f
11. f
12. f
13. t
14. t
15. t
16. f
17. t
18. f
19. f

Multiple Choice Questions

1. d ( p. 203)
2. a  (p. 207)
3. c  (p. 209)

**Ethical and Legal Aspects of Group
Work**

True or False Statements

1. t
2. f
3. t
4. t
5. t
6. f
7. f
8. f
9. t
10. t
11. f
12. f
13. f
14. f
15. f

Multiple Choice Questions

1. a (p. 224)
2. d (p. 226)
3. c (p. 231)
4. c (p. 229)
5. a (p. 234)
6. d (p. 239)

## CHAPTER 11

### Groups for Children

True or False Statements
1. f
2. t
3. t
4. t
5. f
6. f
7. f
8. f
9. f
10. f
11. t
12. t
13. t

Multiple Choice Questions
1. d (p. 255)
2. b (p. 258)
3. c (p. 266)

## CHAPTER 12

### Groups for Adolescents

True or False Statements
1. t
2. t
3. f
4. t
5. t
6. f
7. f
8. f
9. t
10. f
11. t
12. f
13. f
14. t
15. f

Multiple Choice Questions
1. c (p. 275)
2. a (p. 278)
3. a (p. 284)

## CHAPTER 13

### Groups for Adults

True or False Statements
1. f
2. t
3. t
4. t
5. f
6. f
7. t
8. t
9. f
10. f
11. f
12. t
13. t
14. f
15. t
16. t

Multiple Choice Questions
1. d (p. 302)
2. d (p. 302)
3. b (p. 306)

## CHAPTER 14

### Groups for the Elderly

True or False Statements
1. t
2. f
3. t
4. t
5. f
6. f
7. t
8. f
9. f
10. f
11. t
12. t
13. t
14. f

Multiple Choice Questions
1. b (p. 329)
2. a (p. 335)
3. d (p. 339)